The Ionians and Hellenism

States and Cities
of Ancient Greece

Edited by
R. F. WILLETTS

The Ionians and Hellenism

A study of the cultural achievement of
the early Greek inhabitants of Asia Minor

C. J. Emlyn-Jones

Routledge & Kegan Paul
London, Boston and Henley

First published in 1980
by Routledge & Kegan Paul Ltd
39 Store Street,
London WC1E 7DD,
9 Park Street,
Boston, Mass. 02108, USA and
Broadway House,
Newtown Road,
Henley-on-Thames,
Oxon RG9 1EN

Printed in Great Britain by
Redwood Burn Ltd Trowbridge and Esher
© C. J. Emlyn-Jones 1980

British Library Cataloguing in Publication Data

Emlyn-Jones, C J
The Ionians and Hellenism.
1. Ionians
I. Title
938   DF136.I6   80-41143

ISBN 0-7100-0470-2

For RFW

Contents

Illustrations

Between pages 50-51

1 'Wild Goat' style oinochoe: height 36 cm. British Museum 67-5-8.928. c.625–600 BC. Reproduced by courtesy of the Trustees of the British Museum.

2 'Fikellura' amphora: height 34 cm. Running Man painter. British Museum 64.10–7.156. Third quarter of sixth century BC from Kameiros. Reproduced by courtesy of the Trustees of the British Museum.

3 East Greek Black Figure cup 'Bird Nester': diameter 23.5 cm (without handles). Louvre F.68. c.550 BC. Photo: Louvre Museum.

4 Ivory statuette 'Spinning Woman': height 10.5 cm. Istanbul. Early sixth century BC, from Ephesos. Photo: Istanbul Museum.

5 Ivory statuette 'Eunuch Priest': height 11 cm. Istanbul. Early sixth century BC, from Ephesos. Photo: Istanbul Museum.

6 Ivory statuette 'Hawk Priestess': height 10.5 cm. Istanbul. 570–560 BC, from Ephesos. Photo: Istanbul Museum.

7 Marble statue 'Cheramyes Hera': height 1.82 m. Louvre MA 686. c.560 BC, from Samos. Photo: Louvre Museum.

8 Marble statue, 'Philippe' from the Geneleos group: height 1.60 m. 560–550 BC, from Samos. Photo: German Archaeological Institute, Athens.

9 Limestone statue, youth from Cape Phoneas: height 1.68 m. 540–530 BC. Photo: German Archaeological Institute, Athens.

10 Marble seated figure from Didyma: height 1.55 m. British Museum B 271. c.570 BC. Reproduced by courtesy of the Trustees of the British Museum.

11 Marble seated female figure from Didyma: height 1.25 m. British Museum B 280. Early fifth century BC. Reproduced by courtesy of the

Trustees of the British Museum.

12 Marble lion from Didyma: length 2.11 m. British Museum B 281. Early sixth century BC. Reproduced by courtesy of the Trustees of the British Museum.

13 Marble maiden's head from the Artemision at Ephesos: height 19 cm. British Museum B 89. c.550 BC. Reproduced by courtesy of the Trustees of the British Museum.

14 Marble head of a maiden, with veil, from a decorated column relief from Didyma: height 16.1 cm. Staatliche Museen, Berlin. c.550 BC. Photo: Preussischer Kulturbesitz.

15 Ionic capital from the Ephesian Artemision (reconstructed): height 1.096 m. British Museum. c.560 BC. Reproduced by courtesy of the Trustees of the British Museum.

16 Kore: 'Berlin Kore' from Attica: height 1.93 m. Staatliche Museen, Berlin. 570–560 BC. Photo: Staatliche Museen.

17 Kore from the Athenian Acropolis, associated with the column bearing a signature of Archermos of Chios: height 55 cm. Acropolis Museum no. 675. Last quarter of sixth century BC. Photo: Athens TAP Service.

18 Caeretan hydria: height 43 cm. Louvre E 701. c.530–525 BC from Cervetri. Photo: Louvre Museum.

Acknowledgments

My thanks are due first and foremost to Ronald Willetts for inspiration, help and encouragement offered over many years. I am grateful to Desmond Costa, Ian Barton and Robert Lock who read all or part of an earlier draft of this book and made many helpful suggestions for improvement. I would also like to record the painstaking efforts of Joyce Kirkpatrick who typed the manuscript, my wife Marga and Kitty Chisholm, who helped in the preparation of the index, Ray Munns who drew the map and Cecilia Powell of Routledge & Kegan Paul editorial department.

Acknowledgment is due to the following museums and organisations for permission to reproduce works of art: The British Museum (Plates 1, 2, 10, 11, 12, 13, 15); Musée du Louvre (Plates 3, 7 and 18); Istanbul Museum (Plates 4, 5 and 6); German Archaeological Institute, Athens (Plates 8 and 9); Bildarchiv Preussischer Kulturbesitz (Plate 14); Staatliche Museen zu Berlin (DDR) (Plate 16); Acropolis Museum (Plate 17).

C. J. Emlyn-Jones
Oxford, May 1980

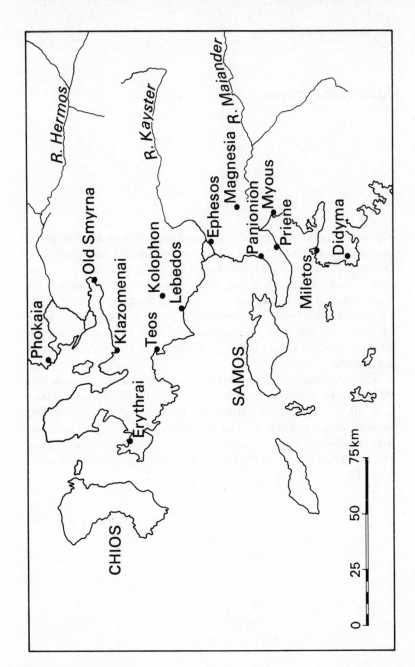

The Ionian cities

Ἰωνικόν

Γιατὶ τὰ σπάσαμε τ'ἀγάλματά των,
γιατὶ τοὺς διώξαμεν ἀπ' τοὺς ναούς των,
διόλου δέν πέθαναν γι' αὐτὸ οἱ θεοί.
῍Ω γὴ τῆς Ἰωνίας, σένα ἀγαποῦν ἀκόμη,
σένα οἱ ψυχές των ἐνθυμοῦνται ἀκόμη.
Σὰν ξημερώνει ἐπάνω σου πρωὶ αὐγουστιάτικο
τὴν ἀτμοσφαίρα σου περνᾶ σφρίγος ἀπ' τὴν ζωή των·
καὶ κάποτ' αἰθερία ἐφηβικὴ μορφή,
ἀόριστη, μὲ διάβα γρήγορο,
ἐπάνω ἀπὸ τοὺς λόφους σου περνᾶ.

C. P. Cavafis (1911)

1 Introduction

> I consider that Asia differs quite markedly from Europe
> both in the nature of all its inhabitants and its
> vegetation; for, in Asia, everything grows far greater
> in beauty and size; the land is gentler than Europe and
> the temperament of the people milder and more easy-
> going. The reason for this is the equability of the
> seasons, since the land lies towards the east midway
> between the risings of the sun and further away from
> the cold than Europe.... It would be fair to liken this
> land very closely to spring, both in its character and
> the moderation of its seasons. But courage, hardihood,
> industry and spirit could not occur in such circum-
> stances, whether among the indigenous population or
> immigrants, but pleasure necessarily reigns supreme.(1)

So writes the unknown author of a Hippocratic treatise
composed probably towards the end of the fifth century BC.
In the work as a whole a systematic attempt is made to
relate human temperament, build, bodily constitution and
typical ailments exclusively to differing types of climate.
The assumptions the author makes in the treatise and the
rigorously schematic nature of his analysis are, of course,
absurdly inadequate by modern ethnographical standards;
yet the work contains a clear realisation of the importance (here, admittedly, exaggerated) of such factors as
water-supply, prevailing winds, soil and the character of
the seasons.

The passage quoted above has a special interest in its
combination of observation, dogma and generalisation which
may well reflect, at a scientific level, a current popular
Greek attitude to the coastal region of Asia Minor
(clearly what the author means by Asia, here) and its
inhabitants. The mildness of the climate was noted by
many ancient writers, including Herodotos and Pausanias,

as well as modern travellers.(2) The picture of the
inhabitants as soft and addicted to pleasure was one which
gradually developed, with some support in early Ionian
sources, into a stereotype after the Ionian Revolt at the
beginning of the fifth century BC and the later incorporation of Ionia into the Athenian Empire. But it was left
to the author of the above passage to make the explicit
correlation between climate and temperament and so fix
the character of the Asia Minor Greeks in the name of
'natural science'.

Part of the author's purpose in the second half of the
treatise is to contrast west and east morally and socially
in terms of Greeks and barbarians, and he makes the traditional observation that eastern races are, on the whole,
feeble, as a result of their government by despots.(3) In
this way the superiority of the Greeks could be put on
what was thought to be a sound scientific basis. In the
treatise as a whole the author is not particularly concerned with the Ionians, and it might be thought that they
sit rather uneasily across the boundary of his neat,
schematic divide, reflecting, perhaps, a perennial Greek
embarrassment with the subject.

Yet within his rigid framework, the writer has room for
accounts of an anthropological nature, reminiscent of
Herodotos. We are told of the Skythians, whose moist
bodily constitution and love of riding produce infertil-
ity, and the mysterious 'Longheads', where the original
social custom of forcing the head to increase in length
has now, the author maintains, 'been aided by nature'.(4)
It is somewhat ironic that the impulse towards this kind of
investigation and even the dialect in which it is written
should have had their origin among a race condemned, on
the Hippocratic theory, to happy mediocrity. The adoption
of the dialect of Greek known as Ionic as the standard
medium for early scientific, medical, historical and
philosophical writings confirms what we know from other
sources, that the systematic observation of the external
world, earthly and heavenly, and the creation of theories
to explain the observations, had their origin among the
Greek peoples of the Asia Minor seaboard. For his basic
scientific premises, especially the symmetrical model of
the world as a combination of blending or hostile opposites, as well as the rational impulse behind his observation
of phenomena, the writer of the 'Airs, Waters, Places' was
indebted, at whatever remove, to the Ionian Greeks.

The focal point of this early scientific activity (and the
region indicated by the term 'Ionian' in this study (5))

was roughly the area specified by the Greek geographer
Strabo in his account of the Ionian cities, from the
boundaries of Karia south of Miletos in the south to the
territory of the small sea-faring city of Phokaia in the
north, just north of the Hermos river.(6) The territory
consisted of a narrow seaboard about ninety miles long and
twenty to thirty miles wide hemmed in by mountains to the
east and south through which passes led to the interior of
Asia Minor. Settlement took place on and around three
major rivers which flowed eastward through the mountains.
In addition two islands, Samos and Chios, contained Ionian
cities and now comprise, incidentally, the only ancient
Ionian territory which is still part of Greece (see map).

Ionia enjoyed a long and eventful history stretching
over a period of more than 2,000 years, from the early
Greek settlement of the post-Mycenaean period to a series
of brilliant cultures which flourished in the large, busy
and affluent cities of the Hellenistic, Roman and Byzantine empires - the 'claras Asiae urbes' which caught the
imagination of the Roman poet of the first century BC,
Catullus,(7) and formed the background for the journeys of
Paul the Apostle a little later.(8) Yet Herodotos' famous
words on the mutability of fortune have never found a more
apt illustration than the Ionian seaboard: 'Of the cities
that were great long ago the majority have become small
and those that were great in my time were small former-
ly.'(9) Factors affecting instability included the gradual
recession of the coastline; Strabo tells us that lawsuits
were brought against the god of the river Maiander for
changing the boundaries of countries on its banks,(10) and
the tendency of this river to silt up led to the decline
of a number of Ionian cities which flourished early, from
tiny Myous to Miletos itself, once a great commercial city
with four harbours, and by the early Middle Ages an abandoned village some miles from the coast. Most cities in
this area had a chequered career; Smyrna, a late entrant
to the Ionian federation from the Aiolic area to the north,
enjoyed a prosperous early history, near eclipse for about
300 years after conquest and destruction by Lydia in the
sixth century BC, and later a flourishing life as a Roman
city, maintained to the present day in its modern Turkish
guise as Izmir. Ephesos, one of the greatest cities of
the area during the Roman period, an important religious
centre and traditionally the last home of the Virgin Mary,
became gradually deserted and the original city was
covered in deep mud by the river Kayster, leaving its
ruins as a quarry for local builders, while the inhabitants moved to a new site. Samos, very important in the
archaic and classical period for its strategic position,

became the head of the Aegean 'theme' under the Byzantine empire and was again prominent in the Greek War of Independence and, even before its reannexation to Greece in 1912, maintained semi-independent status under the Ottoman empire.

The overriding factor for Ionia as a whole has always been her position as a strategic buffer between the east and west which has rendered her often remarkable prosperity precarious. A pattern of invasion and conquest which began with the Lydians and the Persians in the sixth century BC was repeated, one assumes for the last time, in AD 1922, when the Greek occupation of Asia Minor was brought to an abrupt and tragic end by Mustafa Kemal, and a large number of Greek refugees fled from mainland Turkey back to the Greek homeland whence, three millennia earlier, one might say, they had come.

The history of Ionia falls into well-defined periods characterised by the conquest and rule of various imperial masters: the Persians, the Athenians, the Hellenistic monarchs, the Romans and the rulers of the Byzantine and Ottoman empires. The visible remains belong, on the whole, to the later periods. The casual visitor to the ancient site of, for example, Ephesos or Miletos is made immediately aware of the impressive architectural testimony to the grandeur of the past; temples, markets, colonnades, baths, theatres, stadia, gymnasia and, later, churches were built in comprehensively planned city complexes which included extensive private housing set out in the elaborate 'gridiron' pattern (itself an invention attributed to Hippodamos of Miletos, who lived in the fifth century BC (11)).

With the partial exception of Old Smyrna, which was extensively excavated immediately after the Second World War, little of the earliest civilisation of Ionia, the archaic, is visible on the sites, nor does what can be produced offer particularly impressive testimony to what, the guide-book assures us, was a culture in its own way no less magnificent than its successors. In a number of cases the site of the archaic city is still imprecisely known or, as in the case of Ephesos, waterlogged. Very little remains of the large Ionian temples planned and partially executed in the sixth century BC, and a great deal of what the visitor is able to appreciate of the civilisation is anecdotal and confined to the pages of the guide-book. What the tourist lacks with early Ionia, and what he so obviously enjoys with civilisations historically even more remote, such as the Minoan or the Mycenaean, is a physical point of contact. He may even conclude, not entirely without justification, that appreciation of the early Ionians must be essentially a matter for scholars and that stories about Thales and Bias of Priene are no substitute for the so much more substantial realities of the later periods.

It cannot be denied that the dilemma of the layman reflects to some extent that of the scholar. History has not been kind to the Ionians either, as we have already seen, in their subsequent reputation or in the sheer physical survival of their civilisation. It is true, the investigations of Ionia share in some degree the common problems besetting any archaic Greek society - deeply buried archaeological remains and a paucity of written sources, which together make it difficult to enter into a world alien not only to our own but, in some respects, to its classical successor. Yet with Ionia, the problems are particularly acute owing largely to an absence of cultural continuity on all but the most basic levels. Especially in the fifth and early fourth centuries BC, vital for the transmission, and, in many cases, preservation of the accumulated culture of centuries, the Ionian cities sank, in almost all respects, to quite a low level, resulting in the undoubted loss of a great deal of their earlier heritage. When the area regained some of its prosperity during the later fourth century BC, the situation was very different; the centre of power lay further south in Karia, where Hellenised dynasts exercised authority shortly to be superseded by the conquests of Alexander the Great. Ionia was by this time part of the cultural 'commonwealth' of post-classical Greece, and any individuality it possessed had largely disappeared.

As a result, evidence from archaic Ionia is fragmentary in all areas. Consequently, a synthesis of the subject which seeks to advance beyond anecdote or a mere collation of the sources must clearly pose certain fundamental questions about method and, in particular, the degree to which we are actually able to penetrate, figuratively and literally, the Hellenistic and Roman façade.

Yet it has become increasingly obvious that Ionian civilisation is worth the effort. In looking at the foundations of classical Greek culture it is impossible to avoid the conclusion that the Ionians must have played a decisive part. The origins of philosophy, natural science, history, geography, and a major contribution to poetry and classical architecture are all associated in the Greek tradition with Ionia. And this tradition is sound; we cannot imagine the Parthenon without the stylistic influence of the sixth-century BC Ionian temples, Greek tragedy without Homer, Sokrates and Plato without Anaximander, Herakleitos or Anaxagoras; or possibly even

Herodotos without the Ionian geographers and historians. Furthermore, in studying the intellectual revolution by which, in Ionia, the foundations of rational thought and scientific enquiry were laid, modern man has the unique opportunity to see the conceptual framework of his own world in the making. Moreover, it is arguable (and the thesis will be advanced in this book) that it was in Ionia, in the poetry of Homer and the cosmology of the Milesians that, for the first time in history, man took the centre of the stage as a thinking and feeling individual - an assumption upon which western culture has subsequently rested. It is hardly coincidental, too, that it was at about this time, in the eastern part of Greece, if not in Ionia itself, that events of great significance for man's future took place - the invention of the alphabet, the development of literacy and the introduction of coinage.

Yet it is not really sufficient to see the Ionians merely as inspired originators, laying foundations upon which others were privileged to build. In the culturally diverse Greek world of the archaic period, outlying Greek communities tended to produce art, for example, which, while distinctly Greek, owed a great deal to the influence of non-Greek neighbours. In this, the Ionians were no exception; their geographical position enabled them to create an artistic style which was, to some extent, a synthesis of east and west - a meeting of native Greek rigour and intellect with the more conservative and decorative Orient. It is, as one might expect, in visual art that this quality is most immediately perceived - in the early sixth-century BC Ephesian ivories in Istanbul or the 'Cheramyes Hera' in the Louvre, for example (see Chapter 3 pp. 47-9) - a synthesis in which the stylistic influence, in details as well as general conception, of Hittite, Assyrian and Egyptian art is clear. Yet, in Ionia, the influence of the non-Greek element is not really confined to visual art. Early Mesopotamian and Egyptian creation-myths had an undoubted influence on early Greek cosmology and, at a more mundane level, inscriptions in languages other than Greek in the Ionian cities themselves, as well as non-Greek personal names, testify to the strong influence, from an early period, of immediate neighbours such as Karians and Lydians. All this gives some substance to the contention of G.M.A. Hanfmann that 'for the Ionian, the barbarian was never far from the gates.'(12) Whether, with E. Akurgal, we are prepared to assume that Ionian art largely took its character and originality from the long drawn-out contact with Anatolian culture is another question; but strong influence there undoubtedly was.(13)

    An account of the early Ionians which seeks to emphasise
their achievement and even to suggest that, for a time,
they reached a cultural level higher than anywhere else in
the Greek world, is always open to the charge of reviving
the, now rather unfashionable, heresy of 'Panionismus' -
the belief, current at about the beginning of this century
and later, that Ionia was the cradle of Greek culture, the
source of its political and economic, as well as its literary and philosophical riches. The Ionians were displayed
as the great middle-men of Greek civilisation, assimilating
and adapting the riches of the east for their less-advanced
fellow-Greeks, and fertilising the stolid and unimaginative
mainland with their intellect and humour. For example, the
distinguished scholar Wilamowitz was able to regard the
early sixth-century BC inscription from the island of
Chios, revealing a progressive constitution, as significant
in making us realise the primacy of Ionia in laying the
foundation for the organisation of Greek society and the
Greek state, exactly as it did also for philosophy and
poetry.(14) This equation of originality in cultural
developments with progressive social systems received
stimulus from the nineteenth- and early twentieth-century
rediscovery of the Ionians associated with the major
German editions of the Presocratic philosophers and the
British and German excavations at Ephesos and Miletos
respectively.(15)

    The extravagance of these claims has been effectively
countered in the post-war period. In 1946, R.M. Cook, in
an influential article, exploded the chronological basis
upon which the existing view of the primacy of Ionia was
based and, in particular, questioned current attitudes to
the ancient chronology with regard to the dates for the
founding of Ionian colonies. His general conclusion was
that, whatever her position in literature and thought,
Ionia was, if anything, late in developing economically
and socially.(16) Since Cook's thorough reassessment of
the evidence, study of Ionia has proceeded with much
greater caution; yet it may be thought that the pendulum
has now swung too far in the other direction. It was
perhaps ironic that Cook's article should appear on the
eve of the epoch-making excavations of Old Smyrna, which
revealed the remains of some of the oldest post-Mycenaean
Greek houses and a seventh-century BC city complex of some
magnitude.(17) It is now thought that urbanisation occurred, for a variety of reasons, earlier in Ionia than on
the mainland of Greece. More recently, excavation of the
lower levels of archaic civilisation in almost all the
Ionian cities has substantially raised the date at which

we may assume the Ionian migrations from the Greek mainland took place.(18)   Finally, it can be argued that the
idiosyncratic development of Ionian art has for too long
been judged by the standards of Greek art as a whole,
thereby obscuring its originality in its own context.
Proper concern to deny the automatic equation of literary
and philosophical originality with social and economic
innovation has sometimes led to an overall picture of lop-
sided development, which is itself no more convincing than
the perspective it replaces.   It is important to recognise
that the Ionians, whether behind or in front of their
fellow Greeks, were undoubtedly different.

In the modern, as in the ancient, world, the Ionians
still occupy an equivocal place in the hierarchy of
cultures.   The picture of the soft, sensual, unambitious,
pleasure-loving East Greeks competes with the undoubted
evidence for their intellectual boldness, their reputation
as intrepid explorers and advanced engineers, and, when
forced to it, brave defenders of their country.   The
present state of research on Ionia makes it unlikely that
this picture will be radically altered in the near future.
Progress in archaeological excavation is steady if un-
spectacular and the attention of excavators is naturally
concentrated more upon the rewarding finds of the Hellenistic and later periods.   After the initial discoveries of
the lowest level of Greek inhabitation it seems improbable
that further exploration of the archaic levels of the
Ionian cities will reveal anything radically new.(19)
Much the same applies to the written historical sources,
the evidence of which has been applied as fully as their
nature permits.(20)   Art and architecture has been the
subject of detailed study, especially in its relations
with the Orient.(21)   In literature, on the other hand,
since the war each of the Ionian philosophers has been the
subject of detailed investigation and the whole question
of the origins of philosophy fully ventilated.(22)   The
historical background and poetic technique of the Ionian
poet Homer have been radically reassessed.(23)

The time for a major synthesis has not yet come (if it
ever does).   Yet, the position of Ionia, split up between
different detailed specialisms, is not a happy one, though
the prudence of such a procedure, given the state of the
evidence, is not hard to appreciate.   The present study,
however, is written in the belief that the various products of Ionian artistic, literary, scientific and philosophical genius do exhibit common links which reflect a
unified vision both unique and influential.   This is the

primary justification for a book which sets out to discuss Ionian culture as a whole and to consider, in some measure, its influence on later Hellenism.

2 The Ionian cities

Owing to the limitations of the archaeological evidence we
are unusually dependent upon literary sources for a reconstruction of the history of the early Ionian cities.
Almost the only near-contemporary literary source for
early Ionia is Herodotos, whose account forms part of his
general history of the conflict between the Greeks and the
Persians. The only other extant sources of any length are
the much later accounts of the historian and geographer
Strabo (first century BC) and the traveller Pausanias
(second century AD) who both deal with Ionia in some
detail in the course of general surveys of the Greek
world. This evidence may be supplemented on the one hand
by occasional scraps of information and inferences from
early Ionian writers themselves (though this source is
uncertain and the return meagre) and, on the other, by
numerous pieces of evidence which can be found dotted
around in a variety of late authors, ranging from
Athenaios, Plutarch and Eusebios to Stephanos of Byzantium.
  We have also some information on the sources used by
our major authorities. Strabo used Pherekydes of Athens
(c. 500 BC), the author of the earliest surviving account
of the early migrations from mainland Greece;(1) Pausanias
does not name his chief source but, in his account of
Chios, uses Ion of Chios (fifth century BC)(2) of whose
prose account of the founding of Chios we possess one
fragment. The case of Herodotos is more complicated. As
he does not name his sources, the origin of his Ionian
excursus and the Persian conquest of Ionia in Book I,(3)
as well as his history of the Ionian Revolt in Books V and
VI,(4) is a matter of conjecture. For the latter events
he may well have used the mid-fifth-century BC historian
Charon of Lampsakos, and the prominence of the Karians in
his account of the latter part of the Revolt could be due
to his use of the Karian, Skylax of Karyanda, who wrote a

biographical essay on Herakleides, tyrant of Mylasa, in
the 470s BC. Yet it has become of late increasingly clear
that there was no major literary historian before Herodotos; a great deal of his information came from oral
sources and as the result of personal research *in situ*.(5)

There remains, however, the tantalising problem of the
early Ionian writers of whom little survives but their
names, for example, Kadmos of Miletos, who is said to have
composed an account of the founding of Miletos and the
whole of Ionia in four books,(6) Dionysios, also of
Miletos, an even more shadowy figure, and Asios, an early
native of Samos, six of whose verses on the luxury of the
Samians are quoted by Athenaios,(7) and who wrote a genealogical epic consulted by Pausanias.(8) We are unable,
by the very nature of the evidence, to advance much
further along these lines, except to note that a number of
prominent individuals, such as Xenophanes of Kolophon, the
philosopher and Mimnermos the elegiac poet (also of
Kolophon or, more likely, Smyrna) were alleged to have
written historical works on the founding of their own city,
and that Panyassis, the fifth-century epic poet from
Halikarnassos in Karia, is said to have written an Ionic
poem in six books on the Ionian migration. Despite the
scepticism of F. Jacoby(9) there is no *a priori* reason for
not believing that those works existed and that our extant
authorities profited by them.

Finally, mention must briefly be made of the late sixth-
century BC geographer Hekataios of Miletos who, among his
other works, wrote an invaluable geographical description
(περιήγησις) of the known world. The absence of much of
the material on Greek Asia Minor, leaving the names of
cities in catalogue form preserved by Stephanos of Byzantium, is one of the great losses to scholarship on this
subject.(10)

The extent and nature of the literary sources govern,
to a degree considerable even for archaic Greece, the way
in which early Ionia is presented to us. Our authorities
direct a powerful but narrow beam of light which illumin-
ates quite limited areas both historically and geographic-
ally. Our knowledge of the Ionian migrations is full,
from a personal and genealogical standpoint which possibly
reflects the known predeliction of early historians for
local κτίσεις (foundation stories). At the other end of
our period, from the rise of Lydia at the end of the
seventh century BC, we have the more historical Herodotos.
The intervening period, however, is scantily covered in
the case of most cities. Moreover, in the case of
individual cities, even Herodotos' account is highly
selective; while we learn a considerable amount about e.g.

Samos and Miletos, other cities such as Phokaia or Chios
tend to figure only when they take the stage.

The nature and contribution of archaeological data is
much less easy to summarise, and will therefore be
mentioned only in the course of the historical summary
below. But it is, of course, true to say that, like the
literary sources, the evidence from archaeology is scanty
and uneven.

In marked contrast to the western Greeks of Magna Graecia
and Sicily, those on the eastern extremity of the Hellenic
world had the misfortune to carve out their early existence in a land destined to become a first line of defence
(expendable by both sides, as it happened) in the major
clash between the Greeks and the last and most formidable
of a series of eastern neighbours, the Persians. Clinging,
as it were, to the seaboard of a large and mountainous
land inhabited by powerful peoples, and only partially
protected by their geographical position, the Ionians were
always extremely vulnerable to attack and conquest by
vastly superior forces. This, coupled with the perennial
inability of Greek city-states to combine effectively,
even in the face of immediate and common danger, led to
their reduction, after a brief revolt early in the fifth
century BC and transformation within a couple of generations from centres of major importance into a backwater.
Ionia appears again at the end of the century as a theatre
of war in the final struggle between Athens and Sparta,(11)
and during the early fourth century BC as a pawn in the
shifting diplomatic positions of the Greeks and Persians,
between whom, as masters, there was probably little to
choose. 'Liberation' from the Persians came later in the
century with the invasion of Alexander the Great.

Under what circumstances, one might well ask, did
Greeks come to be occupying so precarious a position in
the Aegean world? The general picture of early migration
is fairly clear. In the wake of the collapse of the
Mycenaean civilisation and subsequent invasion from the
north, a number of Greek migrations eastward across the
Aegean took place, first of Aiolians to north Asia Minor,
then of Ionians to the middle area, and finally Dorians,
who settled in the south.(12) It is the second of these
three migrations which is of principal interest because
it went further inland and, in subsequent centuries, the
Ionians expanded at the expense of their Greek neighbours
to north and south. For example, Smyrna and Phokaia were
absorbed into the Ionic area at an early stage, and, in
the south, Dorian Halikarnassos seems in the archaic and

classical periods to have been in many respects an Ionian
city, albeit with a strong native Karian element. Indeed,
the comparative silence of the Aeolians (apart from
Lesbos) and Dorians in the subsequent history of Asia
Minor (at least until the fourth century BC and the rise
of Rhodes and Halikarnassos) has led to the general
tendency to refer to all the early Greek inhabitants of
West Asia Minor under the name 'Ionian' (a practice which
will *not* be followed here).

Relative chronology for the migrations is easy to
establish, but absolute dating for the Ionian settlement
is more problematic. The major authorities (see above,
p. 10) largely agree in describing the Ionian migration as
a uniform event originating from Athens, which traditionally held out against Dorian invaders. The organisers of
this event and the founders of the various Ionian cities
were sons of the Athenian king Kodros who was of Pylian
descent.(13) The prominence of Athens in the tradition
and the predictably schematic nature of the record have
led to doubts about its validity and especially how far it
reflects the real historical role of Athens in the
migration. Three basic questions initially present themselves: who were the Ionians, when did they occupy the
Asia Minor coast and why?

Herodotos' famous definition of 'Ionian' as a name
which applies to all who originated from Athens and kept
the festival of the Apatouria(14) begs a number of
questions, not least the degree to which he and the fifth-
century Athenians were projecting into the past their
position as champion and mother-city of the Ionians.(15)
Despite considerable scepticism in the past,(16) modern
research has largely vindicated the ancient traditions in
so far as they give prominence to Athens in the migration.
Observations of common essentials of calendar, cult and
tribal system(17) have very recently been strengthened by
evidence from archaeology, which shows the very close
dependence stylistically of the sub-Mycenaean and Protogeometric pottery of Ionia on Athens, as opposed to the
more adventurous Dodecanese.(18) The history of the
migration settlement itself is another question. Archaeology has revealed small sites which clearly failed to
achieve sufficient importance to be included in the
canonical twelve cities of the Ionian league.(19) It
might well be that foundation by a son of Kodros and even
participation in a single act of colonisation was an
honour bestowed retrospectively on those cities whose
later status justified their inclusion in the Ionian
league.(20)

The question of the racial identity of the migrants

is not of major importance. Quite apart from the obscurity of Herodotos' references to Ionians in the Peloponnese
before the migrations and the controversial question of
the date of the development of the Ionic dialect,(21)
Herodotos himself makes it clear that an Ionian claim of
racial purity would be absurd since 'not the least part of
them were Abantes from Euboia...and mingled with them
Minyans from Orchomenos, Kadmeians, Dryopians, Phokians
separated off from the parent race, Molossians, Pelasgian
Arkadians, Dorians from Epidauros and many other peoples
all mixed in.'(22)

The second question has proved the most controversial:
when did the Ionians occupy the Asia Minor coast? Once
again, the most recent archaeological finds have tended to
rescue the ancient traditions from the scepticism of
previous generations. At Miletos and Old Smyrna a
distinct sub-Mycenaean layer in the stratification of the
sites is clear evidence of new foundation which probably
dates back to the eleventh century BC.(23) On the
question of whether the Greeks had occupied the area
during the Mycenaean period, doubt exists. It has been
suggested that Greek settlement of Asia Minor was an
achievement of the Mycenaean period,(24) but there is no
evidence to suppose that the presence of Mycenaean pottery
in Asia Minor indicates more than a trading connection.(25)
If the reference to a place called Milawata in the
fourteenth-century BC Hittite archives is to Miletos (and
this remains a matter of dispute) then clearly it was
within the sphere of Achaian influence, since the ruler of
the Achaians is mentioned as its overlord.(26) But
against Greek settlement before the migrations we have the
historical tradition and the absence from the Ionic epic
poet Homer of any reference to the presence of Greeks in
Bronze Age Asia Minor; on the contrary, Miletos, the only
place on the Ionian coast mentioned by Homer, is inhabited
not by Greeks but by native Karians. Admittedly, Homer
maintains a similar silence with regard to the Hittites,
and we are aware that the poet is only trying to reproduce,
as far as he can, the conditions of pre-migration Greece.
Yet, at the very least, the unanimous silence of the
literary tradition proves that the Greeks themselves were
not conscious of any cultural continuity, which itself
concedes the major point. On the other hand, the raising
of dates for the earliest migration to Ionia *after* the
fall of the Mycenaean civilisation, as a result of
archaeological excavation, is a matter of great significance, which may prove to have a profound effect upon
hypotheses concerning the Ionian contribution to Greek
culture and especially the size of the Ionian contribution

to the Homeric poems which, it will be maintained
below,(27) has sometimes been underestimated.

The reason why the migration took place is not precisely known. However, like the slightly earlier Aiolian
migration, it was undoubtedly connected with disturbances
brought about by the Dorian Invasions. The prestige
accorded to Athens as the founding city may well reflect
the relative stability of Attica as a refuge for the dispossessed. According to Thukydides, the migration was a
direct result of the resulting overpopulation.(28)

In view of the distinctiveness of later Ionian culture,
it would be useful if one could point to factors which, at
an early stage, affected the direction in which Ionia
subsequently travelled. Unfortunately, this is far from
being the case. It must be admitted that the vital Dark
Age centuries are perhaps even darker for Ionia than for
mainland Greece. The literary migration accounts were
clearly composed under the influence of the mainland
pattern which personalised the downfall of the kingship
and the development of aristocratic government as the
result of feuds and violence between members of the
leading families. In Miletos, about which we have the
fullest information, a tradition was preserved of the
overthrow of the kingship, precipitated by a
dispute between Leodamas and Amphitres, the latter a
member of the royal clan of the Neleids (descendants of
the founder Neleus, son of Kodros), the outcome of which
was the appointment by the people of an 'aisymnetes'
(elective ruler) to restore order.(29) In Ephesos, the
founder Androklos, according to Strabo, led the colonisation of Ionia and consequently the royal seat of the
Ionians was established there.(30) The rivalry of Ephesos
with Miletos for primacy in the tradition (reflecting,
possibly, their conflicting later claims for leadership of
the Ionian league) is the only major discrepancy between
Strabo and Pausanias. Androklos is said to have driven
native inhabitants, Karians and Leleges, from the upper
city of Ephesos, and died in a war helping the citizens of
Priene against the Karians of Mykale.(31) The Samians
under their king Leogoros, son of the founder Prokles,
were also victims of the Ephesian Androklos, who made war
on them for conspiring with the Karians against the
Ionians, expelling them from their island, to which they
returned only after ten years.(32) Prominent in Chios
were Hektor, grandson of the founder, who made war on
native elements in the island(33) and Hippolochos, who was
killed in the course of a squabble with neighbouring
Erythrai over land.(34)

The literary traditions are detailed but, from our

point of view, random and rather uninformative. They give
us no help, for example, in attempting to date external
influences on culture which, in the course of time, led to
Ionia's idiosyncratic contribution to art and literature.
Are these influences to be dated to the early Dark Ages or
do they date from Ionia's later contact with her eastern
neighbours? What of the various pre-Greek inhabitants of
the area whom the Greeks encountered? Karians had
inhabited Miletos, where they united with incoming Cretans
to found the city, an event which archaeology dates to the
seventeenth or sixteenth century BC.(35) The degree to
which Karians are to be associated with the Mycenaean
remains in Asia Minor is doubtful (see above, p.14). At
the time of the Greek migrations, however, Herodotos tells
us that the Ionians of Miletos 'did not bring wives with
them to their settlements, but married Karian women whose
parents they had put to death. For this slaughter these
women made a custom and bound themselves on oath (which
they handed down to their daughters) never to sit at meat
with their husbands nor address them by name, because the
husbands had slain their fathers, their former husbands
and sons, and then taken them as wives.'(36) This degree
of intermarriage, even if not paralleled elsewhere in
Ionia, would imply racial, if not cultural influence on
the Greeks. That this was the case is indicated by the
existence of six tribes in Miletos (two more than the
Attic four) which, though not attested for the earliest
period of settlement, probably implied the necessity of
incorporating not only the non-Ionian leaders and followers of the original migration into the citizen body, but
also the native Anatolian population.(37) This may well
also have been the case at Ephesos where, at a period
possibly before 600 BC, as a further development the six
Ionian tribes were reduced in status and the citizen body
increased from outside.(38) The existence of marked
physical differences between mainland and East Greeks (if
the evidence of their artistic portayal of the human body
is to be believed) might not be merely the result of
physical indulgence(39) or oriental stylistic influence
but also a consequence of racially inherited.bodily
characteristics. The rather odd and unexplained appearance of two Phrygians to bring about the end of the
Milesian royal dispute (see above, p.15)(40) suggests
that the whole episode might belong to a later period,
perhaps the eighth century BC when the Ionians began to
have definite links with the interior of Asia Minor,
although certainty is impossible. We may conclude by
pointing out the almost complete absence of any chronological framework, even the haziest, for the above events.

Furthermore the Ionians, while undoubtedly influenced by
native inhabitants, were entering what might be termed a
political and cultural vacuum caused by the major
destruction and dispersal of the Bronze Age civilisations
of Asia Minor. A marked absence of powerful or culturally
sophisticated neighbours is apparent. The archaeological
evidence, such as it is,(41) suggests that the early
Ionian cities, at the beginning of their development, were
to be regarded more as provincial followers of Athens than
assimilators of native ideas.

It is impossible to say precisely when the twelve cities
became a formally organised federation (in a sense this
never happened). The loose federation known as the Ionian
league was probably religious in origin and had its head-
quarters on Mount Mykale, north of Miletos, where there
was a sanctuary to Poseidon Helikonios. There is late
evidence for the early destruction of a thirteenth member,
the city of Melie, to whom the site of the Panionion
belonged, 'because of the arrogance of her citizens', and
the redistribution of her territory.(42) It has commonly
been supposed that the destruction of Melie marked the
beginning of the league proper, although this view is not
universal.(43) The site of the Panionion has been discovered and investigated, but unfortunately, with the
exception of an archaic altar, all evidence as to its use
and function dates to a period when the festival was being
revived after Persian domination.(44) The first evidence
we have that the league was functioning politically comes
only from the time of the Persian conquest of Ionia, when
a meeting was held at the Panionion to decide what to do,
at which the Milesians were conspicuous by their absence,
having made their own terms with Cyrus, the Persian king.
(45) The evidence suggests that, until the Ionian Revolt
in 499 BC, the league was a fairly loose federation which
accomplished little more than *ad hoc* proposals at times of
crisis. Moreover, proposals for joint action like those of
Bias of Priene or Thales of Miletos made, apparently, at
these meetings, were the inspiration of remarkable individuals rather than the expression of a general desire.
Even during the Revolt, at which time we may suppose co-
operation never to have been greater, little is heard of
Ephesos or Kolophon, and the former may have defected to
Persia quite early on. (The state of the league during
the Revolt, and the probable motivation for the Ionian
Revolt will be briefly discussed below, pp. 32-4.)

The character of each city was distinctive and resulted
in radical differences of direction in later periods.
Miletos, generally regarded as the earliest foundation,
and in the sixth century BC the most important of the

Ionian cities, lay on a peninsula on the southern shore of
the Gulf of Latmos. The original settlement was made on a
hill, Kalabaktepe, to the south of the archaic city.
Miletos was the southernmost of the three major cities
commanding the mouths of the main rivers flowing eastward
(the other two being Ephesos and Smyrna, the latter
originally an Aeolic city and only later admitted to the
league). Miletos on the Maiander, unlike the other two,
was protected from the hinterland of Asia Minor by
mountains. This comparative isolation, coupled with the
absence of room for much territorial expansion, gave
Miletos its character as a sea-going, trading and colonising city. Its comparative inaccessibility, too, enabled
the city to survive successive attacks by powerful eastern
armies, while its northern neighbours succumbed. It is
significant that the fall of Miletos in 494 BC marked not
only the success of the Persian repression of the Ionian
Revolt but also the end of Ionia as an independent entity.
Its power and the reputation of its citizens is perhaps
indicated by the rather back-handed compliment bestowed on
it (first found in Anakreon, the lyric poet attached to
the court of Polykrates, tyrant of Samos after an
unsuccessful war with the latter over Priene during the
later sixth century BC): παλαὶ ποτ᾽ ἦσαν ἄλκιμοι Μιλήσιοι
(once, long ago, the Milesians were powerful), a phrase
which became proverbial for indicating faded glory.(46)
In the classical period, Miletos was famous for its
furniture, the quality of its wool and a dye made from a
purple found on the Karian coast.(47) Culturally, it was
the centre of the philosophic and scientific tradition
which gave Ionia its ancient fame and which probably
received great stimulus from the city's overseas connections. The city produced little poetry, as far as the
extant evidence allows us to judge; the few fragments of
the mid-sixth-century elegist Phokylides do not constitute
evidence of an exceptionally lively tradition.(48) Artistically, Miletos is famous for the series of seated
sculptures that lined the Sacred Way leading from the city
to its oracular shrine and temple at Didyma, to the south
(see below, Chapter 3, p.50). Didyma was the site of a
massive temple in the sixth century (two others were at
Ephesos and Samos) served by priests known as the
Branchidai (after an eponymous ancestor). The sanctuary of
Apollo and the oracle were probably much older than the
Ionian migration and the name of a Greek god was imported
and attached to a native cult, probably Karian, the
influence of which, no doubt, persisted in later times.(49)
The temple received the offering by the Pharaoh Necho of
his battle dress in which he won a victory at Megiddo in

the late seventh century BC, from which period an early
stoa has been discovered.(50)   The temple was sacked along
with Miletos in 494 BC, followed by the flight of medising
priests to Sogdiana.(51)

Ephesos, on the river Kayster represents a major contrast to Miletos.   The city commanded the extensive
territory of the Kolophonian plain to the north; lacking
the natural protection of Miletos and lying close to the
Lydian capital of Sardis, Ephesos tended to look eastward
from an early stage and by the sixth century BC (and
undoubtedly far earlier) had close associations with Lydia
both in population and religious cult.   In the late
seventh century, the tyrant Melas was the son-in-law of
Alyattes, ruler of Lydia, and this close association was
continued after Croesus' attack and subjugation of the
city.(52)   Croesus later helped in the building of the
sixth-century Artemision, Ephesos' large Ionic temple, and
dedicated the majority of the pillars, as Herodotos and
the inscriptions on the column bases (which can be seen in
the British Museum) tell us.(53)   The cult of Artemis (St.
Paul's 'Diana of the Ephesians') was thought to be even
more ancient than that of Didyma, and cultivated by the
pre-Ionian native inhabitants.(54)   Later the shrine had
close Lydian connections, as cult objects carried by a
priest and priestess, fashioned as ivories, tell us.   In
particular priestly worship in Ephesos appears to have
been connected with a bee cult which had strong Anatolian
connections.(55)   The Lydian influence in the city during
the sixth century is perhaps illustrated by the satiric
poet Hipponax, whose language contains many words of
Lydian origin.(56)   Ephesos took no part in the colonial
expansion of Ionia in the late seventh and sixth centuries
BC.   Moreover, Herodotos also informs us that Ephesos and
its neighbour Kolophon were excluded from the common
festival of the Apatouria, 'by reason', he adds cryptic-
ally, 'of a certain deed of blood'.(57)

The two offshore islands, Samos and Chios, were
strategically much less vulnerable than their mainland
neighbours, and always provided a large part of the naval
force of Ionia.   Samos' position on a trade route between
Greece and the Levant gave the island an early prominence
reflected in a number of colonies planted well before the
main Ionian wave of colonisation.   Samian prosperity can
also be detected in the quantity and quality of Geometric
pottery discovered in the Heraion, itself one of the most
important sanctuaries of the Greek world, containing the
remains of what may be the earliest Greek temple.(58)   In
this particular case the absence of a break in Bronze Age -
Dark Age cult practice has received archaeological

support.(59) Politically, there is evidence that the downfall of a tyranny in c. 600 BC led to an oligarchy of
aristocratic landowners, the Geomoroi. In the latter part
of the century a tyrant, Polykrates, dominated Ionia with
the aid of a powerful navy. Herodotos, in his lengthy
account of Polykrates, mentions what he regards as three
of the greatest building and engineering feats of the
Greek world, the famous tunnel and pipeline through a
mountain of limestone rock nearly 1,000 ft long, an artificial harbour and the Heraion itself.(60) Samos was an
important artistic centre in the archaic period, particularly in the field of sculpture and bronze-casting (see
further below, Chapter 3). Asios, a poet of archaic Samos,
in lines preserved by Athenaios,(61) describes Samian
nobles attending the Heraion, and gives us a rare glimpse
of a colourful and luxurious world:

οἱ δ' αὔτως φοίτεσκον ὅπως πλοκάμους κτενίσαιντο
εἰς Ἥρας τέμενος, πεπυκασμένοι εἵμασι καλοῖς,
χιονέοισι χιτῶσι πέδον χθονὸς εὐρέος εἶχον·
χρύσειαι δὲ κορύμβαι ἐπ' αὐτῶν τέττιγες ὣς·
χαῖται δ' ἠωρεῦντ' ἀνέμῳ χρυσέοις ἐνὶ δεσμοῖς,
δαιδάλεοι δὲ χλιδῶνες ἄρ' ἀμφὶ βραχίοσιν ἦσαν.

(And they, just so, used to frequent the precinct of
Hera whenever they had combed their locks, swathed in
beautiful robes, and sweeping the floor of wide earth
with their snow-white tunics; and golden hair-brooches
surmounted them, like grasshoppers; their flowing
tresses, held by golden bands, swayed about in the
breeze, and intricately decorated bracelets encircled
their arms.)(62)

    Chios, Samos' northern island neighbour, is less well
known in its earlier history, despite its considerable
wealth derived from trade in wine and slaves. The internal
political development of the island, however, is known in
limited but for this period unexpectedly detailed fashion
through the discovery of an inscription in the southern
part of the island at Tholopotami. Originally dated
c. 600 BC but now recently lowered with greater probability
to mid-century, this inscription is unique in archaic
Ionia in the information it provides concerning the working
of what appears to be an advanced form of government, the
notable feature of which is the reference to a βουλὴ
δημοσίη (citizens' council), to which those sentenced by a
magistrate may appeal; the council appears to be elective,
meets regularly and has considerable powers. Furthermore
the existence of δήμαρχοι (chief citizens) who function

alongside the traditional aristocratic kings, suggests
considerable modification of the aristocratic governing
procedure, for which we have no direct evidence elsewhere
in Ionia.(63) Although the constitution (as was not
appreciated earlier)(64) almost definitely postdates that
of Solon, it still reflects an enlightened prosperity
which may be appropriately reflected much later in one of
the rare personal commendations of the later fifth-century
BC historian Thukydides in an epitaph, as it were, upon
the Chians, who had the bad luck to back the wrong side in
the last stages of the Peloponnesian War. 'The Chians
alone of all the peoples I have known, with the exception
of the Lakedaimonians, have succeeded in combining prosperity with prudence, and the greater their city grew, the
more firmly they ordered their government.'(65)

Of the cities of Panionic status that failed to attain
the front rank, Priene, on the north shore of the Maiander,
was uncomfortably close to Miletos and Samos and, in the
archaic period, the victim of territorial disputes. The
later Hellenistic city was a major undertaking on the
Hippodameian plan, but little is known about the archaic
city.(66) The early population contained a strong Theban
element from its foundation and had close connections with
Boiotia in names and cults.(67) Priene seems to have
possessed authority in the league, nevertheless, and owed
her position as administrator of the Panionion for the
league not only to geographical proximity to Mount Mykale
but also to her political acumen, embodied in the statesman Bias, one of the seven wise men, who wins the approval
even of the dismissive Ephesian philosopher Herakleitos
for his saying that 'most men are bad.'(68) In a more
positive vein, two of his successful exploits were a peace
treaty with Alyattes of Lydia and the direction of a
successful defence against Croesus. His advice at the
time of the Persian capture of Lydia, unhappily ignored,
was that the Ionians should abandon Asia Minor, unite and
sail for the western island of Sardinia, 'useful advice',
says Herodotos with a pardonable degree of hindsight,
'which had they followed, they might have been the most
prosperous of the Greeks'.(69)

Kolophon, to the north of Ephesos, traditionally was
occupied early; a later migration settlement under
Andraimon, a Pylian, may have by-passed Athens. A later
arrival from Athens of Ionians under Prometheus and
Damasichthon, said to be the sons of Kodros, sounds rather
like a belated attempt to 'clean up the record'.(70)
Later, citizens from Kolophon were instrumental in the
capture of the Aiolic city of Smyrna. The citizens of
Kolophon possessed, according to Aristotle, extensive

estates before their defeat and near-capture by the
Lydians under Gyges, a fate which was averted by Kolophon's
famous cavalry.(71) The city clearly inclined towards
Ephesos rather than Miletos and shared with the former the
possession of extensive territory. Kolophon went into an
early decline and took no recorded part in the Ionian
Revolt. The city was distinguished in the possession of
an elegiac poet, Mimnermos (on whom see below, Chapter 4)
and a philosopher, Xenophanes. Composing in the sixth
century BC Xenophanes paints a rather unflattering picture
of the Kolophonian aristocracy:

> ἁβροσύνας δὲ μαθόντες ἀνωφελέας παρὰ Λυδῶν,
>   ὄφρα τυραννίης ἦσαν ἄνευ στυγερῆς,
> ἦσαν εἰς ἀγορὴν παναλουργέα φάρε' ἔχοντες,
>   οὐ μείους ὥσπερ χίλιοι εἰς ἐπίπαν,
> αὐχαλέοι, χαίτησιν ἀγάλμενοι εὐπρεπέεσσιν,
>   ἀσκητοῖσ' ὀδμὴν χρίμασι δευόμενοι.

(Having learned useless luxury from the Lydians while
they were free from hateful tyranny, they went into the
assembly wearing purple-dyed cloaks, not less than a
thousand in all, boastful, glorying in their fair-
flowing tresses, soaked in the perfume of artifical
unguents.)(72)

This fragment, from a near-contemporary observer, has
been much used to demonstrate the corrupting effeminacy of
the Ionians and its inevitable political consequences.
However, Xenophanes was writing from a specific moral and
philosophical standpoint in which tyranny was the inevitable price paid for luxury.(73) If we momentarily
disregard the moral slant, Xenophanes' picture, not
unattractive, is reminiscent of Asios on the Samians (see
above, p.20).(74)
Near to Kolophon, towards the coast, lay the oracular
shrine of Klaros, mentioned in the Homeric 'Hymn to the
Delian Apollo'.(75) In the early period it was clearly
less important than Didyma, and there is no record of its
activity before Hellenistic times, apart from a legend
recorded by Strabo.(76) Some archaic finds have been
made, however.(77)
Phokaia was the northernmost city of the league and
originally, as archaeological pottery finds testify,(78)
lay within the Aiolic area of Asia Minor. Unlike Smyrna,
there is no record of its incorporation, although, as with
Kolophon, a reflection of its legitimisation may be the
tradition that Kodrid princes were later brought in to
rule.(79) Its prominence in our sources seems out of all

proportion to its size; this may be explained by the great
naval skill of its citizens which led to pioneering
exploration and trade.   The Phokaians explored the Adriatic
Sea and founded prominent colonies in the far west,
including Massalia (Marseilles) and Tartessos in Spain.(80)
A Phokaian, Euthymenes of Massalia, was reputed to have
explored the west coast of Africa.   Herodotos recounts
with sympathy their heroic decision, at the time of the
Persian capture of Ionia, to abandon their city and sail
to Corsica:

> Harpagos marched against their city and besieged it,
> but he made overtures, and said that he would be satis-
> fied if the Phokaians would demolish one bastion of the
> wall and dedicate one house.   But the Phokaians, very
> angry at the thought of slavery, said they wished to
> deliberate for a day and then give an answer; but while
> they were counselling, Harpagos must, they demanded,
> withdraw his army from the walls.   Harpagos said that
> he knew what they planned to do, but that nevertheless
> he would allow them to deliberate.   While Harpagos
> withdrew his army from the walls, the Phokaians
> launched their fifty-oared ships, placed in them their
> children and women and all movable goods, besides the
> statues from the temples and all things therein
> dedicated apart from bronze or stonework or painting;
> then they themselves embarked and set sail for Chios;
> and the Persians took Phokaia, thus left uninhabited.

Herodotos continues the story, in which the Chians refuse
to give the Phokaians a home near at hand; so they turn
their thoughts to Corsica.   He concludes:

> While making ready for their voyage, they first sailed
> to Phokaia, where they slew the Persian guard to whom
> Harpagos had entrusted the defence of the city; this
> being done, they called down mighty curses on whom-
> soever of themselves should stay behind while the rest
> sailed.   Not only this, but they sank in the sea a mass
> of iron, and swore never to return to Phokaia before
> the iron should reappear.   But while preparing to set
> out, more than half the citizens were taken with a
> longing and a pitiful sorrow for the city and the life
> of their land, and they broke their oath and sailed
> back to Phokaia.(81)

This passage, while giving us a glimpse of the turbulence
and irresolution which were characteristic of small Greek
states, also demonstrates heroism against a mighty empire

which was to be so emphatically displayed in the later
Persian Wars in Greece. Migration westward was not confined to Phokaia, and may account for later decline.

The minor cities also had their part to play. In Teos,
a mixed body of settlers was later joined by Athenians and
Boiotians,(82) and evidence of settlement has been
detected, by a Turkish excavation, from Protogeometric to
Roman times, although little survives from the earliest
period.(83)   Thales of Miletos, the famous philosopher and
scientist, is credited with the proposal that the Ionians
should federate in the face of the Persians, with a common
centre of government at Teos (chosen, perhaps, for its
insignificance).(84) A reputation for letting the world
go by is partly belied by the Teians' decision, like their
northern neighbours, the Phokaians, to migrate to Thrace
'being unable to bear the insolence of the Persians'.(85)
Like the Phokaians also, some of them later returned.
Teos was no mean city, playing some part in trade and
colonisation; its greatest claim to renown was as the
birthplace of the famous sixth-century BC lyric poet,
Anakreon, who later lived in Samos at the court of
Polykrates. Later inscriptional evidence suggests also
that, like the Kolophonians, the Teians possessed substantial landed estates.(86)

Klazomenai, lying on the southern shore of the gulf of
Smyrna, was, from the archaeological record, an early
settlement which later obtained a leader from Kolophon,
thereby, perhaps, securing its entry into the league.(87)
The hoplites of the city distinguished themselves against
Alyattes and the Lydians, but after the Persians conquered
Ionia, or perhaps after the Ionian Revolt, the city was
transferred to an island opposite the mainland site; it
remained throughout the classical period an island city
until a causeway was built by Alexander the Great.(88)

Erythrai, a pastoral community facing the island of
Chios, is chiefly known to history through its internal
political development, recorded by Aristotle and reflected
elsewhere, in which the rulers, the Basilidai, although
governing well, were overthrown through a general reaction
against oligarchical government.(89)

Of the two smallest cities little is known. Myous at
the head of the Latmian gulf owes its place in history
mainly to its status as part of the gift given by the
Persian king to the Athenian statesman, Themistokles, as
his price for defection: 'for bread, Magnesia, for wine,
Lampsakos ... and Myous for his meat'.(90) Lebedos, the
last of the twelve cities, hardly figures. One may
perhaps venture to suppose that the ability of these small
cities to maintain their status in the league amid fierce

competition derived not a little from their traditional
claim to foundation by a son (albeit, in the case of Myous,
a bastard) of Kodros.

Any consideration of Ionia must include Smyrna,
although the city, unlike its northern neighbour, Phokaia,
was a late entry to the league. Originally an Aiolic city,
it was taken by Ionian refugees from Kolophon who, so the
story goes, watched until the inhabitants vacated the city
to celebrate a festival and then proceeded to shut them
out. In an arrangement displaying priorities of a realistic nature, the Ionians arranged to hand over movable
goods, but refused to surrender the city.(91) Excavation
suggests that Ionian Protogeometric became more plentiful
than local monochrome ware in the ninth century, thereby
dating the historical take-over earlier than had previously been supposed.(92) Until the destruction by Alyattes
c. 600 BC Smyrna was a city of major importance. Quite
apart from very early buildings, Smyrna in the seventh
century BC presents a picture of planned urbanisation
with the earliest Greek anticipation of the 'Hippodameian'
gridiron city layout and massive city-walls of remarkably
sophisticated construction.(93) After its capture and
destruction the city practically ceased to exist as such
for 300 years until, in the Hellenistic period, it was
refounded on a new site.(94)

From the foregoing it will be clear that a unified picture
of the earlier Ionian centuries is unattainable.(95)
Externally, the Ionians were clearly engaged in consolid-
ating the migration(96) and marking out their territory in
opposition to the native inhabitants and each other.
Politically, the literary sources, somewhat predictably,
show Ionian development on the mainland Greek pattern,
with the early elimination of the kingship in favour of
aristocratic rule which comprised or included members of
the regal family. From very early on, as in other parts
of the Greek world, the Ionian cities were city-states
(πόλεις), reproducing with remarkable exactitude that
preference for small self-governing communities which gave
Greek civilisation as a whole its distinctive, centrifugal
character, at least until the classical period. The
Ionian cities also suffered all the disadvantages contained in such a situation - internal instability and
continual inter-city strife.

Reliance on the evidence of literary tradition and
pottery styles alone might lead to the conclusion that the
Ionians were content to follow the mainland as provincial
communities. Yet there are some indications of the

future; early urbanisation at Smyrna, leading to the
advanced city complex of the seventh century, suggests
that external pressure and an absence of mainland tradition
may have led to an unusually early civic consolidation.
This is certainly the view of J.M. Cook, who sees the
Ionian city as 'the first certain and unambiguous appar-
ition of the organized Hellenic polis'.(97)   More significant still was the development of the Homeric poems, the
end product of which (c. 750 BC) presupposed a rich oral
tradition in Ionia stretching back for many generations,
and an ethos which must partly derive from the Ionian
cities themselves. Of the Ionian cities contending for
the honour of rearing the greatest Greek poet, Smyrna has,
perhaps, the best claim.(98)

We have already remarked upon the basic difference
between coastal cities like Miletos with limited room for
territorial expansion, which turned early to trade and
colonisation, and inland foundations like Kolophon, whose
dependence on large agricultural estates was reflected in
a more conservative government often, as at Ephesos, with
oriental connections. This absence of common economic
interest may have been one factor in Ionia's later
vulnerability in the face of the enemy, especially the
Persians, whose great success at 'divide and rule' was
later demonstrated so clearly on the Greek mainland.

The Ionians emerge, in the first half of the seventh
century BC, into the somewhat flickering light of the
earliest history. This century saw the end of Ionia's
fortunate isolation from powerful neighbours and the rise
of a threat which was to overshadow the remainder of her
independent existence, conquest by one of the powers which
inhabited the interior of Asia Minor. The relationship of
Ionia to her eastern neighbours was always ambivalent - a
source of wealth, power and artistic inspiration but at
the same time a threat to independence. The attitude of
eastern potentates to the Greeks had a similar character,
genuine philhellenism and intermarriage alternating with
invasion and conquest.

There is some evidence of Ionian contact with the mid-
Anatolian power of Phrygia before this, although trade
links do not appear before the seventh century.(99)   One
of the most significant Phrygian (or Lydian) gifts to
Greece may have been the musical scale and the seven-
string lyre (although the latter may have been an
independent Greek development) associated with the name of
Terpander of Lesbos; this lyre is strikingly illustrated
in a 'dinos' sherd from Old Smyrna of approximately the
same date.(100)   A possible return gift may have been the
Greek alphabet, although recent opinion is that the

alphabet came from north Syria independently to Phrygia and Ionia.(101)   At all events it is likely that the Ionians were among the early recipients of the alphabet, introduced towards the end of the eighth century BC (see further, Chapter 4).

Towards the middle of the seventh century arose the power of Lydia, Ionia's immediate eastern neighbour, which was to dominate her for approximately 100 years. Under a dynastic usurper, Gyges, Ionia was invaded, Kolophon's lower city captured, Smyrna and Miletos attacked. This pressure was continued under Gyges' successors; in the meantime Ionia, in common with her eastern neighbours, suffered from the attack of a northerly tribal people, the Kimmerians, who swept down into Asia Minor, attacked the Ionian cities and created much devastation. By the end of the seventh century BC relations between Lydia and Ionia must have been particularly close. Herodotos' account of the invasions of Alyattes and Milesian strategies against him is highly entertaining and probably reflects that ambivalence in relationship mentioned above:

> In the twelfth year of depredation by burning of the [Ionian] crops by the [Lydian] army, the following event occurred; as soon as the fire had taken hold, it was driven by the wind and set alight the temple of Athene at Assesos and burned it down.... when the army returned to Sardis, Alyattes fell ill.

The Lydian king was compelled by the Delphic oracle to rebuild the temple, and so regained his health. Herodotos makes it clear that Thrasyboulos, tyrant of Miletos at the time, had very good intelligence through his friend Periander, tyrant of Korinth, and could anticipate Alyattes' moves:

> Alyattes, when these things [the Delphic message] had been reported to him, immediately sent a herald to Miletos with the desire of making a truce with Thrasyboulos and the Milesians until the temple could be rebuilt. The herald set off; meanwhile Thrasyboulos, forewarned and anticipating what Alyattes was likely to do, acted as follows; he ordered the Milesians to collect all the grain, his own and private stores, in the agora and, when he gave the signal, to start eating, drinking and having a good time.(102)

As a result of finding the Milesians apparently so prosperous, the Lydian monarch concluded peace. Behind Herodotos' typically personal presentation we can perhaps

detect the inherent strength of Miletos and her comparative imperviousness to land invasion owing to the growing
strength of her navy, and overseas contacts. We also see
the consultation of a Greek oracle by a Lydian monarch (as
Croesus was to do later with much more fateful consequences) as an obvious example of the good relationships
demonstrated in the Ephesian political marriage mentioned
above (p.19).

More concretely, there existed under the foundations of
the Ephesian Artemision a coin deposit - probably the
earliest in the Greek world - to be dated not later than
the first decade of the sixth century BC. Herodotos
informs us that the Lydians were the first to use gold and
silver currency; this can probably be dated to the time of
Gyges, when the mines owned by the Lydian royal family
were first exploited.(103) The existence of the deposit
implies not only close economic co-operation between the
Lydians and Greeks but also a considerably advanced state
of trade in the Ionian cities themselves. It is to the
latter that we must now turn.

Perhaps the most decisive and enduring conclusion of
the modern reassessment of the place of Ionia in Hellenism
is the discovery that, despite geographical proximity to
the east, Ionia lagged behind mainland Greece in exposure
to eastern influence. Mainland Ionia in the early seventh
century BC lay neither at the end of a major caravan route
across Anatolia (as was at one time supposed(104)) nor on
the direct sea route from mainland Greece to the Levant.
This fact is particularly significant (as we shall see,
below, Chapter 3) in the history of Ionian art. At the
same time close trade links (as opposed to casual contact)
between Ionia and the hinterland of Anatolia during the
eighth - early seventh century BC are very hard to
establish. The picture, right up to the middle of the
seventh century, is of comparative isolation and cultural
self-sufficiency.(105)

Yet, from the beginning of the century, gradual
expansion to the south had begun, especially among the
coastal cities. Samos, as its position would indicate
(see above, p.19) led, but by the mid-seventh century
other cities had expanded beyond Rhodes and Cyprus to the
Levant and Egypt. Absence of strong evidence for land
shortage in Ionia and the nature of the area into which the
Ionians initially moved both indicate that trade rather
than colonisation provided the initial impetus at this
stage. During the reign of Psammetichos I of Egypt (664-
610 BC), a sanctuary called the Hellenion was established
at Naukratis in common by Teos, Phokaia and Klazomenai and
other Aiolic and Doric cities; the Milesians (along with

the Aeginetans and the Samians) had their own sanctuaries
also.(106)   The main imports to Ionia were wheat, linen
and, in a way most significant of all, papyrus, which at
this time generally replaced leather as the chief writing
material of the Greek world.   The Ionians also needed to
import metals, of which there was a dearth: tin and bronze
from the far west, iron and copper from Syria and Cyprus
and gold and silver from Lydia.(107)

This movement grew from modest beginnings.   At the same
time, contact with diverse cultures coupled with a sharp
growth in prosperity towards the end of the seventh
century BC laid the foundations for that receptivity to
new ideas which, in the following generations, burst forth
in the truly astonishing *Blütezeit* of the Ionian sixth
century BC when for a few generations it is no exaggeration to say that Ionia led the Hellenic world.

The major external manifestation of this period was the
far-reaching expansion, led by the Milesians, to the north
along the coasts of Thrace and the region of the Propontis,
reaching the Black Sea at the beginning of the sixth
century BC and, during the following fifty years or so,
establishing colonies all around the Black Sea shore,
providing trade links with the north shore of Asia Minor,
the Danube estuary and the extensive wheat-growing area
of South Russia.   The foundation dates of the various
colonies and the picture of economic development which
they presuppose have suffered considerable chronological
revision recently, mainly in a downward direction, as
archaeological evidence has corrected the literary
traditions of Strabo, pseudo-Skymnos and Eusebios, the
three major sources for the colonisation.(108)   Nevertheless, the general picture and the enormous resources
which it presupposed on the part of the Milesians who were
largely responsible for it, can hardly be exaggerated.   In
many cases a trading-post preceded the founding of a
colony;(109) the main imports were fish, wheat and timber.
Yet more extensive sources of metals were found in northern Asia Minor and the region of the Caucasus, for which
the famous Trapezous (later Trebizond) and Phasis at the
eastern end of the Black Sea, were important.   Pliny the
Elder's legendary estimate of ninety colonies planted by
the Milesians alone is undoubtedly too high, but not
altogether a hopeless exaggeration.(110)

Towards the end of the seventh century BC the historical record becomes more coherent for the Greek world in
general and, for Ionia, Herodotos' expansive and leisurely
narrative becomes more connected.   Internally, the
evidence we have is fullest for Miletos where, c. 630 BC,
a tyranny arose (a universal phase in the political

development of the Ionian, as of the Greek world generally), in this case reflecting changes in society from land
ownership to mercantile interests and not, as in Solonian
Athens, under pressure from a poor and dispossessed
peasantry, for which movement there is no clear evidence.
(111) Moreover, as Aristotle informs us, the tyranny
arose somewhat differently in Miletos, namely from pro-
longation of the chief magistracy, the 'prytaneia', which
may have reflected the power given to the 'aisymnetes' at
the time of the fall of the kingship (see above, p. 15).
We have already met one Milesian tyrant, Thrasyboulos, who
was ruthless and effective in the defence of the city
against Lydia (see above, p. 27). His friendship with
Periander, tyrant of Korinth, is immortalised in the
advice given by Thrasyboulos to the latter when he sent a
messenger to Miletos to ask Thrasyboulos how to maintain
power. Thrasyboulos took the messenger into a cornfield
and decapitated any stalk which stood out above the rest
and told the messenger to return to Periander and tell him
what he had seen.(112) This friendship implied also
coinciding interests in the far west; it is known that
Miletos had particularly close trading relations with the
south Italian town of Sybaris, at the destruction of
which, according to Herodotos, 'the whole male population
of Miletos from the youths upwards, had shaved their heads
and exhibited great grief.'(113)

In contrast, at Erythrai, for example, the regal family,
the Basilidai, survived long in power. In Ephesos, the
Androklids were overthrown c. 600 BC by a tyrant called
Pythagoras whose successors had close family ties with
Lydia (see above, p. 19). However, the connection of
tyranny with eastern support was not invariable; Pindaros,
a later tyrant of Ephesos, was nephew of the Lydian king
Croesus, although head of a patriotic party; in the
general submission to Lydia, Pindaros' banishment was part
of Ephesos' peace terms.(114) At Samos, on the other hand,
more extensive land for cultivation was reflected in the
power of the aristocratic landowners, the Geomoroi, who
overthrew a tyrant named Demoteles, only to succumb themselves, in the later sixth century, to the more powerful
and effective Polykrates.

The political situation which followed the deposition
of tyrants is again most clearly recorded for Miletos.
After Thrasyboulos, power was held by a party led by Thoas
and Damasenor. Their removal led to particularly ruthless
and bloody civil strife between ἡ πλουτίς and χειρομάχα
(for which we may accept the gloss of Herakleides of
Pontos: 'people of property' and the 'dêmos'(115)). If we
are to believe Athenaios, revolting atrocities were

committed on both sides:

> At first the people prevailed and, after they had
> thrown the rich out, they assembled even the children
> of the fugitives on the threshing-floors, had oxen
> trample on them and destroyed them in the most terrible
> manner. Thereupon the rich, again getting control,
> tarred and burned to death all whom they could get hold
> of, along with their children.(116)

Such atrocities are all too familiar in the vicious
struggles of the early 'polis', and, as the above episode
illustrates, the Ionians were no exception. Herodotos
tells us that this civil strife, which lasted about sixty
years and weakened the state considerably, was concluded
by men from the island of Paros who were invited to
arbitrate and gave power to those whose estates were well
cultivated, which probably represented a return to government by a landowning oligarchy.(117) This government
cannot long have outlasted the Persian conquest of Ionia,
although it is impossible to estimate how far the Persians
interfered in internal political arrangements initially,
especially in Miletos, which received preferential treatment. There is little more one can make of the Milesian
political situation, however unsatisfactory from a historical point of view our evidence is; Phokylides, an elegiac
poet of mid-sixth-century Miletos, was no Solon, and
fragmentary statements emphasising the importance of
choosing the 'middle way' lack any explicit reference to
events(118) and appear to echo the gnomic clichés of early
elegy. This is particularly unfortunate in view of the
fact that the period of strife coincides almost exactly
with the lifetime of the greatest of the Milesian thinkers
and the first western philosopher, Anaximander, whose
pronouncements on the nature of the universe, the first of
their kind ever to be made, reflect very definite legal
and political preconceptions.(119)

Externally, the eastern grip on the Ionians grew
tighter with the reign of Croesus, son of Alyattes. He
made war on the cities individually and subdued them,
forcing them to pay tribute. Herodotos is not informative
about the extent of the Lydian control, beyond stating
categorically that before Croesus' reign all Greeks had
been free.(120) Certainly Croesus' overlordship did not
extend to direct political interference; moreover Croesus
was a philhellene who gave rich presents to the oracular
shrines at Delphi and Branchidai, among others.(121) His
presentation to Ephesos has already been mentioned (above,
p. 19). He also made friends with the Ionian islanders,

abandoning his intention of attacking them, according to
Herodotos, from lack of a sufficient navy.

Croesus' downfall, enthrallingly if improbably
recounted by Herodotos as an example of the fatal consequences of excessive pride and overconfident interpretation of an ambiguous oracle,(122) removed Lydia from the
scene and exposed Ionia to the much less congenial power
of the Persian empire under Cyrus the Great. Soon after
the fall of the Lydian capital Sardis in 546 BC the king
turned his attention to the conquest of Ionia, informing
the various cities that they should have 'danced to his
tune' earlier, and that it was too late for deputations.
(123) A meeting was called at the Panionion (the first
recorded, see above, p.17) where resistance to the
Persians was decided upon; the Milesians were absent,
having made their own, more favourable, terms with Cyrus,
possibly because of their long record of resistance to
Lydia.(124) The Persian general, Harpagos, had little
difficulty in subduing the Ionian cities, many of them
showing much less aversion to their conquerors than the
heroic Phokaians (see above, pp. 22-4). The Milesian
oracle demonstrated its partisanship by ordering the
surrender to the Persians of a renegade Lydian called
Paktyes whom Cyrus had entrusted with Lydian treasure,
although Paktyes was a suppliant at Kyme.(125)

With the Persian conquest, Ionia enters the last phase of
her early existence. Her loss of freedom may not
initially have been great in either political or economic
terms. There is certainly no sudden falling-off; on the
contrary, the absence of competitors may have resulted in
a positive gain for some cities. The gradual predominance
of Athenian pottery at Al Mina in the Levant and Naukratis
in Egypt does not necessarily imply a corresponding
Athenian presence and Boardman conjectures that most of
the trade was still run by East Greeks.(126) Considerable
prosperity is presupposed by the remarkable architectural
and sculptural achievements of the second half of the
century, especially at Samos which was not yet subject to
Persia, where Polykrates, its tyrant, built up a
formidable navy and undertook a number of large projects
at home.(127)

Politically, the Persians seem to have been, initially
at least, tolerant masters, interfering only sporadically
with the internal political affairs of the Ionian cities.
Yet this must, at some time, have changed. By the time of
the Persian king Dareios' expedition against Skythia
(c. 513 BC) we know from Herodotos that the Ionian cities

were ruled by pro-Persian tyrants, who guarded the Persians' vital passage across the Bosphorus.(128) The economic evidence is less clear. There was an undoubted increase in the activity of mainland Greece, especially Athens, in areas which had hitherto been largely Ionian, for example the Black Sea, and it is probable that the removal of Sybaris in 510 BC, and the Milesians' great grief at this, testifies to the loss of valuable western trade. The Persians imposed a heavy tribute (400 talents of silver to be paid by the Ionians, Magnesians in Asia, the Aiolians, Karians, Lykians, Milyans and Pamphylians(129)) which could have caused great hardship, especially if payments had to be maintained by a population reduced in number by frequent mass emigration, as at Teos and Phokaia (see above, pp. 22-4). Against all this we have to consider Herodotos' assertion that, at the beginning of the Ionian Revolt, Miletos had reached the peak of its prosperity; the size of the fleet produced at the final battle of the Ionian Revolt (Herodotos estimates 353 ships), even if seen as a desperate massing of forces, compares favourably with any mainland Greek force before 480 BC.(130)

Lack of firm evidence here is all the more unfortunate in view of Herodotos' presentation of the Ionian Revolt of 499-494 BC. It is his clear intention to depict the abortive struggle as a hopeless and discreditable manoeuvre inspired solely by the personal and highly disreputable ambitions of one or two adventurers, chiefly Histiaios, tyrant of Miletos, and his son-in-law Aristagoras. Moreover, Herodotos has a dramatic purpose in depicting the revolt as the ἀρχὴ κακῶν (beginning of misfortune) for the Greek world in general - an unfortunate escapade in which Athens got herself regretably involved. In taking this line he fails to consider the obvious readiness of the Ionians to revolt and their achievement in sustaining such action against a mighty empire for five years. There must have been great pressure on them to motivate the throwing-off of a yoke which they had borne for almost fifty years. Herodotos remarks cynically that Aristagoras, short of money and rebelling for want of a better solution, 'made a pretence of abdicating his own position in favour of democratic government (ἰσονομίη) and subsequently did likewise in the rest of Ionia, expelling the tyrants.'(131) Yet, whatever Aristagoras' motives really were (and these are beyond recovery)(132) Herodotos does not conceal the fact that the system of tyrants under the local satrapy, initially not resented unduly, was, two generations after Cyrus' conquest of Ionia, an anachronism in the Hellenic world generally, where tyranny had long been in retreat.

Herodotos' account of the revolt is unsatisfactory in other ways. Possibly as a result of his sources (see above, pp. 10ff.) as well as his bias as a Dorian from neighbouring Halikarnassos,(133) his account lacks continuity. Between the account of the initial adventures of his villains, Histiaios and Aristagoras, and the final battle of Lade in 494 BC Herodotos fills in only three major events: the burning of Sardis by the Athenians (persuaded to help by Aristogoras) and the Eretrians, a campaign in Cyprus and, towards the end, desperate fighting in the Karian mountains. It is not surprising that historians experience trouble in filling the quite considerable period of time with events.(134)

There is evidence that the revolt was serious and organised. Military strategy was co-ordinated by generals specially appointed and the league issued a common silver coinage.(135) Yet is is probable that the length of the resistance can only be explained in terms of the time it took the Persians to concentrate their forces. At the battle of Lade (the small island guarding the entrance to Miletos) the enemy was able to concentrate its four great naval powers, Phoenicia, Egypt, Cilicia and Cyprus against the largest force the Ionians could muster. Herodotos' account of the battle shows the Ionians in no better light than his treatment of the previous happenings. After a refusal to serve under a Phokaian admiral, Dionysios, because his city was providing only three ships and they were unused to hard work, the Ionians, especially the Samians (whom Herodotos is at pains to excuse) proved unable to stand together in the face of tempting individual offers from the enemy.(136)

In the summer of 494 BC, following defeat in the sea-battle (in which some contingents, notably the Chians, had fought bravely) Miletos was captured and enslaved by the Persians after a short siege. Herodotos doubtless exaggerates when he states that the city was emptied of its inhabitants;(137) later, when the Greeks 'liberated' Ionia at the battle of Mykale in 479 BC, there were certainly enough Milesians available to desert their masters and play a decisive part in the battle.(138) On the other hand, in the city itself, a burnt layer almost everywhere suggests extensive destruction and, significantly perhaps, the seaport quarter was not rebuilt after the collapse.(139) Milesian survivors were transported to Ampe on the Persian Gulf,(140) and the Persians assigned the interior parts of Miletos' territory to the Karians of nearby Pedasos.(141)

Whatever the facts of the destruction, in retrospect it

was the fall of Miletos which symbolised for Greece not only a barbarian triumph but the decisive end for the Ionians themselves. At the same time the subsequent decades saw the passing of the archaic cultural world, in which the Ionians had shared and made their distinctive contribution, into the wider and more homogeneous milieu of classical Greece.

3 The character of Ionian art

In any attempt to isolate the distinctive qualities of
Ionian culture, art forms an obvious point of departure.
For the modern investigator the remains of Ionian vase-
painting, architecture and sculpture - scanty in comparison
with the surviving objects from mainland Greece - present
the most direct and immediate contact with the values and
spirit of the Ionians themselves. Within the limitations
imposed by contemporary conventions and techniques, Ionian
art speaks for itself in a way which cuts through the
accretions of later interpretation and prejudice.

Taken as a whole, Ionian art occupies a somewhat
ambivalent position in the general history of Greek art.
A casual acquaintance with the remains is enough to
convince one that they differ in certain important
respects from the art of other parts of the Greek world.
Ionia has traditionally been regarded as pursuing an
idiosyncratic and frequently provincial path in comparison
with the more sophisticated, accomplished and innovatory
mainland of Greece. Yet a considerable debt to Ionia is
owed by classical Greek art. To mention briefly only two
obvious examples: the classical Athenian temple undoubtedly owes a great deal of its conception, not to mention
detailed decoration and proportions, to the large-scale
Ionian temples (regrettably not surviving) of the sixth
century BC at Ephesos, Samos and Miletos; second, the mid-
sixth century development in Ionia of the large-scale
clothed female figure know as the 'kore' (the maiden)
contributed much, in spirit and conception as well as
style of dress, to the more numerous and illustrious
examples found on the Athenian Acropolis.

Failure to give these influences their due weight in
some recent studies(1) reflects the difficulties involved
in any assessment of the position. Chief among these is
the absence of substantial remains for purposes of

comparison. In the case of Athens, a large quantity of
statuary and pottery of the archaic period was stored away
in pits on the Acropolis when it was destroyed by the
Persians in 480 BC. Ionia had no such luck; the
depredations of successive invaders, the neglect of time
and the limited opportunity for modern excavation until
quite recently has resulted in a comparatively small
amount of material being available. This is especially
true of the deepest layers; a full history of Ionian
Geometric pottery remains to be written.(2) In the case
of later periods, especially the mid-sixth century,
Ionia's acknowledged zenith, the question arises whether
such masterpieces as, for example, the Louvre 'Bird Nester'
kylix (see below, p. 44) or the 'Cheramyes Hera' from
the Samian Heraion (also in the Louvre; see below, p. 49)
are unique in their quality or merely the survivors of
a more substantial tradition. Modern scholarship has
usually inclined to the former conclusion.(3)

Another factor of importance is the Ionian 'diaspora';
a number of important artistic centres owed a great deal
to Ionian influence or even immigrant Ionian craftsmen,
for example Etruria, Egypt, Persia, Skythia and even
Athens. The case of Etruria is particularly crucial; can
one claim as Ionian the series of famous and outstanding
Black Figure vases produced at Caere in Etruria, which
reflect Ionian styles of painting but exceed the
indigenous product in quality?(4)

This leads to a further, fundamental question - the
definition of 'Ionian' in an artistic context. In the
archaic period Ionia proper is usually seen as part of the
larger area of eastern Greece, which includes the Cycladic
islands, Rhodes, Cyprus and the northern part of Asia
Minor, including Lesbos. For much of the time Ionia was
not the centre of the major developments in East Greek
art; in the Geometric and early Orientalising period the
dominant centre appears to have been Rhodes, and it was
only in the sixth century BC that the mainland cities of
Ionia came into their own, and, for a short time,
flourished. Yet, while Ionia obviously cannot be considered in isolation from her neighbours, Greek and
'barbarian', the basic conception of Ionian art does (it
will here be argued) differ enough from others to justify
separate treatment.

All these problems are, however, subordinate to one
which runs right through the present study - that is, the
question of historical perspective. Ionian art has never
entirely escaped censure as 'provincial' in its failure to
conform to the standards of craftsmanship and design
accepted in the mainland Greek world. Artistically the

Ionians appear to have lagged behind their neighbours and
to have remained indifferent to some of the major artistic
developments pioneered by Korinth and Athens during the
seventh century BC, in particular the development of the
portrayal of the human figure in pottery decoration and
the consequent introduction of the pictorial narrative of
traditional scenes and stories from epic and other sources,
literary and oral. In sculpture, the generalised design
and soft contours given to the human body can be contrasted
with the greater feeling for the anatomical structure of
the human figure further west. In architecture the comparison of the sixth-century Ionian temples with the more
perfect Athenian temples, whose virtuosity was subordinated
to a concern for overall proportion and balance, has often
been made, to the disadvantage of the former. It is
arguable that in all three cases a value judgment presupposes an arbitrary viewpoint imposed by the more
obvious and striking qualities of mainland, and especially
Athenian, art. The Athenians, in art as in other things,
were swift to assimilate and transform external influences,
to the extent that the debt often remained unacknowledged,
or even unperceived, by the beneficiaries.

It is perhaps more profitable to see Ionian art not
merely as inferior Greek workmanship but as the product of
the synthesis of Greek values and influences of a different
kind. A tendency to repeat decorative patterns, common in
oriental art, is combined in Ionian vase-painting, for
example, with a feel for abstract design and the capacity
for lively observation typical of the Greeks. In sculpture
an apparent assimilation of many of the static, hieratic
conventions and styles of the east overlies an intellectual
rigour and directness, not to mention humour, which has
always been associated with Hellenic culture. It is this
pull of opposing values, varying in strength and tendency
at different periods and with different media, which gives
Ionian art its distinctive stamp.(5) In comparison with
the mainland, the geographical proximity of Ionia to
central Anatolia, the Levant and Egypt led to an oriental
influence which, though, paradoxically, later assimilated
than the mainland influence, was much more pronounced when
it came. Yet this influence never overwhelmed the Ionians,
nor, at the other extreme, did they merely introduce
oriental elements as such. Commenting on assimilation of
the artistic heritage of the older civilisations by the
Greeks generally, Boardman observes that the contribution
of the Near East and Egypt 'was made, not by the imposition
of their arts and ideals, but...by the deliberate and dis-
criminate choice of the Greeks themselves.'(6) This
observation applies a *fortiori* to the Ionians; faced with

possibly greater cultural pressure than their fellows
across the Aegean, they nevertheless developed an idiom
which, superficially alien, was nevertheless their own.

Ancient art critics sensed that Ionian art had its own
particular character. Vitruvius, the Roman writer on
architecture at the time of Augustus, described the
invention of the Ionic column as an attempt to imitate the
slender, graceful appearance of a woman, as opposed to the
more manly Doric which was strong and unadorned.(7) This
descriptive analogy clearly has significance beyond
Vitruvius' immediate context; G.M.A. Richter sharply distinguishes the heavier, softer eastern types of 'kouros'
(unadorned male figure, counterpart to the 'kore') from the
more slender, sturdier western types.(8) In the latter the
interest in anatomical structure and detail is much greater
than in the former, which are open to the charge of crudity
and shapelessness. Richter considers this to be in part a
consequence of the physical difference between the races;
the reputed softness of the Ionians and the physical manifestations of this in plump bodies and effeminate dress is
satirised by Hermippos, quoted by Athenaios, in the case of
the inhabitants of Abydos, who were Milesian colonists:

χαῖρ᾽, ὦ διαπόντιον
στράτευμα, τί πράττομεν·
τὰ μὲν πρὸς ὄψιν μαλακῶς
ἔχειν ἀπὸ σώματος,
κόμῃ τε νεανικῇ
σφρίγει τε βραχιόνων.
ἤσθου τὸν Ἀβυδόθ᾽ ὡς
ἀνὴρ γεγένηται;

(Hail, army from across the sea, how goes it? Judging
from appearances, you're soft of body, with youthful
tresses and plumpness of arms. Have you ever noticed
a native of Abydos showing himself as a man?)(9)

Hermippos reflects a standard Greek prejudice that the
Ionians were fat because of over-indulgence, in which
there may have been some substance.(10) Yet it seems more
likely that Ionian sculptural convention reflects not so
much racial characteristics (which would hardly have been
worthy of imitation, or, if they were, have been so
marked) as Ionian lack of interest in the anatomical
details of the body as such and far greater concern with
exploring the possibilities of abstract design, mass and
decorative pattern (compare Plates 10 and 11).

The above general considerations are intended to aid the
more detailed historical picture which follows. As a
brief preliminary, three main characteristics of Ionian
art as a whole may be listed - characteristics which, it
is hoped, will be adequately illustrated below: first, a
concern with the cumulative effect of decorative patterns
for their own sake - an element strongly influenced by
eastern conventions but, in Ionia, modified and strengthened by the second element, a definite feeling for
abstract form, line and mass. The final characteristic -
the most important and pervasive - is a sense of liveliness, urbanity, humour and intelligence - qualities which
one scholar, G.M.A. Hanfmann, has explicitly related to an
Ionian 'eager inquisitive attitude to life' which can be
detected in much sixth-century Ionian sculpture.(11) He
concludes: 'Altogether, the Ionian works of the late
archaic period constitute a triumphant assertion of the
Ionian character; these men and women seem to proclaim by
their exotic beauty and quickened liveliness that they are
"like only unto themselves" and different from all other
Greeks.'(12) The author is here talking about the later
sixth-century BC heads of temple-maidens from Didyma (see
below, p. 52) and the argument that these qualities only
came later to maturity in Ionia is fundamental to his
thesis. Yet it is possible to see these qualities much
earlier than the late archaic and to argue that something
of the quality which pervades the distinguished masterpieces may be detected in Ionian art as a whole. It is to
this subject we now turn, considering first vase-painting,
then sculpture and finally architecture.

   The beginnings of Ionian vase-painting were not, as
far as we can judge from the limited evidence, auspicious.
The earliest post-Mycenaean remains correspond to the
various phases of the Athenian-inspired Geometric style
and clearly coincide with the earliest period of mainland
Greek settlement in Asia Minor (see chapter 2, pp. 12-17).
Finds have not been substantial, especially in the earliest
phases, transitional between sub-Mycenaean and Protogeometric.(13) Of the major Ionian cities, only Miletos and
Smyrna have yielded anything like substantial quantities,
so that stylistic comments are somewhat provisional.
However, all finds to date lend further weight to the
established view that Ionian Geometric was much less
ambitious in conception than that of the mainland and
considerably inferior in execution.(14) There is a marked
absence of large-scale composition and a total absence of
the organisation and coherence found in, e.g., Attic
examples. This becomes, in the later stages of the phase,
yet more obvious, if one compares the magnificent Athenian

pots, mostly from the Dipylon cemetery, with the best examples that Ionia can offer.(15)   The close connection of Ionian Geometric with Athens, as opposed to other areas, which show greater independence, has already been noted (see above, chapter 2, p.13).   Yet, technically, the Ionian repertoire of Geometric conventions is much more limited and, on the whole, poorly executed.   More ambitious individual schools arose in Chios and, more notably, Samos, where the Heraion has yielded almost the only attempt at depicting the human figure, in a 'prothesis' (laying out of a dead body).(16)   However, the crudity of the style of this and other attempts at figure drawing makes it impossible to suppose that there was any regular tradition of figure drawing even in the late Geometric period of the early seventh century BC.(17) This early absence of the human figure is a tendency which remains with Ionian vase-painting; it may be thought paradoxical that such a tendency should exist in a culture which was at roughly the same time establishing the fundamentals of what was to become a model for later Greek and European humanism, namely the Homeric view of man (on this see further, chapter 4).

The general impression, therefore, is of provincial imitation, and poor at that.   Yet this is not the only possible interpretation.   What Hanfmann describes as the blurring of the 'inherent strictness and discipline of the Greek Geometric heritage',(18) may owe something to the influence of non-Greek elements in Anatolia.   The monochrome grey 'Bucchero' ware, characteristic of the Aiolic area and found on some Greek sites, akin to similar Phrygian ware, tells us little, but Phrygian vases found at sites such as Boğazköy in mid-Anatolia, decorated in a manner akin to the Greek Geometric, suggest a degree of cultural contact which may have influenced the Ionians; 'barbarisation' may, as Hanfmann also suggests, have had its positive side in giving artists a 'more receptive attitude toward observation of reality'.(19)   In view of the lack of evidence it is important not to exaggerate the likelihood of this possibility; however its very existence serves to illustrate the ambiguity of so much in Ionian art - seen from the mainland as inferior and conservative but also possibly reflecting close contacts with non-Greeks in Asia Minor, for which inscriptional and literary evidence gives some support.(20)

Consequently it is perhaps barely coincidence that the most striking Geometric sherd from Smyrna should be from a 'dinos' illustrating for the first time in Greece the seven-stringed lyre, which became the standard Greek instrument.   The question of whether the Greeks invented the instrument or imported it is controversial. It is, however, significant that tradition ascribes the invention to Terpander of Lesbos who was thought to have obtained the idea from the Lydians.(21)   The design of the sherd is also interesting; the 'imprecision' of the small fragment of hatched triangles on the sherd suggests either care-lessness and lack of ability or a greater sense of freedom and life - a development away from the Geometric conven-tion rather than a debasement of it (see Plate 1).

The 'dinos' sherd comes from the latest stage of the Geometric period in Ionia, the early seventh century BC. The lateness of this date illustrates the backwardness of the Ionians; a Phoenician bronze bowl dated to the late ninth century BC has been found in a tomb in the Kerameikos at Athens and native Greek ivories inspired by Syrian originals have been located in the Dipylon cemetery, dated to the late eighth century BC.(22)   During the first half of the seventh century Athens experienced the full orientalising of her art; Korinth may have been earlier. It was not, however, until c. 650 BC that the Ionians began to move away from a stagnant sub-Geometric. It may seem paradoxical that Ionia, whose proximity to Syria and Phoenicia might be supposed to render her more susceptible to eastern influences, should follow behind the mainland of Greece. One explanation is the stagnation of Ionia in the early seventh century and loss of contact with the mainland, possibly owing to the beginning of pressure from the east; at the same time, contact between the Levant and Greece tended to be by the sea-route which by-passed main-land Ionia (see chapter 2, p. 28); finds at Al Mina, the Phoenician entrepôt in the eastern Mediterranean, show that the earliest Greek interest was from the Cyclades and Euboia in the eighth century BC, whereas indications of an East Greek presence are decidedly later.(23)

After a sub-Geometric of some individuality, revealed chiefly in Rhodian Bird bowls (of a greatly superior quality to mainland Ionic),(24) Ionian orientalising took the form, in the mid-seventh century, of a 'Wild Goat' style - one of the most characteristic of East Greek ceramic products. These vases were probably produced throughout the Ionian world, and notable examples are found from Rhodes itself and as far north as Smyrna.(25)   The main elements of 'Wild Goat' were continuous friezes of animals (goats were predominant, although the lion, boar, dog, hare, sphinx and goose are also found) chasing each other around the body of the pot, which was divided into horizontal zones. The other characteristic was regular floral and abstract decoration, which covered the remain-ing surface area of the pot. Despite the regular nature of

these patterns, 'Wild Goat' does not come from Geometric;
the stimulus for the content and design seems to come from
east Anatolian art: Urartian and Neo-Hittite, possibly at
second hand through the medium of mainland Greek copies.
In the best of these vases, the effect of the running
animals is one of energetic life and observant details;
the decoration is freshly coloured, and, above all, the
carpet-like effect of the repeated decorative patterns
(arguably derived from embroidery design in the east)
against the fresh glaze, gives the surface, as E. Buschor
remarks, a magic quality.(26)   As in most Ionian art, the
details and idea may be eastern, but the conception and
execution is unmistakably Greek (see Plate 1).

    'Wild Goat' has on occasion been overpraised;(27) it
failed to develop, and, looking back with the later
accomplishments of Athenian Black Figure in mind, it
reveals clear limitations, not the least being the failure
to develop incision technique.   Its quality, however,
depends not on human figures or pictorial narrative, in
which the Ionians never felt much interest, but upon the
careful articulation of rich ornamentation for its own
sake and a preoccupation with pattern - qualities which
were destined to appear elsewhere in their art.

    During the sixth century, East Greece continued its
very separate development from the mainland by evolving
distinct mature Black Figure styles.   In the north,
distinctive developments were associated with Chios.
Early in the sixth century Chios developed an individual
Black Figure style known as the Chalice style (the
predominant shape of pot on which examples of this style
are preserved); unusually for Ionia, human figures are
represented in compositions of battles, dances, proces-
sions and even one or two mythological scenes.   Until
recently, Naukratis was considered the main site for this
pottery; but recent excavations on the site of Chios
itself have revealed considerable finds.(28)   In the south,
from Rhodes to Samos, pottery was dominated by 'Fikellura'
(which takes its name from a cemetery in Rhodes in which
some of the earliest examples of this style have been
found.(29)   'Fikellura' was a development from 'Wild Goat'
and was prevalent in the southern part of the East Greek
region from c. 575 BC until the end of the sixth century
BC.   Although never able to compete with Attic, even on
its own territory, 'Fikellura' has features which are
worth noting, especially 'free field' decoration, which
occurs in some examples that are preserved; this style
makes a daring use of space by ignoring the traditional
articulation and zoning of the surface of the pot, and
hence suspending its figures in space, as it were.   A

notable example is an amphora depicting a running man (see
Plate 2).(30)

The most remarkable product of Ionian vase-painting was
the series of cups, of 'Fikellura' type, but painted under
the influence of Attic Black Figure, known as the Ionian
Little Masters. These are very small in number, relatively
isolated, but forming a group which is recognisably Ionian
in character, but outstanding, by any standards, in
quality. Much of the material from which judgment can be
made is fragmentary; yet examples from the Samian Heraion,
Naukratis, Aegina and Italy, give clear evidence of the
qualities we have so far noticed - lively observation of
animals, exquisite detail and a rhythmic handling of
decorative pattern.(31) Pride of place must go to the
'Bird Nester' kylix, arguably the finest product of Ionian
vase-painting.(32) The cup has been considered Attic, but
is now firmly placed in the Ionian category.(33) The
inside of the cup carries the more important design. The
centre of the composition is a man whose function has been
variously interpreted as bird-catching, vine-picking or
grasshopper hunting.(34) The most remarkable feature,
however, is the tree, which rises from its base horizon-
tally on either side of the man towards the edges of the
cup. The remainder of the surface is filled with a
pattern of branches and leaves which droop, willow-like,
from the apex of the tree on either side. In the branches,
one can detect small creatures, a snake, a grasshopper and
a bird returning with food for its young. Detail is
reserved, albeit minutely, rather than incised - in this
it follows the standard East Greek convention (see
Plate 3).

The cup is closely related in style to Fikellura and
shares this style's bold and imaginative use of spatial
relationships, while going yet further away from the
conventional; the man is the centre of the composition,
but his suspension in nothing is deliberately emphasised
by the tree which defies both logic and perspective by
stretching at right angles to the human figure. The
branches, defying gravity, sweep out in ever widening arcs
round the edge of the bowl in four main segments. The
effect, however, is far from chaotic; the central figure
is well balanced by the tree(s), whose branches push out
towards the edges of the cup, to make a clearly articulated composition. While this feeling for balance and
symmetry clearly takes precedence over normal perspective,
there is freedom and diversity, especially in the branches
and leaves, whose springy rhythm and diverse patterning
prevent monotony. The rhythm and execution of the leaves
is continued as an abstract pattern on the outside of the

cup, with leaves of a different kind.

Paradoxically, the general impression is one of vitality and lively observation, detectable not only in the exquisite little animals and insects and the energetic pose of the hunter, but also in the sure sense of line and the curves of the tree and branches. An intellectual experiment with perspective, balance and line is combined with realism and humour.

The execution of this masterpiece is daring and accomplished, and also suggests apparent opposites; the bird carrying food to its young irresistably recalls the formal yet minutely observed world of the Homeric simile; Achilles complains that his efforts for the Greeks have gone unrewarded:

ὡς δ' ὄρνις ἀπτῆσι νεοσσοῖσι προφέρῃσι
μάστακ', ἐπεί κε λάβῃσι, κακῶς δ' ἄρα οἱ πέλει αὐτῇ.

(As a bird gives up morsels to her unfledged young, whenever she gathers them, and it goes hard with her.)(35)

On the other hand, the composition suggests intellectual power and control, and reminds us, in the words of G.M.A. Richter, that 'artists, no less than philosophers, enquired into the nature of things.'(36) It is perhaps not irrelevant to mention that the subordination of perceptible reality to abstract design was one of the major preoccupations of the early Ionian thinkers (see further, chapter 5), whose work was roughly contemporary with the mid-sixth-century painter of the Louvre kylix.

Ionian vase-painting never gained much currency outside its own territory (the exceptions will be noted below, pp. 56-9) and even within it, met hard competition from the generally superior Korinthian and later, Attic ware. It is, in an objective sense, provincial. The situation with sculpture is different. From the end of the seventh century BC until the end of the sixth, the Ionians produced works in ivory, stone and bronze that equalled and often exceeded in quality those of the mainland, and exerted considerable stylistic influence on it. The survival rate is not a great deal higher than for vase-painting, but what does remain has a much greater impact.

The origins of large-scale sculpture in Greece lie in the mid-seventh century BC, and the earliest sculptures, of the style known as Daedalic, take their inspiration from the east. From about the middle of the century Greeks

settled and traded around the Nile delta and they are
thought to have adopted certain conventions from the
colossal statuary of Egypt, as well as the practice of
using hard stone. In particular the standing naked youth
('kouros') has obvious parallels in Egypt, although the
borrowers created something more life-like and anatomically
sensitive.(37)

The claim of Ionia as the originator of Greek sculpture,
based on little more than a general belief in the prominence of early Ionia, would not now be so strongly
maintained,(38) if only because early examples from Ionia
are entirely absent. More likely candidates are the
Nikandrê statue from Delos (640-630) or the series of
early 'kouroi' from the mainland (c. 600).(39) For Ionian
examples we have to wait until the early to mid-sixth
century BC. Again, as in vase-painting, there seems to be,
at first sight, a characteristic lag between Ionia and the
mainland of Greece, connected, as we have seen, with
Ionia's position away from the main routes of commerce.

Yet the term lag is misleading and has relevance only
if we are considering monumental sculpture; the excellence
of early Ionian sculpture lies in its miniatures, in
bronze, wood and, above all, ivory. An early bronze
statuette from Smyrna (late seventh century) already
betrays individuality in the soft contours of the modelling and an early concern for facial features, which
become characteristically Ionian in the sixth century -
almond-shaped eyes, crooked mouth, broad nose, thickset
body, sloping shoulders and stylisation of the hair.(40)
Even at this early stage the emphasis on curves, surfaces
and what has been called 'generalised modelling', is
notable. A wooden group from Samos (c. 625-600 BC), of
Zeus and Hera embracing in a 'sacred marriage', also foreshadows later Ionian sculptural style; the facial features
are not Greek, but the attitudes and modelling, as well as
Hera's clothing, are.(41)

The most important Ionian miniature work, however, is
in ivory and comes from Ephesos. Here, again, the mainland is probably earlier, at least with depictions of the
human figure; examples from the mid-seventh century have
been found at the temple of Artemis Orthia in Sparta and
in the Kerameikos cemetery at Athens.(42) The earliest
Ephesian examples have recently been down-dated,(43) and
were probably made in the early sixth century. They can
immediately be sharply distinguished from the mainland
examples by the absence of detailed anatomical modelling
of the human body, especially the lower half which has a
cylindrical ξόανον (image carved of wood) look, associated
with very early Greek statuary.(44) The art of ivory-

carving had close Anatolian associations for the Greeks
and it has been suggested that Phrygia may have been an
intermediary for Hittite and Urartian traditions. We know
from Homer that there was a Karian or Lydian school of
ivory-carving in the early period; he creates an extraordinary simile (surely from personal experience) to
describe the thigh of Menelaos, hit by an arrow:

ὡς δ' ὅτε τίς τ' ἐλέφαντα γυνὴ φοίνικι μιήνῃ
Μῃονὶς ἠὲ Κάειρα, παρήϊον ἔμμεναι ἵππων·
κεῖται δ' ἐν θαλάμῳ, πολέες τέ μιν ἠρήσαντο
ἱππῆες φορέειν· βασιλῆϊ δὲ κεῖται ἄγαλμα,
ἀμφότερον, κόσμος θ' ἵππῳ ἐλατῆρί τε κῦδος.

(As when some Maionian or Karian woman stains ivory
with dye, to be a cheekpiece for horses; it lies in
in store, and many horsemen desire to carry if off; but
it lies, an ornament for a king, both as an adornment
for his horse and as an honour for his charioteer.)(45)

Many examples of native Anatolian work have been found
in Ionia and there was an oriental workshop in Ephesos
itself; this in itself makes the distinction between
Greek and non-Greek work often difficult, and in many
cases academic.(46) This is certainly not the case,
however, with the most important, which will now be
discussed.

One of the earliest is the 'Spinning Woman', who wears
a long garment which, in its lower half, becomes an almost
perfect cylinder with the feet and almost all anatomical
features absent.(47) The right hand is made to conform to
the prevailing shape as far as possible, but not without
clearly indicating the tools of her craft, the spindle and
thread, which pass down from the distaff, held in the left
hand at waist level, under the right hand, to hang suspended against her clothes. Her dress, jewellery and hat are
non-Greek (Lydian or Hittite), as is the style of some of
the incised features of the face. Yet the mouth curves in
a characteristically Greek way to give the face a quizzical
expression not found in eastern work. Three main elements
seem to be present: the oriental model, superficially
present in the details of adornment and features; second
the Ionian feel for shape and the way detail is made to
conform to this element; finally, a depiction of an
everyday action, skilfully incorporated into a abstract
outline, and a clear sign of personality in the face.
Again, a paradoxical combination of natural and abstract,
hieratic and everyday (see Plate 4).

The 'Eunuch Priest', also from Ephesos, is slightly

later in date. Strabo tells us that Artemis of Ephesos
was served by priests called Megabyzoi who enjoyed
elevated semi-royal status and were associated with a cult
of pre-Greek, and possibly Hittite origin.(48) As in the
previous example, dress and ornament are Phrygian (the hat
is reminiscent of that worn by king Urpalla in a rock
sculpture at Ivriz, in the Taurus Mountains.(49) But the
conception is Greek.(50) This is particularly noticeable
in the face, where the mouth and eyes form what may be the
earliest example of the archaic smile, which is possibly
of Syrian origin (see further below, p.56). The smile
gives radiance, serenity and humour to the whole face,
here still lacking the sinister, almost mocking quality
detectable in later Ionian examples (see Plate 5 and below,
p. 56).

A veiled woman in ivory (c. 580 BC) represents a
development from the 'Spinning Woman' (see above, p. 47);
the conception is more lifelike without, it may be noted,
conceding anything to the demands of natural representation
beyond the modelling of the top half of the body. Distinctive in this statuette are the subtle hint of a smile
in the curve of the lips, giving the whole great serenity
associated with her probable religious calling; second,
the wearing of a 'himation' (an outer garment which was
later traditionally worn by Greek 'korai') which affords
the artists the opportunity of executing curves around the
waist, and allowing the disproportionately large hands to
curve against the body at right angles, in a similar
manner.(51)

All these tendencies culminate in the masterpiece of
this series, the 'Hawk Priestess' (c. 570-560 BC) – so
called from the long pole attached to her head, on top of
which sits a hawk.(52) This statuette has no equal in the
Greek world in this particular field. The cylindrical
shape of the lower half of the body is maintained, but
with great elaboration; the feet are revealed in an arc of
the hem of the dress, there is a distinctive pattern of
folds at the front and the upper half of the body curves
voluptuously. The stylised hair is very elaborate, with
long pigtails between the arms and breasts at the front.
The face gives a serenity and joyfulness which is hinted at
by the earlier statuettes. The feeling for curve and line
is here successfully integrated with a sensual portrayal
of the female body (see Plate 6).

This statuette occupies a key position in Ionian
sculpture; it represents a culmination of existing trends
and, at the same time, anticipates many of the characteristics of Ionian monumental statues. In examining these
miniatures, closely interconnected stylistically, yet

utterly distinct from contemporary mainland Greek work, we are conscious of the development, within archaic conventions, of a conception of the human figure which may reasonably be termed 'Ionian'. The Anatolian borrowing (see further below, pp. 55f.) does not really go far to explain the extraordinary qualities of these statuettes, which have a sureness of design and a sophistication only later achieved in mainland Greece, and only then, it might be argued, with Ionian help.

The continuity of style between Ionian miniature and large-scale sculpture is most cogently demonstrated in one of the most famous of all Ionian sculptures, the 'Cheramyes Hera' from the Samian Heraion (c. 560 BC),(53) a headless statue which takes its name from the dedication: Χηραμύης μ' ἀνέθηκεν τῆρηι ἄγαλμα (Cheramyes dedicated me as a gift to Hera). The cylindrical lower half of the body is broken only by the arc at the hem of the 'chiton' (underlying tunic) which allows the feet to be displayed. The top half of the body is covered by an Ionic 'himation' in which diagonal folds (gradually becoming vertical as the 'himation' stretches down on the right side of the body to the lower half of the figure) sweep across the breast in a wave-like movement. The preoccupation with patterns and flexible curves is here very marked; the sheer unrelieved vertical folds of the 'chiton' are balanced by the less regular diagonal folds of the 'himation'. The delicacy and poise of the surface treatment belies the apparent rigidity and absence of bodily detail to give a composition which is both dignified and life-like. Above all, the control of patterns and curves reminds one irresistably *mutatis mutandis* of the Louvre kylix (see above, pp. 44-5). As we shall see (below, p. 56) artistic portrayal of garment-folds is something that the Ionians introduced from the east, and made their own (see Plate 7).

This achievement, and the precarious nature of the balance between dignity and fussiness is demonstrated by a near contemporary statue, the 'Philippe' of the Geneleos group (a number of statues on bases still *in situ* in the Samian Heraion).(54) Here the folds are incised rather than carved, and the effect of the vertical lines of the covering 'himation' is less realistic. Realism is attempted, however, in the folds of the 'chiton' which are drawn up into the right hand, with consequent dislocation of the lines of the folds and lower hem of the garment - an element which became a stylistic formula much more effectively executed in the slightly later thickset youth from Cape Phoneas (c. 540 BC)(55) where the folds have reached a high degree of realism, especially in the layering of the drapery hanging from the shoulder (see Plates

8 and 9).

Enough examples survive, either whole or in fragments, to show that the earlier 'korai' were a major stylistic influence;(56) in general the stylistic traits in folds and hems became more intricate and life-like, but virtuosity tended to make its own confusion, and the result is loss of monumentality and impact; it is fairly generally agreed that the quality of the 'Cheramyes Hera' (see above, p. 49) was not equalled again in Ionian sculpture.(57)

The qualities perceived in the above statues have been met before in this chapter; a feeling for line, decoration and mass which has reached a high level of abstraction; a softness and an eye for detail without surrendering the coherence and rhythm of the whole. An observation by Miss G.M.A. Richter on Greek archaic sculpture in general might be thought to apply particularly to Ionia - she isolates the 'ability to discern form and reason without surrendering full receptivity to the immediate and concrete' - a quality not confined, as we shall see, to art.(58)

The works of art discussed above have been drawn from the finds in the shrines of Artemis at Ephesos and Hera on Samos. Miletos too made a great contribution to sculpture. A series of seated figures originally lined the Sacred Way from Miletos to its shrine at Didyma. Ten of these are extant and five (removed in the later nineteenth century) occupy a permanent position in the British Museum. These massive, bulky figures, brought to England by C.T. Newton in 1858, span about seventy or eighty years and, owing to their similarity, give a very clear picture of the development of Ionian sculpture. The earliest (c. 580 BC)(59) is the only one which still possesses a head although the features are almost entirely absent. The masses of the body and chair are undifferentiated, relieved only by the simple sweeping layered folds of the upper garment. The effect is massive but lacking in detail. The next oldest, the statue of 'Eudemos' (c. 570-560), so-called from the inscription on it indicating the sculptor,(60) shows signs of development. The figure is to some extent separate from the chair on which he sits and individual limbs are visible. The folds of the garment are more intricately portrayed with a feeling for the depth of a zig-zag pattern (an earlier anticipation of the figure from Cape Phoneas, see above, p. 49), and the feet are just visible.

Two slightly later examples advance still further.(61) Folds are still more pronounced and the central vertical strip of folds (observed originally on the Ephesian ivory 'Hawk Priestess', see above, pp. 48-9) is clearly articulated. The latest of the statues dates from much later

1 'Wild Goat' oinochoe: height 36 cm. c.625-600 BC.

2 'Fikellura' amphora: height 34 cm. Third quarter of sixth century BC.

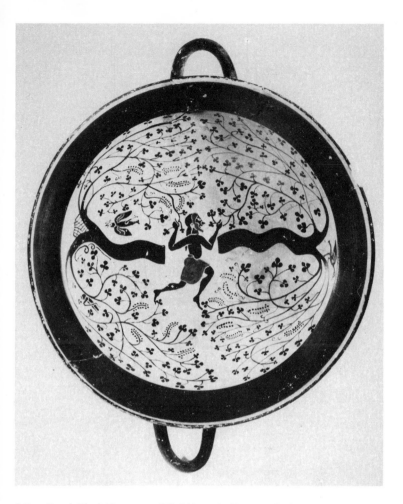

3 East Greek Black Figure cup 'Bird Nester': diameter 23.5 cm. c.550 BC.

4 'Spinning Woman' (ivory): height
10.5 cm. Early sixth century BC.

5 'Eunuch Priest' (ivory): height
11 cm. Early sixth century BC.

6 'Hawk Priestess' (ivory): height 10.5 cm. 570-560 BC.

7 'Cheramyes Hera' (marble): height 1.82 m. c.560 BC.

8 'Philippe' (marble): height 1.60 m.
560-550 BC.

9 Youth from Cape Phoneas (limestone): height 1.68 m. 540-530 BC.

10 Seated figure from Didyma (marble): height 1.55 m. c.570 BC.

11 Seated female figure from Didyma (marble): height 1.25 m. Early fifth
century BC.

12 Lion from Didyma (marble): length 2.11 m. Early sixth century BC.

13 Maiden's head from Ephesos (marble): height 19 cm. c.550 BC.

14 Veiled head of a maiden from Didyma (marble): height 16.1 cm. c.550
BC.

15 Ionic capital from Ephesian Artemision (reconstructed): height 1.096 m.
c.560 BC.

16 'Berlin Kore' from Attica: height 1.93 m. 570-560 BC.

17 Kore from the Athenian Acropolis: height 55 cm. Last quarter of sixth century BC.

18 Caeretan hydria: height 43 cm. c.530-525 BC.

(the beginning of the fifth century BC)(62) and reveals a
multiplication of folds, considerably increased in depth
and executed with much greater fluency; the body seated in
the chair has much greater individuality and poise. We
are here on the verge of the classical period, in which a
distinctive Ionian style was largely merged into an all-
embracing classical mode (see Plates 10 and 11).

Also from Miletos, and prominent in the British Museum,
is a recumbent lion, one of the most impressive of Ionian
sculptures.(63) The lion had been a notable feature of
Hittite, Assyrian and Egyptian art and a number of ivories
from the late seventh and early sixth centuries BC were
executed in the oriental tradition at Smyrna and Ephesos.
The British Museum lion contains on its body an inscription
revealing that the 'sons of Orion dedicated it to Apollo';
the style of the lettering reveals that the lion dates
from the late seventh or early sixth century BC, and
therefore represents the oldest monumental sculptural
style of Greek Asia Minor.(64) The influence is Egyptian,
but the conception characteristically Ionian. Although
the head is unfortunately missing, the modelling of the
forepaws and hind legs gives the sculptor the opportunity
to exploit curve and mass to full advantage. The smooth
body surfaces can be contrasted with what remains of the
mane, which is stylised in a manner somewhat reminiscent
of drapery folds (see Plate 12). A later lion of the
same type (c. 550 BC) in Berlin,(65) reveals the style of
face; the animal is in a watchful pose. The later lion
shows greater realism, especially in the articulation of
skin folds, but much less intellectual power behind the
articulation of the masses. Yet the achievement of the
Ionians may be appreciated by comparing them both with an
oriental lion from Sardis, the Lydian capital (c. 540 BC)
(66) where the effect is static and lifeless; the sculptor
has command of all the techniques of his Greek neighbour,
but not the conception.

Since almost all Ionian large-scale sculpture is headless, it is not possible to say much about the development
of the facial features of Ionian 'korai', except in
Athenian examples (on which, see below). However, there
do survive a number of heads from the temples at Ephesos
and Didyma, where the Ionians, copying, possibly, the
Egyptians, decorated the columns of their temples with
figured relief sculptures (see below, p. 56). At Ephesos,
where Croesus of Lydia dedicated most of the columns of
the archaic temple,(67) a number of heads were carved, a
few of which have survived. The most remarkable of these
is a fragmentary head (the features without part of the
right side) found near the temple and now in the British

Museum.(68) The features are broad and fleshy and the
calm, smiling remoteness of expression (and the illusion,
fortuitous from our point of view, that the eyes are
actually closed) recalls Indian or Chinese models. The
beauty of the chin and lips (which contain just the
suggestion of a smile) combined with the flowing curves of
nose, eyelids and eyebrows, gives this face a dreamy
serenity quite unparalleled in mainland art; however a
direct link can be traced back to the facial type of the
Ephesian ivories, in which these characteristics are found
in embryo (see Plate 13). Another head of similar type,
also in the British Museum, is not quite so striking in
its impact, but does allow us to observe the elaborately
stylised hair which again recalls the prominence of this
feature in the Ephesian 'Hawk Priestess' (p. 48).(69)
Enough similar heads, male and female, have been discovered to make it clear that we are dealing with a widely
disseminated Ionian type.(70)

Turning to Didyma, we have the remains of decorated
column reliefs from a temple to Apollo roughly contemporary with the Artemis temple in Ephesos. Two heads of
maidens (the work of the same artist) show more angular
features than the Ephesos heads, but the same broad
features and smile (for one of these, see Plate 14).(71)

The smile of these maidens, not without a hint of irony,
reminds one of Sappho's Aphrodite - μειδιαίσαισ' ἀθανάτῳ
προσώπῳ (smiling with immortal countenance) when she play-
fully enquires from the lovesick poetess what ails her
this time.(72) These elements, along with others we have
isolated, are not the idiosyncracy of one artist, but
reveal a spirit which on the one hand seems to be reflected
in Ionian sculpture generally and the area which came under
its influence, and on the other, remains utterly distinct
from that of other Greeks. This spirit, which undoubtedly
reflected something in the life of the people, also
ultimately lent a great deal to the perfection of classical
art.

Little mention has been made of statues in bronze.
Although Rhoikos and Theodoros, the architects of the early
sixth-century BC Samian Heraion, are credited by Pausanias
with the invention of hollow bronze-casting,(73) few full-
scale bronzes from east Greece survive. It has been con-
jectured(74) that melting down of bronze statues may
account for the absence of Samian statues from the time of
Polykrates; it was certainly about this time that the new
process of bronze-casting became prevalent.

In assessing the part played by the Ionians in architecture,

we are in a difficult position, since almost all archaic
Ionic architectural remains have disappeared below Hellenistic and Roman successors, by whom ambitious' archaic
projects were often continued, and sometimes finished.
For the sanctuaries of the early period, we have to depend
largely upon reconstruction from ground plans. A partial
exception to this is Old Smyrna, whose site, owing largely
to being abandoned, proved more easily accessible.(75) A
very early house was discovered,(76) oval in shape, made
of brick and consisting of a single room. The building
has been reconstructed to a height of three layers of
bricks. A number of other houses of rectangular shape
have been uncovered, dating to the ninth century BC(77)
and, in the middle of the eighth century, there was a new
phase of building following some kind of catastrophe,
possibly the Kolophonian capture of the city (see chapter
2, p. 25). Taken as a whole this is valuable evidence for
the comparatively advanced state of at least one part of
Ionia in the early archaic period. During the late Geometric period (mid-eighth century - mid-seventh), there
are more oval, rectangular and, notably, apsidal houses
and, in addition, certain circular buildings which lie
with their lower half in the earth, remarkably like the
'tholoi' mentioned in the 'Odyssey', and utilised as
store-houses. They lie inside the house-complex. In
'Odyssey', XXII, 457-60, Telemachos rounds up the disloyal
maidservants for execution in a place from which there was
no escape:

μεσσηγύς τε θόλου καὶ ἀμύμονος ἔρκεος αὐλῆς

(between the round building and the fine wall of the
courtyard).(78)

By the end of the seventh century BC when Smyrna was
finally attacked and destroyed by Alyattes, it was powerful and well built. The discovery of a terracotta bath in
one of a series of stone houses with several rooms
testifies to high living standards. Extensive housing had
been laid out in regular patterns, apparently anticipating
the 'Hippodameian' gridiron system, surrounded by a newly
rebuilt town wall, in places 50 ft thick, made from fine
polygonal stones.(79) The discoveries also include the
base of what was planned as one of the earliest monumental
stone temples of the Greek world.(80) The fate of Smyrna
after the sack of Alyattes - almost total destruction with
its population dispersed in villages (see Chapter 2,
n. 94) - illustrates quite as effectively as that of
Miletos, 100 years later, the precarious basis of great

wealth and prosperity.

Of the three major sanctuaries of the Ionian world, disappointingly little survives; two points, however, are clear: these temples exceeded in size and elaboration any previous or contemporary Greek achievements and, second, the manner of their design gave an 'Ionic' order to the Greek world, which had a profound influence on later classical architectural style.

The sanctuary of Hera at Samos was situated on a site which the Ionians probably took over from a native cult, about four miles from the city. The earliest temple dates from the eighth century BC; it was long and narrow and consisted of mud-brick on a foundation of stone. The great sixth-century temple designed by Rhoikos and Theodoros was singled out by Herodotos as one of the three greatest building and engineering feats of the Greek world. Destroyed by fire (c. 530 BC), its rebuilding was initiated by Polykrates but never finished.(81)

As in the case of Samos, so with the Ephesian Artemision, the site suggests what in fact the historical tradition records, that the Ionians took over the site of a native cult (see chapter 2, p. 19, nn.53-5). The temple, for which Croesus contributed funds, was begun mid-sixth century BC, but never properly finished. It was rebuilt in the fourth century BC after being burned down by a madman, Herostratos, who, desirous of immortality, thus effectively secured it. The sanctuary at Didyma, ten miles south of Miletos, was deliberately destroyed by the Persians and the cult statue taken back to Ecbatana by Dareios. The temple of which remains survive was started in the fourth century BC.(82)

All these temples exhibited ambitious design (the absence of funds to complete them may be a sign of the increasing poverty of late sixth-century Ionia under the Persians(83)) and a willingness to let decoration 'break up' the line of columns and the entablature, in sharp contrast to the Doric style which was less adorned. The Ionian column had more slender proportions, but the design as a whole exhibited less discipline and subordination of parts to the whole.

The scale of Ionian architectural undertakings may possibly point to Egyptian inspiration; yet the style owes little or nothing to this source. Although the main features of the Ionic order - arguably the most influential creation of the Ionian Greeks - reached a fixed form in the classical temple of fifth-century Athens, the remains of sixth-century Ionian architecture exhibit a considerable variety of features of diverse, and often doubtful origin.

We have already referred to the characteristic tendency
to decorate the column bases of temples with figured
relief sculpture (see above, p. 51), a feature which,
repeated on the parapet along the edge of the roof, is the
forerunner of the classical sculptured marble frieze. The
introduction of the full entablature with a frieze between
architrave and cornice was effected in the Siphnian
treasury at Delphi, probably with the aim of increasing
the height of the entablature.(84)
  The Ionic capital was the ultimate survivor of a number
of different types of column-capital current in the early
sixth-century BC Ionian world. The leaf-capital was
prominent in the treasury of the Phokaians of Massalia
(Marseilles, an early trading colony) at Delphi; the
survival of remarkable leaf-capitals from Smyrna and
Phokaia suggest that this was a northern Ionian characteristic.(85) Similar in design are the elaborate 'egg-and-
tongue' and 'leaf-and-dart' mouldings, prominent in the
Massalian treasury and in early fragmentary survivals from
the Ephesian Artemision.(86) The Aiolic capital (e.g. the
Troad temple at Neandria (early sixth century BC))(87)
which exhibits the characteristic volutes and mouldings of
Ionic, was probably designed originally for free-standing
monuments. Essentially a specialised variant of the Ionic
capital, it was more at home in miniature art, especially
furniture; its architectural use was limited both in
period and geographical area. Early examples of the
standard Ionic capital have been preserved in the votive
offerings in the sanctuaries of Apollo on Delos and at
Delphi; a mature Ionian example is the reconstructed
capital from the Ephesian Artemision in the British Museum
(see Plate 15).(88)

It has been remarked that, in considering influences from
the east on Greek art in the archaic period, the process
of transformation is more interesting than the original
elements utilised.(89) In Ionia the proximity of non-
Greek craftsmen, often in the city itself, for example
ivory workers at Ephesos,(90) exposed Greek craftsmen to
strong influences, which makes the evolution of a mature
Greek style all the more remarkable, testifying to
something particularly distinctive in the Ionians themselves.
  As we have seen (pp. 41) early Anatolian influence on
Ionian art is debatable, and certainly not to be precisely
formulated. Nevertheless, despite a generally late
reaction to the Orientalising movement (see above, p. 42)
there is evidence of early contact between Phrygia and

Ionia in metalwork; Boardman lists bronze cauldron attach-
ments, belts, fibulae and shallow dishes, one of which is
held by the famous 'Hawk Priestess' (see above, pp. 48-9).
(91)   The marriage of the daughter of the Phrygian king
Midas to Agamemnon of Kyme in Aiolia in the eighth century
BC suggests early contact.

A number of characteristic Ionian elements can be
traced to their supposed eastern models; the artistic
patterning of folds in the drapery of clothed statues is
anticipated in Aramean work of the mid-eighth century BC
(92) and may have spread from Babylonian art even earlier.
Yet these eastern folds, unlike the Ionian, are incised
rather than layered and they lack the rhythm and feeling
for pattern of their western imitators. Another example
is the famous 'archaic smile'; this is undoubtedly an
Ionic introduction into the Greek world, probably derived
from Syria, a notable example being that of a woman's
head ornamentally carved on a piece of furniture from
Nimrud.(93) What begins as a pure detail becomes in the
earliest Ionian examples (the ivory 'Spinning Woman' and
the 'Eunuch Priest', see pp. 47-8) an effect of the whole
face; the earlier 'model' only curves the lips, the Greeks
give the eyes expression also, which makes it difficult to
suppose that we are dealing merely with an acquired convention. Likewise, patterns of carpets, details of jewellery and furniture ornament become more disciplined and
lively. The still, somewhat hieratic poses of figures
take on a life and energy withoutlosing their poise. Yet
the synthesis was not mechanical; while it is true to say
that the east contributed something, in conception as well
as detail, to Ionian art, the result is almost always
thoroughly assimilated and internally coherent.

So much for what the Ionians took; more important, in
many ways, is what they gave. Historically by far the
most important influence was the brief, but decisive
influence of Ionian sculpture on mainland Attica. In
terms of priority, Attica certainly developed monumental
sculpture earlier than Ionia, or so it would seem from the
extant evidence; yet her earliest sculptors lacked a vital
quality of grace, vitality and delicacy of design, which
the Ionians supplied. A comparison of two masterpieces is
instructive: the famous Attic maiden in Berlin(94) and the
'Cheramyes Hera' (see above, p.49). In one sense the
comparison is unfair since the Ionian statue is headless,
but no other near-contemporary complete Ionian work
survives for comparison. Yet the strengths and weaknesses
of each are clear. The Attic work has strength and clear
lines: the feet and body show much more concern for human
anatomy and the drapery folds are decisively executed.

Yet the overall effect is somewhat stiff; the figure is
more schematic and lacks graceful proportions; ,the folds
of the clothing lack the sinuous rhythm and line of the
'Cheramyes Hera'. If the Attic head is compared with the
slightly later Ionian female heads from Ephesos and Didyma
(see pp. 51-2) the differences are striking: the Attic
head, though strong, serene and smiling, lacks the fine
modelling and the enigmatic, voluptuous quality of the
Ionian. This is especially noticeable around the mouth,
which, in the Ionian heads, contributes a great deal of
the expression, and the eyes, which are narrower and more
carefully matched by the line of nose and eyebrows (see
Plates 7 and 16).

When the later Attic 'korai' are examined, Ionian
influence may be associated historically with connections
between the Athenian tyrant, Peisistratos, and his Ionian
counterparts. One of the best examples of this is the
'Peplos kore' from the Acropolis.(95) It is most probable
that some of the Attic ' korai' of this period (c. 530 BC)
are the work of immigrant Ionian craftsmen. The famous
Acropolis 'kore' (c. 520-510) associated with a column
bearing a signature of Archermos of Chios, has been
thought an Ionian importation. More concretely, after the
mid-sixth century, Ionic drapery, the 'chiton' with short
'himation', was introduced to Attica as the traditional
dress for 'korai'; this ousted the 'peplos', which nevertheless returned into fashion again after the Persian Wars,
perhaps as a general reaction against the eastern fashions
(see Plate 17).(96)

Other influences were various. While, as we have seen,
in the Geometric period, Ionia was on the periphery of an
area whose centre lay in Rhodes, Cyprus and the Cyclades,
by the sixth century BC the major Ionian cities were the
artistic centre of a sculptural tradition which extended
into the hinterland of Anatolia and to Rhodes and Cyprus,
not to mention Ionian colonies in the north, such as
Kyzikos.(97) Close relationships with Cyprus are to be
deduced from the fine 'kouros' in marble of East Greek
workmanship in the British Museum.(98) In the field of
vase painting the seventh-century BC presence of Ionians
in Egypt is revealed by a great deal of pottery, mainly of
the 'Wild Goat' style, and especially some fine Chian ware,
some of which is possibly the work of Chian potters in
Naukratis itself.(99) Other Ionian towns also made a
major contribution to the East Greek presence in Egypt,
revealed by the pottery remains.

The long drawn out Ionian diaspora was particularly
significant for the west. Sixth-century Chian wine jars
have been discovered at Syracuse and Marseilles, Samian

or Rhodian 'Fikellura' at Gela and Syracuse; but the most
important Ionian artistic remains found in the west come
from Etruria. A series of fine Black Figure vases were
made by immigrant Ionians under the influence of Athenian
Black Figure. These are known as the Caeretan Hydriai
(from their place of discovery, Caere in Etruria). Taken
as a whole, they exceed in quality most home-produced
Ionian vases, but are nevertheless regarded by most
scholars as reflecting Ionian styles.(100) A number of
Ionian traits in stone sculpture and minor bronze works as
well as in tomb paintings and jewellery suggest that the
influence was from an Ionian presence rather than merely
imported models. Boardman, in discussing the transport-
ation of artistic ideas from one part of the Greek world
to another, remarks on the exceptional success of the
Ionians in this respect, especially in the face of the
all-pervasive competition of Attic wares (see Plate 18).(101)

Ionic artistic influence in the west during the archaic
period is not confined to vase-painting. Of the three
temples at Paestum (Poseidonia) on the south-west coast of
Italy, two, the so-called Basilica and the temple of
Demeter, contained marked Ionic features within a general
Doric design. Notable were Ionic-style mouldings on the
capitals of the Basilica and on the architraves of the
temple of Demeter and marked Ionic influences in the
proportion and design of the columns of both temples.
This influence is also marked in the late sixth-century
Doric temple on Corcyra at Kardaki, where the entablature
is ornamented by 'egg-and-dart' moulding and the absence
of a frieze suggests a direct imitation of Ionic.(102)

There is also evidence for the influence of the art of
Ionia on that of Skythia through the Ionian Black Sea
colonies, especially those of Miletos. Owing to the
extensive Milesian colonising of the north coast of the
Black Sea, it is likely that the Greek art with which
these nomadic peoples came into contact was Ionian in
character. But, at the same time, a certain affinity may
be detected between the essentially decorative and
abstract 'animal' style of the Skythians and the Ionian
predilection for the same qualities, albeit in a Greek
context.(103)

While, as we have seen, Ionia obtained a great deal
from the east, there is some evidence of influence in the
reverse direction. Phrygian painted pottery of the mid-
seventh century incorporates motifs from archaic East
Greek vases; these, along with finds of East Greek pottery
on Phrygian sites, shows that the trend of Phrygian
influence on Ionia was at this time being reversed.(104)
Somewhat later, during the Persian period, frescoes have

been discovered, executed in an unmistakably eastern Greek
style, in the old Phrygian city of Gordion. Finally,
there is evidence in the Persian Empire itself of the work
and influence of immigrant Ionian craftsmen from the
reign of Cyrus through to that of Xerxes. Pliny tells of
an immigrant sculptor, Telephanes from Phokaia, who worked
for the Persian monarchs Dareios and Xerxes.(105)   The
Ionic order of architecture is much in evidence at Cyrus'
palace at Pasargadae and here, too, we see a clear
imitation of the typically Ionian patterning of drapery
folds, albeit in a stiff and stylised reproduction of the
original.(106)

Ionian art is an essentially archaic phenomenon; already
at the end of the sixth century and the beginning of the
fifth, the great age of Ionian artistic achievement was
over. A marble torso of a 'kouros', from the Samian
Heraion, shows a development towards classical anatomical
detail which inevitably marked the end of the characteristic Ionian sculpted figure.(107)   The last individual
Ionian Black-Figure school, that of the Klazomeneian
sarcophagi, represented the final, fairly undistinguished,
manifestation of Ionian painted pottery.(108)   The
characteristic Ionian architectural order, with its
emphasis upon grace and decoration, was already being
married to the Doric to produce the classical synthesis.
Ionian architecture, after a considerable period of near
eclipse, had a second heyday in the fourth century BC in
such notable works as the Halikarnassos Mausoleum, the
temple of Athena in Priene and the famous Alexander
sarcophagus from Sidon.(109)   Yet these were works which
were created in what was largely a common idiom emanating
from the Athenian classical achievement. Whatever Ionia
had contributed to this had long since been assimilated
without trace.

'Πάππα φίλ', οὐκ ἂν δή μοι ἐφοπλίσσειας ἀπήνην
ὑψηλὴν εὔκυκλον, ἵνα κλυτὰ εἵματ' ἄγωμαι
ἐς ποταμὸν πλυνέουσα, τά μοι ῥερυπωμένα κεῖται;
καὶ δὲ σοὶ αὐτῷ ἔοικε μετὰ πρώτοισιν ἐόντα
βουλὰς βουλεύειν καθαρὰ χροῒ εἵματ' ἔχοντα.
πέντε δέ τοι φίλοι υἷες ἐνὶ μεγάροις γεγάασιν,
οἱ δύ' ὀπυίοντες, τρεῖς δ' ἠΐθεοι θαλέθοντες·
οἱ δ' αἰεὶ ἐθέλουσι νεόπλυτα εἵματ' ἔχοντες
ἐς χορὸν ἔρχεσθαι· τὰ δ' ἐμῇ φρενὶ πάντα μέμηλεν.'
ὣς ἔφατ'· αἴδετο γὰρ θαλερὸν γάμον ἐξονομῆναι
πατρὶ φίλῳ· ὁ δὲ πάντα νόει καὶ ἀμείβετο μύθῳ·
'οὔτε τοι ἡμιόνων φθονέω, τέκος, οὔτε τευ ἄλλου.
ἔρχευ· ἀτάρ τοι δμῶες ἐφοπλίσσουσιν ἀπήνην
ὑψηλὴν εὔκυκλον, ὑπερτερίῃ ἀραρυῖαν.'(1)

('Daddy dear, could you not get a waggon fitted out for
me, a high one with good wheels so that I can take the
fine clothes to the river to wash - those which are
lying about dirty? It is only decent for you yourself
too, sitting among the leaders of the state and sharing
counsels, to have clean linen on your back. What is
more, there are five sons of yours who have grown up in
the palace, two married and three merry bachelors; they
are continually wanting newly washed clothing to go to
the dance; all this is my responsibility.'
She spoke thus; for she was ashamed to speak directly
of her joyful marriage to her dear father; but he
understood everything and answered her:
'I do not begrudge you the mules, my child, or anything
else. Go, and the servants will fit out a waggon, a
high one with good wheels, with a hood attached.')(2)

So, in Book VI of Homer's 'Odyssey', the Phaeacian
princess, Nausikaa introduces herself in conversation with

her father, king Alkinoos. The effort of translation
reveals some of the main elements of the Homeric
Kunstsprache: an even, flowing style which makes considerable use of repeated phrase patterns arranged paratactically (juxtaposition of equal, independent clauses and
avoidance of subordination), fixed formulae for indicating
the beginning and ending of speeches and 'ornamental'
epithets.(3) Yet the stylised diction also conveys
immediacy, urbanity and humour. From her oblique initial
request(4) and her disingenuous justification by reference
to Alkinoos' own needs in ℓ.60,(5) to the king's gentle,
teasing(6) reply in ℓℓ.69-70, the scene combines acute-
ness of insight with directness of expression and gentle
irony in a way which belies the formality of the style.
A closer inspection reveals, however, that, far from
succeeding in spite of the stylisation, the effect conveyed
arises naturally and spontaneously out of the language
itself.

Homer's dialogue has always appealed, with a directness
which entirely transcends its historical remoteness, to
the sensibilities and emotions of civilised men. Yet the
playful and often comic ironies of family and wider social
relations are only part of a deeper and more serious
perception of man which runs through the entire Homeric
corpus. It has often been a source of wonder that so
mature and sophisticated a conception of humanity should
lie at the origins of Greek, not to say European, literature as a kind of unattainable model for all that followed it.(7) In judging Homer as their supreme literary
genius, it may be thought that the Greeks were entirely
correct; never again, it could be maintained, did they
quite succeed in combining so all-embracing a vision of
man with this degree of directness and artistry.

Homer's concern for human spiritual and social development in association with, but also sharply independent of,
the gods - what may be termed his humanism - separates
Greek culture right from the beginning from the essentially
god-centred and theologically motivated literature which
was composed during the previous millennium in the technically advanced but politically conservative cultures of
the Near East, chiefly the Mesopotamian, Hittite and
Egyptian. These hieratic societies are to be sharply
contrasted with the early Greek city-state, which was a
small, independent unit, comparatively free from bureaucracy and more secular in its religious outlook.

The Homeric poems are the chief - in fact almost the
only - cultural survival from early Iron Age Greece, and
it is consequently from them that the bulk of our evidence
for early Greek beliefs is derived. Indeed, what may be

called the Greek discovery of man appears to owe so much
to the Homeric poems that subsequent ideas have often been
seen, albeit implicitly, as representing a natural and
almost preordained development from Homer. More recently
there has been recognition of the contrast as well as the
continuity between Homer and his successors.(8) At the
same time, mainly as a result of a greater appreciation of
the true nature of the composition and development of the
Homeric epics, it has been realised that a monolith,
apparently without forbears, was really the culmination of
a poetic tradition of unique richness and complexity
stretching back many hundreds of years.

The 'Iliad' and 'Odyssey' narrate events which purport
to have taken place at the end of the Greek Bronze Age,
namely a short episode from the Greek war against Troy and
the wanderings and return home of Odysseus, a Greek hero.
It is known that there were other poems on subjects connected with the Trojan war and its aftermath which,
together with the 'Iliad' and 'Odyssey', comprise the
Trojan cycle. These other poems survive only in short
fragments and citations, as do traces from other traditions connected with Boiotia, Korinth and other cities.(9)
In particular, we are well acquainted with the details of
the Theban cycle from the large number of occasions on
which its material was utilised by later Greek dramatists.

Yet the Homeric poems alone survive in enough bulk to
be suitable for detailed study. Their historical development is fairly clear in outline. The origins of later
narrative poetry based upon the incidents of the Greek
expedition against Troy, as well as many other semi-
legendary and historical events from the late Bronze Age,
can probably be traced to near-contemporary songs composed
to honour and perpetuate the memory of the life and deeds
of outstanding heroes. In 'Iliad' IX, Agamemnon's
ambassadors discover the estranged Achilles singing of the
κλέα ἀνδρῶν (189) (the renowned deeds of men) and in the
'Odyssey' both the Ithakan and Phaeacian courts have their
professional bards, who sing at the request of their lords
and honoured guests.(10) The Trojan stories must have
travelled back, in whatever form, to Greece with the
Achaians when they returned home, and once more crossed
the Aegean in the early Dark Age with the migrants from
the mainland to Asia Minor (see above, chapter 2, p. 12)
This period of development culminated in the 'Iliad'
and 'Odyssey' composed somewhere in Ionia at about
the middle of the eighth century BC.

The problems involved in going beyond this outline have
usually been considered too great to allow a precise
historical and cultural context for the later development

of the poems. After their final composition, the 'Iliad'
and 'Odyssey' swiftly spread to the rest of Greece to
become the major cultural heritage of all Greeks. As a
consequence the question of what they owed to Ionia in
particular has usually seemed neither answerable nor even
important. The main question to be considered in this
chapter is whether the matter must be left there, with the
'Iliad' and 'Odyssey' suspended, as it were, in the limbo
of early Iron Age Greece or whether the 'Iliad' and
'Odyssey' may be considered as Ionian creations which gave
something distinctive to the rest of archaic Greece.

This question is made more difficult to consder by the
unfortunate fact that the five centuries from the generally
accepted date for the sack of Troy (c. 1240 BC) until the
final composition of the 'Iliad' and 'Odyssey' are by far
the worst documented in the whole of Greek history. The
collapse of the Bronze Age cultures of Greece and Asia
Minor led to an abrupt decline in civilisation to which
the archaeological record bears almost universal witness.
Yet it is clear that the poetic tradition which culminated
in the 'Iliad' and 'Odyssey' must have come through this
period somewhere and in some form. Two major questions
arise: what particular elements are to be assigned to
which particular period within the long tradition? If the
poems were composed in Asia Minor (which is indisputable)
how long had they been there?

To take the second question first: the evidence, such
as it is, seems to point to Ionia as the major formative
influence on the poems. The most conclusive evidence for
this lies in the language which, although a mixture of
several dialects (which together could never have formed
the normal spoken tongue of any group of Greek speakers),
shows clearly the overwhelming preponderance of Ionic,
which, on its own, demonstrates at the very least a number
of generations of Ionian composition. Apart from a small
admixture of Attic (from the post-Ionian transmission of
the poems(11)) and forms akin to Arcado-Cyprian (and
consequently probably traceable to the pre-Dorian Invasion
stage of the epic tradition) the most obvious dialect
influence is that of Aiolic. It has been supposed that
these traces of Aiolic are the remains of an entirely
Aiolic stage in the transmission and that epic poetry,
first practised and elaborated by Aiolian bards, probably
in North Asia Minor, was taken over and adapted to their
own dialect by Ionian singers, an assumption which may
have gained support from the tradition that the Aiolian
migration to Asia Minor preceded the Ionian and Dorian.(12)
Many of the Aiolic forms, though by no means all, survive
in expressions of a stereotyped nature ('formulae' will

be discussed in detail below, p. 71), especially where
a change into Ionic would have affected their suitability
for use within the strict and comparatively inflexible
Homeric hexameter. This seems, at first sight, to support
the theory of a general Aiolic phase in the development of
the poems.(13) That the forms represent a pre-Ionic
vocabulary cannot be denied. Yet the view has been
advanced more recently that the majority of Aiolic forms
in Homer do not refer necessarily to an Aiolic phase in
the development of the poems, but may well be relics of
the pre-Dark Age Achaian language, of which the Linear B
tablets have been supposed to furnish a number of Homeric
examples.(14) This development is of considerable significance since; if the hypothesis is valid, there is
nothing to prevent the assumption that the Ionian phase in
the tradition stretches back to the beginning of the post-
Dorian Invasion period. It is true that very little is
known about the earliest stages of the Homeric epic
tradition and few linguistic elements in the poems can be
traced back to them with absolute certainty;(15) yet it
seems unavoidable that the basic stories on which the
poems grew were preserved by means of some kind of verse
tradition developed within a few generations of the Trojan
War.(16) On the other hand, Aiolic influence cannot be
rejected altogether; clear connections, whether pre- or
post-Dorian Invasion, of the Trojan Cycle with Aiolis are
present in the prominence of Achilles, the chief hero of
the 'Iliad'. It is also highly probable that, in the
Ionic expansion northwards, during the early Dark Ages,
into Aiolic Phokaia and Smyrna (see chapter 2, pp. 22-3 and
25) linguistic elements from the area would be adapted by
peripatetic bards. Yet, at the same time, it is increasingly clear that the mainstream of the tradition was, and
remained, Ionian. Precisely how far back this tradition
may have extended must now be considered.

    That Athens played a part in the pre-Ionian migration
epic tradition is undeniable. The literary tradition that
Athens alone held out against the Dorian invaders is
supported by the archaeological evidence.(17) Moreover it
was the centre for refugees from other parts of Greece and
provided the initial organisation for the migration to
Ionia (see chapter 2, p. 15) A generation ago, when
the Ionian migration was placed as late as the ninth
century BC, the Athenian phase of the epic tradition was
seen as correspondingly long and influential. The importance of the Athenian development of Geometric pottery, the
first post-Mycenaean artistic venture, was felt to reflect
the kind of artistic environment in which epic poetry
might have flourished. This hypothesis was taken to its

extreme by C. Whitman who put forward an elaborate (and, in detail, highly improbable) analogy between the structure of Geometric pottery design and that of the 'Iliad'.(18)

A consequence of the archaeological finds of the last thirty years on the Ionian sites is the considerable up-dating of the probable first arrival of Ionians in Asia Minor to c. 1100 BC (see chapter 2, p.14), which gives a *terminus post quem* for the introduction of the Homeric poems. The hypothesis of a major Athenian phase in the tradition becomes much less tenable in the face of the possibility that this phase of development may have been quite short. It is, of course, impossible to prove that the poems travelled with the earliest migrants, or that the poems did not continue to develop on the Greek main-land. Yet we need go no further than our own 'Beowulf' for· an example of epic flourishing and receiving elaborate treatment among exiles. What more natural than that the Ionians should cling to this symbol of their national and cultural identity in the process of carving out their existence among the non-Greek peoples of west Asia Minor? Furthermore, if a more elaborate tradition of epic poetry was maintained at Athens, it is very surprising that there is no evidence for it. In fact, on the scanty evidence available, Athens seems to come a poor third to Boiotia and Korinth.(19)

The first, and more difficult, question posed above (p.63) concerned the degree to which elements within the tradition may be dated. Owing to the traditional nature of the subject, themes and language, the survival of early elements in the poems is no guarantee of the general antiquity of the immediate context since, as a consequence of their method of composition and artistic aims (on which see below, pp. 70ff.) poets used traditional words and phrases again and again in new contexts or in new ways. Hence, as G.S. Kirk has demonstrated, the existence of Mycenaean cult-titles, artifacts or even vocabulary is not necessarily an indication of the survival, in the final poems, of even a minor degree of Mycenaean poetic com-position.(20) Yet an examination of certain linguistic features seems to reveal a greater certainty. Kirk, in an examination of the evidence for neglect of the digamma in Homer (a sound which disappeared early in Ionic and whose neglect would therefore tend to suggest Ionic composition) and for contraction of vowels (also evidence for later composition), concludes, albeit with some caution, that 'much of the formal expression of the Greek epic as we have it belongs to the period after 1000.'(21) This conclusion, combined with the historical evidence for the migrations, makes it reasonable to suppose that the major

expansion of the poems from relatively crude beginnings
into compositions of great virtuosity of technique and
profundity of conception was the work of Ionian bards
which took place during the period extending from the
migrations until the mid-eighth century BC. The nature of
the evidence makes it unwise to give this hypothesis
greater precision.

Any discussion of the 'Iliad' and 'Odyssey' as Ionian
poems must be qualified by the assumption of non-Ionian
influence. The poems as a whole are a mosaic of elements,
ranging from allusions to full-length stories, derived
from the vast saga tradition of Greece. The whole of the
'Odyssey' contains continual reference to the story of
Agamemnon, Klytemnestra and Orestes, as a kind of perpetual
counterpoint and moral contrast to the chief story of
Odysseus, Penelope and Telemachos. Odysseus' wanderings
contain clear traces of the Argonautic legend as well as
fairy-story and folktale. In the 'Iliad', Boiotian traditions are continually appearing in the references to the
father of Diomedes, Tydeus, and his exploits around Thebes,
and Nestor's extended reminiscences recall Pylos, his home.
It is hardly likely to be coincidence that the literary
tradition on the Ionian migration gives prominence to both
Boiotia and Pylos (see chapter 2, p. 13). These are only
the most prominent of countless references to the furthest
corners of the contemporary known world.

Yet a clear distinction must be made between influence
and composition. Stories from other traditions tend to
appear in highly compressed, unadorned versions or in
lengthy factual narrative,(22) which, to many scholars, is
an indication of their comparative unimportance and subsidiary role in the story. Yet the 'compression' could
also, and perhaps more plausibly,be explained as the
contrast between Homer and comparatively unambitious
poetic traditions elsewhere. Indeed, when the stories are
elaborated, we can perhaps see the original version not
only transformed linguistically into Ionic, but refracted,
as it were, through the powerful lens of Homeric genius.

This falls well short of proof; yet all the fragmentary
evidence of the Trojan epic cycle as well as other legends
leads to the impression that the quality of Homer was not
merely unique but in a completely different class from the
other epic traditions. Clearly the *argumentum e silentio*
is here perhaps not entirely adequate, but the evidence is
cumulative. The argument is often advanced that the bare
survival of odd lines or groups of lines from other epic
traditions, especially those from Boiotia and Korinth,
along with a great deal of supporting evidence from later
writers, shows that the Homeric poets were in close

artistic touch with the mainland. This may have been so;
but that which does survive, including the non-Homeric
epic cycle (attributed to a number of poets both in Ionia
and elsewhere) gives no ground at all for supposing
artistic quality remotely approaching that of the 'Iliad'
and 'Odyssey'. Indeed there is reason to suppose that it
was in his basic conception that Homer surpassed the work
of his epic contemporaries. In a recent article
J. Griffin sharply contrasts the heroic, profound and
technically accomplished Homeric epics with the more
fantastic, miraculous and stylistically looser, less
dramatic poems of the epic cycle.(23) The assumption that
Homer was not part of the general tradition, but unique,
suggests that the major development of the monumental
poems, as Kirk calls them,(24) is a late and mature Ionian
phenomenon. Yet the poems did not emerge from nothing;
the 'Iliad' and 'Odyssey' must owe a great deal both in
dramatic conception and detailed execution to a fairly
long Ionian tradition for which we can find no parallel
elsewhere. Precisely how these qualities are displayed in
the poems will emerge later.

Very little is known about Homer beyond the fact that he
was an Ionian and composed c. 750 BC. A number of cities
claimed to have produced him, the chief candidates being
Smyrna and Chios. The latter city contained a guild of
poets known as the Homeridai as early as the sixth century
BC, who claimed a special relationship with Homer. The
Homeric 'Hymn to Delian Apollo' refers to an Ionian
festival on Delos, the events of which are recounted by a
man who reveals himself as:

τυφλὸς ἀνήρ, οἰκεῖ δὲ Χίῳ ἔνι παιπαλοέσσῃ
τοῦ πᾶσαι μετόπισθεν ἀριστεύουσιν ἀοιδαί.

(A blind man, he dwells in rocky Chios. His songs are
all celebrated for future generations.)(25)

The 'blind man of Chios' was assumed by Thukydides in the
fifth century BC to be Homer himself,(26) but the event
clearly refers to a later period than that in which Homer
performed. Both Chios and Smyrna, however, have strong
claims, between which no certain choice can be made.
    Homer's close association with Ionia only appears
incidentally in the poems, since the tendency of the poet,
in which he is partially successful, is the reproduction
of the historical conditions of the period of the poems -
in this particular case, of pre-migration Ionia. Hence

there are no Greeks at Miletos (see chapter 2, p.14) and
Ionians only appear as a contingent at Troy, associated
with the Boiotians, Lokrians and Phthians in trying to
contain the Trojan hero, Hektor.(27)

Yet evidence of personal knowledge of the landscape of
Asia Minor does occur in the poems, significantly in the
similes. This is important, since the similes have been
shown to belong linguistically to a late period in the
development of Homeric diction,(28) and hence represent
something probably familiar to the poet:

τῶν δ', ὥς τ' ὀρνίθων πετεηνῶν ἔθνεα πολλά,
χηνῶν ἢ γεράνων ἢ κύκνων δουλιχοδείρων,
'Ασίῳ ἐν λειμῶνι, Καῢστρίου ἀμφὶ ῥέεθρα,
ἔνθα καὶ ἔνθα ποτῶνται ἀγαλλόμενα πτερύγεσσι,
κλαγγηδὸν προκαθιζόντων, σμαραγεῖ δὲ τε λειμών,
ὣς τῶν ἔθνεα πολλὰ νεῶν ἄπο καὶ κλισιάων
ἐς πεδίον προχέοντο Σκαμάνδριον· αὐτὰρ ὑπὸ χθὼν
σμερδαλέον κονάβιζε ποδῶν αὐτῶν τε καὶ ἵππων.

(These, as the many flocks of winged birds, of geese,
cranes or long-necked swans, in the Asian meadow around
Kayster's streams, fly hither and thither exulting in
their wings, noisily settling one in front of the
other, and the meadow resounds with their screaming,
so of these the many tribes flowed forth from the
ships and huts on to the plain of Skamandros; and the
earth rumbled horribly under their feet and those of
their horses.)(29)

The river Kayster flows into the sea near Ephesos; the
scene depicted here is imagined with such vividness and
natural detail that it is hard to imagine that the poet
did not see it, or something like it. The acute
observation of προκαθιζόντων (the whole body of birds
moving forward by the advance of single birds who settle
in front of the rest),(30) and the addition of significant
natural detail by means of an accumulation of clauses
paratactically arranged is typical of the exquisite miniature world of the Homeric simile (see further below, pp.
85ff).

Further geographical details betray, almost incidentally, a knowledge of Ionia; earlier in the same book (notable for its simile-clusters) the assembly of Greeks was
shaken by the words of Agamemnon, as on the sea the waves
are driven by the winds near Ikaria, an island off the
coast of Asia Minor beyond Samos.(31) Elsewhere, he
describes the north and west winds blowing from Thrace,(32)
and in Book XXIV, Achilles, in his famous recounting of

the story of Niobe, describes a stone image of her on
Mount Sipylos, near Smyrna.(33)   There are a number of
other minor details which suggest knowledge of Ionia and
also the Troad.(34)

Arguments which seek to relate the society and attitudes
of Homer to those of early Ionia tend to be circular,
since humour, domestic, almost courtly sophistication and
pleasant living are 'Ionian' qualities which, for the
earliest period, derive almost entirely from the evidence
of the poems themselves.(35)   Yet the argument is not
entirely without foundation; the evidence from painted
pottery suggests that in the late eighth and early seventh
centuries BC Ionia was relatively cut off from mainland
Greece and her eastern neighbours(36) (which provides a
possible partial explanation of the relative absence, in
Homer, of religious and mythical elements connected with
Near Eastern stories, compared with Hesiod).(37)   It is by
now well established that in details of social organisation, military tactics and architecture there is radical
discontinuity between the Mycenaean age and Homer.(38)
While it is difficult to pinpoint any of the above
elements within a 500 year period, it does seem likely
that the tradition would reflect, especially in social
organisation, the somewhat isolated, but nevertheless
materially well advanced 'poleis' of early Ionia.   Possibly
owing to the external pressure from non-Greek enemies, the
Ionian settlements formed themselves early into distinct
communities, sited on easily defensible coastal positions,
often surrounded by elaborate fortifications, as the
remains of Smyrna have shown.   Furthermore, the function
of Homeric kings possibly reflects more closely than anything else that of the local Ionian 'kings', and the
relatively informal social structure which forms such a
startling contrast to what we know of Mycenaean palace
organisation.(39)

Consequently it is possible, without establishing a
watertight case, to conclude that the informal but
delicately sophisticated world of Homer, especially in the
'Odyssey', probably reflects many elements in the life of
the eighth-century BC Ionian 'polis'.(40)   It is
certainly true that many elements which later distinguish
Ionian culture find their first expression in Homer.   In
view of the accumulation of evidence, it may not be going
too far to describe Homer's humanism as a product, largely,
of Ionian soil.

The above argument has attempted to suggest ('prove' is
not an appropriate word here) that the major inspiration

for the Homeric poems is Ionian. The argument is
partly linguistic, partly historical, and relies upon
the overwhelming probabilities of the case. It has
also been based upon the automatic assumption that it is
valid to make a distinction between a tradition, the
heritage of diverse periods and sources of material, and
the working within, or even beyond it, of individual
singers. In order to clarify what is meant by 'tradition'
in the Homeric case, it is necessary briefly to consider
a major, and still controversial question, the nature of
Homeric composition.

The question can, and usually has been, approached from
one of two angles. The absence of writing during the
Greek Dark Age and the apparent problem this posed for
Homeric composition was already recognised at the end of
the eighteenth century by F.A. Wolf,(41) whose work led to
the nineteenth-century 'Homeric Question'. The impossibility, as it was then thought, of extensive composition
without the aid of writing, produced a hypothesis of
numerous short lays composed at various periods and later
combined rather in the manner of the contemporary scholarly
editor of the Finnish national epic, the 'Kalevala'. The
diversity of the linguistic and cultural reference in the
poems, as well as definite and inescapable problems of
structure in both poems, gave support to the great
erudition which went into the construction of probable
hypotheses for the composition of the 'Iliad' and
'Odyssey', bewildering in their complexity.(42)

The other approach, which has ultimately proved more
fruitful, started out with the text of the poems themselves. Alexander Pope, one of Homer's most distinguished
English translators, long ago observed that Homer's
diction was aided by the regularity with which he repeated
large and small units in his verse, using the same words
on each occasion to represent the same idea or action.
For example, when heroes die, the mist of death always
closes round their eyes and their armour clashes around
them (two of a fairly small number of set formulae for
warriors' deaths). Much of the diction, especially
descriptive epithets, seems to be repeated, often with
little regard for its suitability in various contexts.
Homer did not search for 'le mot juste'; he seemed long
ago to have found it, and, moreover, to be perfectly happy
with it.

It was the great achievement of the sadly short-lived
American scholar, Milman Parry, to unite the two basic
approaches, historical and aesthetic, into a theory which
completely changed the nature of research into Homeric
language and style. The editor of his collected works,

A. Parry(43) has clearly shown how most of the elements of Milman Parry's theory were already present in the work of his predecessors; it was left to Parry himself to make the imaginative leap which provided the hypothesis by which the data could be explained.

Parry began by analysing closely the incidence of regularly recurring words in the Homeric hexameter, especially 'fixed' epithets. He successfully demonstrated that, taken as a whole, these constitute an elaborate system designed to facilitate composition.(44)   Each of the major heroes figuring in the poems has a series of epithets which can be used with the name of the individual in almost every metrical or syntactical situation likely to occur. Hence Odysseus may be described as 'godlike', 'resourceful' or 'much-enduring', depending upon the metrical context, since each of these formulae (as Parry called them) occupies a different metrical position in the Homeric hexameter. In the case of the Greek word for 'ship',(45) Parry showed that the selection of an epithet to describe it, e.g. 'black', 'blue-prowed', 'swift', or 'many-thwarted', appears to be governed entirely by the case-inflexion of the words involved and the position they are required to take up in the hexameter. Other such formulae, notably of the type 'he, answering, said' (with all the possible variations of accompanying words) exhibit similar patterns. Moreover, all the repeated elements show a marked tendency to appear in a fixed position in the verse, even when the exigencies of metre do not theoretically exclude alternatives.

If Parry had gone no further, he would merely have demonstrated that the language of the poems made use of repeated, formulaic elements derived probably from a bardic tradition and also that the conservative placing of these elements within the Homeric hexameter closely reflected the exigencies of this comparatively strict metre - all of which would have represented a useful synthesis of existing knowledge. But he went much further, by demonstrating in a series of impressive analyses(46) that the epithets and other formulaic phrases constituted a vast and intricate system characterised by what he called 'length' and 'thrift'(47) - that is, every, or almost every metrical or syntactical possibility appeared to have been covered by the formulae and, at the same time, there were very few expressions which fulfilled an identical function in any one case. Parry drew two conclusions from his findings which constitute the bedrock of his argument (and which much legitimate detailed criticism of Parry has never really shaken): first, the enormous intricacy yet flexibility of the diction must have been

far beyond the capacity of a single composer working in
isolation and creating on his own; it must, therefore, be
the product of a tradition of great richness and
complexity evolving over generations of poets.(48)   His
second conclusion was that the necessity of evolving such
a poetic diction could not be explained by conventional
poetic composition; he showed statistically that for later
'literary' epic poets, no such analysis could be done.(49)
Bringing in, at this point, the historical datum, namely
the absence of writing from the period of Homeric development, he connected the two by showing that the only kind
of composition which made formulaic diction necessary or
even possible, was oral composition - that is, improvisation without the aid of writing, using a vast heritage of
linguistic and thematic material. The absence of a script
shaped and determined the nature of Homeric composition
throughout its development.(50)

Towards the end of his short career, Parry found
startling confirmation of his Homeric hypothesis in the
study of living oral traditions in Yugoslavia and his work
has been carried on by pupils, notably A.B. Lord.(51)
Much of the physical circumstances of composition and the
style of poetry in modern Serbo-Croat oral epic has a
great deal in common with the Homeric epics. Insight has
been gained into the question, by definition unanswerable
in Homer, of how an oral tradition evolves and how an
individual poet is related to his predecessors and contemporaries in the tradition. Especially valuable is the
proof that oral singers are capable of producing poems of
the length of the 'Iliad' and 'Odyssey'.

The forty years since Parry's death have been fruitful
for the development and modification of his hypotheses.
His work has proved to have vast implications for every
aspect of Homer, most of which his early death did not
allow him to pursue. An extension of formulaic analysis
to the theme (an aspect relatively neglected in his own
researches) has revealed that a considerable proportion of
Homeric thematic material might be considered as formulae
'writ large', i.e. standard traditional elements in the
story capable of great flexibility as to length, treatment,
etc. but nevertheless consciously and repeatedly utilised
in the large-scale composition of the poems. The battle
poetry of the 'Iliad', especially, has been the subject of
recent detailed studies by B. Fenik(52) and T. Krisher,(53)
in which the essentially generic nature of the material
has emerged. At the same time, detailed analysis of the
smaller units of composition has corrected the earlier
misapprehension (never fostered by Parry himself) that
oral poetry consisted largely of free composition held

together by a traditional framework of epithets and
traditional 'fixed' lines. The further analysis goes, the
more convincingly is Parry's original hypothesis (that
Homeric language was totally formulaic) vindicated.(54)
The basic distinction between a poet and his tradition
does not really hold in the case of Homer, since his whole
diction constituted a special language inherited from his
predecessors in the tradition. He might innovate, but
would have done so entirely on the basis of the existing
formulaic structure.(55)

Some attempt has been made to discover the history of
formulaic composition from the texts themselves - how
formulae may have been built up and developed by means of
analogy and modification. Prominent in this field have
been J.B. Hainsworth(56) and A. Hoekstra.(57) Perhaps the
most remarkable development from Parry has been contributed
by Lord, on the basis of his experience of comparative
oral traditions. It now seems likely that the Homeric
poet did not consciously select at high speed from a
mental 'card-index' of expressions suitable for use, but
composed in a language learned like any other in which, as
in ordinary discourse, the manner of composition was
largely unconscious. The bard, who is illiterate (on this
point see below, pp. 88ff.) and may therefore have little
idea of what a 'word' or 'phrase' is, concentrates largely
upon his story, the selection and rejection of different
pathways through it, the best way of saying what he wishes
to say and the artistic effect and proportion of the
whole. The matching of formulae, to us so intricate a
task, would not be carried out at a conscious level by the
skilled bard. This obviously remains speculative, but it
has two points to recommend it: first, it restores an
artistic and creative role to the poet which was in danger
of disappearing on any hypothesis of mechanical formulae-
selection; second, it accords closely with descriptions in
the poems themselves of the art of poetic composition,
which concentrate not on the details but on the nature of
the story and the pathway (οἴμη) through it chosen by the
performer.(58)

Problems remain. The limitations of the comparative
evidence from other oral traditions must be appreciated.
As Hainsworth has pointed out,(59) the real proof of the
oral hypothesis is entirely internal to the Homeric poems
themselves. Furthermore, the behaviour of Serbo-Croat
'guslars' remains strictly an analogy as far as Homer is
concerned; we can only obtain information about what is
known, or suspected, about the Homeric period, from first-
hand evidence. Moreover, even the analogy can be a
dangerous one. The modern oral society, on the wane and

existing alongside a highly developed, literate,
industrial society, cannot safely be used to discover what
archaic Greek oral society was really like. A further
problem which has always worried Homerists is the enormous
gap in quality between Homer and Yugoslav epics, even the
best yet discovered.(60) The Serbo-Croat songs recorded
before and after the Second World War represent, it is
clear, the fag-end of a tradition relentlessly encroached
on by modern industrial society. Were the earlier ones
better, and were they really as good as Homer?

A further problem, possibly the new 'Homeric Question',
concerns the degree to which conventional 'literary'
criteria of judgment may be applied to Homer. A.B. Lord
has laboured to produce an 'oral poetics' which tends to
reject any attempt to apply literary criteria to Homer.
Concern for large-scale structure, proportion or artistic
unity, individualistic treatment of language, 'significant'
epithets and suchlike, are, it is maintained, alien to the
oral poet.(61)

It may, however, be maintained that the Homeric poems
exceed their modern counterparts so much in quality that
aesthetic criteria based upon experience of modern epics
has very limited value; as a matter of observation and
detailed textual study, the poems do show signs of all the
qualities apparently forbidden them, which leads in the
direction of assuming as a fundamental hypothesis an
individual poet who was both part of the tradition and
yet, at the same time, great enough to be considered as a
creative poet in his own right. This hypothesis is quite
compatible with the idea of the 'Iliad' and 'Odyssey' as
oral compositions (for Homer and writing, see below, pp.
88ff.).(62)

It is clear that the composition of the Homeric epics,
far from being undervalued by recent developments, has
been revealed as one of the most remarkable achievements
of early civilised man. It is also probable that the bulk
of this unique development was largely the unaided
achievement of Ionian poets. It was also from Ionia that
Homeric epic diction spread as a type of early poetic
'koine' suitable for use by the other Cyclic poets,
Boiotian Hesiod, the authors of the 'Homeric Hymns' and,
with modifications, early elegy and lyric. Ionia gave
Homer and the epic language to Greece, and, in doing so,
partly determined the lines upon which Greek poetic
composition was destined to develop.

We now turn from the technique to the poems themselves.
At the beginning of this chapter it was emphasised how

great was the advance made by Homer on his predecessors.
The term 'advance' must be clearly understood. Much of
the literature of the Near East originating in the second
millennium BC does not lack technical brilliance and
sophistication as well as profundity of conception. In
particular the 'Epic of Gilgamesh', in its Akkadian
version, stands out as a work which begins to explore much
of the spiritual territory later appropriated by Homer.
Although the text largely dates from the first millennium
BC, there are Hittite and Old Babylonian versions extant
which date back to the first part of the second millennium,
thereby establishing a tradition of great antiquity.(63)
The epic is secular in the sense that the poet's emphasis
is placed as much upon the earthly and spiritual development of the hero, Gilgamesh, as upon the gods who made him
and now control his fate. Gilgamesh is a hero; he has
strength, endurance and nobility as well as a capacity for
love, friendship and despair. The death of his friend
Enkidu, with whom he has shared adventures and heroic
trials of strength, is decreed by the gods as punishment for Gilgamesh because he spurned the love of the
goddess Ishtar. The death of Enkidu leads Gilgamesh
towards the struggle to change his own fate, conquer death
and learn the secret of his own existence. His long and
difficult journey, with wasted cheeks and sunken face,
ends ultimately in failure. In the course of his journey,
attempts are made to dissuade him from further pursuing
his goal:

>   'Gilgamesh, whither rovest thou?
>   The life thou pursuest thou shalt not find.
>   When the gods created mankind,
>   Death for mankind they set aside,
>   Life in their own hands retaining.
>   Thou Gilgamesh, let full be thy belly,
>   Make thou merry by day and night.
>   Of each day make thou a feast of rejoicing,
>   Day and night dance thou and play!'(64)

This fatalism in the face of the all-powerful gods can
be found on numerous occasions in Homer,(65) and is part
of a pessimism deeply ingrained in the heroic outlook.
Yet is is not accepted by Gilgamesh; despite his ultimate
acceptance of failure, his relationship with the gods
reveals an ambiguity which links him directly with the
Homeric hero; while accepting the ultimate power of the
gods, Gilgamesh believes in self-determination. He speaks
to Enkidu:

'Who, my friend, can scale heaven?
Only the gods live forever under the sun.
As for mankind, numbered are their days.
Whatever they achieve is but the wind!
Even here thou art not afraid of death.
What of thy heroic might?
Let me go then before thee,
Let thy mouth call to me, "Advance, fear not!"
Should I fall, I shall have made me a name:
"Gilgamesh" - they will say - "against fierce Huwawa
Has fallen!"'(66)

It is this self-assertion and desire for renown in the face of unalterable fate which marks the beginning of man's freedom from total subordination to the gods - a freedom without which there is no recognition of man's humanity and development of 'Geist'.(67)

In this respect 'Gilgamesh' went further than any other pre-Greek literature. Yet we must be quite clear about its limitations. While its attitude anticipates a great deal in Homer it lacks the sublety, nuance and imagination of the Greek epic. Furthermore, Gilgamesh's personal struggle is depicted largely in terms of his relationship with the gods. Personalities are strongly drawn, but lack the depth and complexity which arises from a situation in which the centre of the stage is occupied by the conflict of human relationships. It is this which mankind owes to Homer.

Attempts to describe the historical development of the Homeric poems are all, by definition, hypothetical, since the finished product is our only direct source of evidence. A great deal has been done in an attempt to discover earlier stages in the development of the story of the 'Iliad', and especially hypothetical prototypes for characters and situations in the final poem. Most of this is very speculative and usually helpful in reverse proportion to the detail of the particular thesis propounded.(68) Yet, provided the limitations of the evidence are clearly acknowledged, certain lines of development are probable.

Our knowledge of other heroic poems suggests that the 'Iliad' and 'Odyssey' developed from a comparatively simple and perhaps crude and celebratory account of the events of the Trojan War and its aftermath, designed to preserve the memory of great deeds performed by outstanding heroes.(69) At the same time A.B. Lord has demonstrated that the 'withdrawal' theme of the 'Iliad' and its attendant circumstances is a common theme of traditional poetry in diverse cultures.(70) There are a

number of indications in the 'Iliad' that an older
tradition existed in the course of oral development in
which the insult offered to Achilles - the appropriation
of his girl Briseis by Agamemnon in Book I - was ultimately
resolved by Agamemnon's offer of compensation. This
relatively simple solution (sufficient compensation for
injury restored the heroic equilibrium)(71) seems to be
implied both by the Proem of the poem (I, 1-7, in which
there is no mention of the development of the second half
of the poem) and by the remarks of Athene (I, 210-14) when
she prevents Achilles from taking his sword to Agamemnon by
pointing out that, if he restrains himself, he will obtain
threefold compensation for the injury received. 'Iliad'
IX, the book in which Achilles refuses compensation and
reinforces his refusal to fight, fits badly into its
context, a fact which has always preoccupied critics.(72)
In Book XIX, where Achilles is mourning the recent death
of Patroklos, he appears scarcely to notice Agamemnon's
long explanation and excuse for the quarrel and accepts
compensation this time without demur, partly because by
this time the whole question of insult and withdrawal no
longer has any meaning for him in the face of the much
greater tragedy of the unnecessary death of his friend.
    While the precise development cannot be unravelled, the
above facts do suggest that, without losing their grip on
the essential heroic story, the Ionian bards gradually(73)
built up a more complex and sophisticated plot in which
Achilles' withdrawal is only the First Act, so to speak,
of a more complex tale which incorporates the fateful
'aristeia' and death of Patroklos, Achilles' dearest
friend.
    The expansion of the poem and the greater complexity of
the plot entailed its development into a profound and wide-
ranging composition involving a greater insight into the
nature of heroic values; the basic code of the hero is
explicitly rejected (albeit temporarily) by Achilles:

ἴση μοῖρα μένοντι, καὶ εἰ μάλα τις πολεμίζοι·
ἐν δὲ ἰῇ τιμῇ ἠμὲν κακὸς ἠδὲ καὶ ἐσθλός·
κάτθαν' ὁμῶς ὅ τ' ἀεργὸς ἀνὴρ ὅ τε πολλὰ ἐοργώς.
οὐδὲ τί μοι περίκειται, ἐπεὶ πάθον ἄλγεα θυμῷ,
αἰεὶ ἐμὴν ψυχὴν παραβαλλόμενος πολεμίζειν.

('The same share awaits the man who shirks and he who
fights hard. The coward and the brave man are held in
the same honour. Death comes alike to one who has done
nothing and one who has worked hard. Nothing is left
over for me, though I have suffered afflictions in my
heart, always risking my life in battle.')(74)

Later in the same long episode, Achilles can reject all
the arguments brought by Phoinix, and especially the suggestion that he may eventually find himself 'without
gifts', by denying the whole basis of the heroic code in
mutual social esteem:

Φοῖνιξ, ἄττα γεραιέ, διοτρεφές, οὔ τί με ταύτης
χρεὼ τιμῆς· φρονέω δετετιμῆσθαι Διὸς αἴσῃ
ἥ μ' ἕξει παρὰ νηυσὶ κορωνίσιν εἰς ὅ κ' ἀϋτμὴ
ἐν στήθεσσι μένη καὶ μοι φίλα γούνατ' ὀρώρῃ.

('Phoinix, old father, fostered by Zeus, I have no need
of that honour; I think that I am honoured in the
dispensation of Zeus, which will hold me by the beaked
ships as long as breath remains in my chest and my
knees stir beneath me.')(75)

Achilles' predicament brings him to the necessity of
examining himself and his values in a way unknown to the
heroes of the Serbo-Croat or most other oral traditions.
It is important not to overstate the case; there is a
tendency, prevalent among some modern scholars, to turn
Achilles' experience into a tragedy, involving some kind
of intellectual or spiritual regeneration, nothing of
which has any support in the text.(76) Yet it cannot be
denied that the story of Achilles and Patroklos does
contain elements which foreshadow the later development of
Greek tragedy, principally, dramatic irony.
   The quarrel between Agamemnon and Achilles suggests an
advanced stage in the development of heroic society, in
which its basis is beginning to break down in the face of
more questioning and individualistic patterns of
behaviour. It is perhaps possible to see, in the poem
itself, the tension between new and old in the character
and behaviour of the heroes. The most striking example of
this is Agamemnon, the leader of the Greek fleet, whose
behaviour ranges unpredictably from that befitting a great
hero, towards defeatism and melancholy. It may be that as
a representative of an older and more straightforward
morality he undoubtedly suffers by the side of Achilles,
whose personal and social dilemma tends to eclipse the
more limited situation of his leader. One might also
conjecture that the inconsistency of Agamemnon's conduct
arises less from the limitations of character development
inherent in oral poetry, than from the change in emphasis
arising from the deepening and broadening of the poem's
themes; certainly this is one, not implausible, explanation of the apparent dislocation of events at the beginning of 'Iliad' II, when an attempt by Agamemnon, at the

bidding of a deceptive dream from Zeus, to arm the
Achaians, turns, for no apparent reason, into a test of
their loyalty.(77) Homer's sensibility owes a great deal
to the development of the non-combatant participants in
the poem, whose major achievement is to throw a somewhat
questioning light on the automatic assumptions of heroic
combat. Chief among these are Priam, the aged king of
Troy, Helen, who has been abducted by Paris, and
Andromache, the wife of the Trojan leader, Hektor.

We catch glimpses of Priam throughout the poem; in
Book III on the walls of Troy treating Helen, the cause of
all his misfortunes, with respect and gentleness,(78) and
later in the same book, his horror and refusal to witness
the fight of his son (the ultimate cause of all his
trouble) with Menelaos. In Book XXII he pleads abjectly
with Hektor not to face Achilles.(79) In these passages,
which show an individuality not always present in the
heroic combat, we are aware of a depth of insight coupled
with an economy of means which supports a widely held view
that the major development of Priam's part in the poem was
a recent one in the tradition. Certainly Book XXIV, in
which Priam is the main character, shows signs, linguistic
and theological, of being late, though not an addition to
the main poem.(80) The meeting of Priam and Achilles, one
of the profound moments of the poem, seems to suggest a
new insight:

τοὺς δ' ἔλαθ' εἰσελθὼν Πρίαμος μέγας. ἄγχι δ' ἄρα στὰς
χερσὶν 'Αχιλλῆος λάβε γούνατα καὶ κύσε χεῖρας
δεινὰς ἀνδροφόνους, αἴ οἱ πολέας κτάνον υἷας.
ὡς δ' ὅτ' ἂν ἄνδρ' ἄτη πυκινὴ λάβῃ, ὅς τ' ἐνὶ πάτρῃ
φῶτα κατακτείνας ἄλλων ἐξίκετο δῆμον,
ἀνδρὸς ἐς ἀφνειοῦ, θάμβος δ' ἔχει εἰσορόωντας,
ὣς 'Αχιλεὺς θάμβησεν ἰδὼν Πρίαμον θεοειδέα·
θάμβησαν δὲ καὶ ἄλλοι, ἐς ἀλλήλους δὲ ἴδοντο.

(Tall Priam escaped their notice as he came in and,
standing near, took the knees of Achilles in his arms
and kissed the hands, terrible, manslaughtering, which
had killed so many of his sons. Just as when sore(81)
disaster takes a man who, after killing a man in his
own land, comes to the country of others, to a rich
man's abode, and wonder holds those looking at him, so
Achilles wondered as he looked at godlike Priam; the
others wondered too and looked at each other.)(82)

The qualities of this passage, and of the Book in general,
hardly need emphasis. What is significant is the way in
which the poet, without putting either of his characters

through a radical transformation which would take them
beyond the limitations of their own morality,(83) nevertheless creates a scene of great power and pathos which
temporarily cuts across the narrow and exclusive
restrictions of society and allows two adversaries to
recognise their common humanity.

The above incident can be compared to Book VI, where
Diomedes and Glaukos, though enemies on the battlefield,
call a private truce and exchange gifts because of
ancestral guest-friendship;(84) in this instance, however,
the act is merely part of the stately formality of the
heroic code. The meeting between Priam and Achilles is
much more than this, and the act, between men of their
status, exceptional, though not generally without pre-
cedent.(85) Certain details, too, mark out the manner of
description. The sudden detail of Priam's stature
emphasises his dignity and pathos; the simile emphasises
the emotion felt by the bystanders and Achilles himself
(although it reverses the situation – Achilles is the
murderer). Yet the most significant effect of all, the
description of 'manslaughtering hands' is achieved by
means of an ornamental epithet, used once elsewhere of
Achilles' hands and on numerous occasions in other
contexts.(86) It is hard to suppose here (as on numerous
other occasions) that the epithet is not intended to
convey added pathos or irony.(87) However, much more
important than this is the fact that the effect of the
passage arises not from any special departures from normal
composition. The whole passage is in a traditional style
(noticeably paratactic in construction) and demonstrates
how far, at its most effective, Homer's story arose
naturally and spontaneously from the oral tradition of
which he was still a part. The style is smooth and
objective; emotions and reactions are conveyed both by
implication and by means of the long and intimate dialogue
which follows the above passage.(88)

The 'Odyssey' has suffered in critical estimation by
the side of the more serious 'Iliad'.(89) Its strengths
lie in a different direction, as the quotation at the head
of this chapter indicated. Odysseus' heroism consists in
his ability to endure alone, while the qualities which
distinguish Telemachos his son and Penelope his wife are
those demanded of rulers in peacetime – authority and tact
in the former case, fidelity and modesty in the latter.
In the course of the poem they well earn their epithets
Τηλέμαχος πεπνυμένος (wise Telemachos) and περίφρων
Πηνελόπεια (prudent Penelope), thereby emphasising the
domestic basis of the poem. Telemachos' travels to Pylos
and Sparta to hear news of his father also serve as a form

of initiation into the adult world of peacetime princes,
with elaborate hospitality and courtesies. It further
enables the poet, through the mouths of Nestor and Menelaos,
to tell elaborate stories, possibly the most underestimated
aspect of the oral poet's art.(90)

Yet the 'Odyssey' also has its profundities, which
rise, in an unexpected way, out of domestic humour. After
he has killed the suitors of his wife, Odysseus is
revealed to Penelope, who finds it impossible to believe
that it is really her husband standing before her.
Finally it is Penelope who tests πολύμητις 'Οδυσσεύς
(Odysseus of the many tricks), a byword for initiative and
resourcefulness, by eliciting information from him about a
bed which he had made before he went to Troy - information
which only the real Odysseus would know. It is at this
point that Odysseus, in anger, convinces Penelope of his
real identity. The whole recognition scene is acute,
humorous, psychologically perceptive, but also profound.
The reconciliation of two mature and long-suffering people
is brought about by a domestic trick; the wily Odysseus is
taken in by the cleverness of Penelope. As C.H. Whitman
acutely observes, the choice of a bed as the 'sign', by
which Penelope earlier tells Telemachos she will know
Odysseus, appears to be a traditional motif used in an
original way; it is also a means for Penelope to recreate
her own role as a wife.(91)

Odysseus' revelation of himself to his father, Laertes,
also exhibits the poet's skill at using the traditional in
an original way.(92) Odysseus' deception of his already
distressed and frail parent has caused critics some
worries. The apparently tasteless humour involved has
been seen as further evidence of the spuriousness of the
end of the poem.(93) Yet, as Lord has shown, the length
of the second half of the 'Odyssey' arises from the
elaboration and reduplication of the recognition motif,
with its traditional elements of deception, sign,
recognition (a sequence which appeared in a special way in
the episode discussed earlier, where it was Penelope who
practised the trick).(94) The deception of Laertes is not
only thematically necessary in the context of oral poetics,
but also illustrates the tendency of the poet of the
'Odyssey' to underline emotionally profound situations
with humour.

The Homeric poems penetrated to people's feelings and
motives in a way which was totally unprecedented in the
history of the human race. The world of the gods was also
humanised, and the individuals of earlier theogonic poetry
were evolved into a social group reflecting in essentials
that of human beings. It has long been remarked that the

scenes in the 'Iliad' which involve the gods contain most
of the humour of the poem and anticipate the domestic
relationships of the 'Odyssey'. The origins of Homer's
Olympian pantheon are diverse and often obscure, and their
existence in Homer as a more or less homogeneous family
probably owes a great deal to the poetic tradition itself,
as Herodotos thought.(95)

The creation of gods not only with human characteristics
but also motivated largely by human desires and ambitions,
is one of Homer's most significant achievements, and the
one, incidentally, that a morally earnest nineteenth-
century AD cultural milieu found it most hard to appreciate.(96) Zeus sets the tone in Book I of the 'Iliad',
when Thetis petitions him on behalf of her son, Achilles:

Τὴν δὲ μέγ' ὀχθήσας προσέφη νεφεληγερέτα Ζεύς·
'Ἦ δὴ λοίγια ἔργ' ὅ τέ μ' ἐχθοδοπῆσαι ἐφήσεις
Ἥρῃ, ὅτ' ἄν μ' ἐρέθῃσιν ὀνειδείοις ἐπέεσσιν·
ἡ δὲ καὶ αὔτως μ' αἰὲν ἐν ἀθανάτοισι θεοῖσι
νεικεῖ, καί τέ μέ φησι μάχῃ Τρώεσσιν ἀρήγειν.
ἀλλὰ σὺ μὲν νῦν αὖτις ἀπόστιχε, μή τι νοήσῃ
Ἥρη· ἐμοὶ δέ κε ταῦτα μελήσεται, ὄφρα τελέσσω·
εἰ δ' ἄγε τοι κεφαλῇ κατανεύσομαι, ὄφρα πεποίθῃς·
τοῦτο γὰρ ἐξ ἐμέθεν γε μετ' ἀθανάτοισι μέγιστον
τέκμωρ· οὐ γὰρ ἐμὸν παλινάγρετον οὐδ' ἀπατηλὸν
οὐδ' ἀτελεύτητον, ὅτι κεν κεφαλῇ κατανεύσω.'
Ἦ καὶ κυανέῃσιν ἐπ' ὀφρύσι νεῦσε Κρονίων·
ἀμβρόσιαι δ' ἄρα χαῖται ἐπερρώσαντο ἄνακτος
κρατὸς ἀπ' ἀθανάτοιο· μέγαν δ' ἐλέλιξεν Ὄλυμπον.

(Deeply vexed, Zeus the cloud-gatherer answered her:
'This is a terrible business, when you get me on the
wrong side of Hera, when she chides me with reproachful
words. Even as it is, she always quarrels with me in
front of the immortal gods and says that I help the
Trojans in battle. But you had better go back again
now, or Hera may see us. I will take care of the
matter and accomplish it. Come now, I will nod my
head, so that you may believe me; for this is the
surest pledge I can give among the immortal gods; for
what I assent to with a nod cannot be taken back,
deceitful or unfulfilled.' He spoke and nodded with
his dark brows. The ambrosial tresses of the King
flowed, waving, from his immortal head. And he shook
all Olympos.)(97)

In Homer's world there was no incongruity in the creation
of powerful and awesome gods who could also be depicted
in amusing, undignified and often disgraceful situations.

In the above passage the poet seems almost deliberately to
contrast the formal dignified introduction and conclusion
of Zeus' speech with his colloquial complaint as the hen-
pecked husband. Homer treats the king of the gods with a
licence he rarely employs with humans – in the 'Iliad' at
least.

Profane treatment of the gods is most obvious in the
story of Ares and Aphrodite, told by the bard Demodokos at
the Phaeacian court to enliven a banquet arranged in
honour of the wandering Odysseus. In this 'performance
within a performance', the singer tells of the secret love
of Ares for Aphrodite and the net fashioned by the out-
raged husband Hephaistos which holds the lovers fast, to
the amusement of the other gods. After pithy comments on
the situation, Apollo turns to Hermes:

> '῾Ερμεία, Διὸς υἱέ, διάκτορε, δῶτορ ἐάων,
> ἦ ῥα κεν ἐν δεσμοῖς ἐθέλοις κρατεροῖσι πιεσθεὶς
> εὕδειν ἐν λέκτροισι παρὰ χρυσέῃ ᾿Αφροδίτῃ;'
> τὸν δ' ἡμείβετ' ἔπειτα διάκτορος ἀργειφόντης·
> 'αἲ γὰρ τοῦτο γένοιτο, ἄναξ ἑκατηβόλ' ᾿Απολλον.
> δεσμοὶ μὲν τρὶς τόσοι ἀπείρονες ἀμφὶς ἔχοιεν,
> ὑμεῖς δ' εἰσορόῳτε θεοὶ πᾶσαί τε θέαιναι,
> αὐτὰρ ἐγὼν εὕδοιμι παρὰ χρυσέῃ ᾿Αφροδίτῃ.'
> ῝Ως ἔφατ', ἐν δὲ γέλως ὦρτ' ἀθανάτοισι θεοῖσιν.

('Hermes, son of Zeus, messenger, giver of good things,
now would you, weighed down by strong chains, want to
sleep in bed by the side of the golden Aphrodite?'
Then the giant-slaying messenger answered him: 'Would
that I might, Lord Apollo, far-shooter. There could
be three times as many chains stretched endlessly
round, and you gods and all the goddesses looking on;
but still I would like to sleep beside golden
Aphrodite.' Thus he spoke, and there arose laughter
among the immortal gods.)(98)

The whole episode is handled with delicacy and wit and
demonstrates just that lack of remoteness and reverence
which distinguishes Homer from his predecessors. Outside
Ionian poetry, it is not until the late fifth-century BC
Aristophanes that the gods are treated with such a sense
of fun. The placing of the story within the larger
framework of the poem suggests that such attitudes towards
the doings of the gods were by no means exceptional at
this time.

Relationships between gods and humans were also close.
In Book III of the 'Iliad', Helen sarcastically enquires
of the disguised Aphrodite whether she has any more plans

for her disillusioned victim and suggests that the goddess
might care to abandon Olympos altogether and become Paris'
slave.(99) On a more harmonious level, Athene establishes
a very personal, bantering relationship with Odysseus when
in 'Odyssey', Book XIII, he spins the disguised goddess
one of his many yarns:

'κερδαλέος κ' εἴη καὶ ἐπίκλοπος ὅς σε παρέλθοι
ἐν πάντεσσι δόλοισι, καὶ εἰ θεὸς ἀντιάσειε.
σχέτλιε, ποικιλομῆτα, δόλων ἇτ' οὐκ ἄρ' ἔμελλες
οὐδ' ἐν σῇ περ ἐὼν γαίῃ, λήξειν ἀπαντάων
μύθων τε κλοπίων, οἵ τοι πεδόθεν φίλοι εἰσίν.'

('He would have to be crafty and wily who wished to get
past you in all your tricks, even if a god were to meet
you. Wretch, fancy schemer, never tired of tricks, not
even in your own land would you leave off lying, tricky
speeches which are dear to you from the bottom of your
nature.')(100)

Odysseus' polite reply to the goddess' mild reproach that
he has not recognised her has just the right degree of
ironic insouciance:

'ἀργαλέον σε, θεά, γνῶναι βροτῷ ἀντιάσαντι,
καὶ μάλ' ἐπισταμένῳ· σὲ γὰρ αὐτὴν παντὶ εἴσκεις.'

('It is hard, goddess, for a mortal to recognise you on
meeting, even a very intelligent one; for you take
the likeness of everything.'(101)

In their relationship with the gods, Homeric heroes, while
not failing to show a proper appreciation of the power of
their deities, are at pains to display themselves as equal
partners in everything else.
      An extended passage which combines many of the above
qualities is Book XIV of the 'Iliad', the Deception of
Zeus. A divine interlude in the long drawn-out fighting
of the second half of the 'Iliad', it contains many
elements not usually found elsewhere in either poem,
especially references to the earlier pre-Olympian state
of the gods, a romantic atmosphere and details at times
verging on the baroque, especially in the love-making of
Zeus and Hera:

Ἦ ῥα, καὶ ἀγκὰς ἔμαρπτε Κρόνου παῖς ἣν παράκοιτιν·
τοῖσι δ' ὑπὸ χθὼν δῖα φύεν νεοθηλέα ποίην,
λωτόν θ' ἑρσήεντα ἰδὲ κρόκον ἠδ' ὑάκινθον
πυκνὸν καὶ μαλακόν, ὃς ἀπὸ χθονὸς ὑψόσ' ἔεργε.

τῷ ἔνι λεξάσθην, ἐπὶ δὲ νεφέλην ἔσσαντο
καλὴν χρυσείην· στιλπναὶ δ' ἀπέπιπτον ἔερσαι.

(He spoke, and the son of Kronos grasped his wife in
his arms. Under them the divine earth brought forth
fresh-sprouting grass, and dewy clover and crocus and
hyacinth, thick and soft, which kept them aloft, away
from the earth. In this they lay, and shrouded themselves with a cloud, beautiful and golden; and
glistening dewdrops fell.)(102)

The ostensible occasion of the love-making, Hera's
beguilement of Zeus to distract his attention from the
battle of Troy, clearly overlays a much older version of
the ἱερὸς γάμος (the sacred marriage) of god and consort
which was intimately connected with the renewal of veget-
ation and cycle of the seasons (cf. the wooden 'sacred
marriage' group from Samos, mentioned above, p.46). The
imposition of a humanising and irreverently domestic ethos
upon age-old, hieratic conceptions of deity and its
functions, is characteristic of Homer's theology. Homer's
gods were Ionian gods in the sense that they were deities
of an immigrant people, detached to some extent from
traditional cult and geographical associations. This
absence of mystery and awe foreshadowed to a large extent
the development, on the same soil as Homer, of the secular
love lyric of Anakreon and the first speculations concerning the origins of the universe in both of which the gods
were relegated to a minor role.
    A possible window on Homer's contemporary world is,
finally, provided by the numerous similes. Their contemporary geographical relevance has already been mentioned
(see above, pp. 68f.). They tend to reflect nature and
life in a pastoral or agricultural community, with humble
people engaged in everyday tasks. Many similes extend
beyond the simple point of comparison and develop the
action for its own sake. The developed simile is unique
to Homer among traditional, oral poetries; however it is
unlikely that it is the invention of the poet or poets of
the 'Iliad' and 'Odyssey', as has sometimes been
suggested.(103) The similes seem, in their own way, to
constitute systems which obey somewhat the same rules of
extension and thrift as the epithets (see above, pp.71f.).
A large number of similes belong to one of several
familiar types - sea on cliffs, snowstorms, rivers in
spate, hunting wild animals, etc. - but there is only one
case of exact repetition in the 'Iliad'.(104) The
individual members of the main classes of similes achieve
their diversity by subtle variation of standard detail.

As with the epithet systems, this degree of variety could
not be the work of one poet. The considerable number of
unique similes may be either the inspiration of an
individual poet or members of other groups not found in
the extant poems. A further argument against the
individual personal creation of the simile by Homer is the
presence, in the similes, of a large number of 'nonce'
words (words not found elsewhere in Homer or even in
extant Greek literature). This could be taken to imply
a large vocabulary of words especially designed for the
similes, of which Homer only used a small part in any one
poem.(105)

The similes exhibit a feeling for balance and form, an
acute and sympathetic observation of nature and a clarity
of detail already encountered in the artists of the 'Bird
Nester' kylix and the British Museum lion from Miletos.
Unusual and memorable pictures are drawn: for example, a
boy at the seaside kicking over a sandcastle in play,(106)
the distant smoke and glare of a besieged city on
fire,(107) an octopus pulled from its hiding place with
pebbles on its suckers.(108) These and many others give
glimpses of a rich, colourful world existing alongside the
more remote heroic past. It is in the similes, very often,
that Homer reaches the extremity of pathos and insight.
In 'Iliad', XI Homer recounts the fate of two minor
heroes, Isos and Antiphos, at the hands of Agamemnon:

ὡς δὲ λέων ἐλάφοιο ταχείης νήπια τέκνα
ῥηϊδίως συνέαξε, λαβὼν κρατεροῖσιν ὀδοῦσιν,
ἐλθὼν εἰς εὐνήν, ἀπαλόν τέ σφ' ἦτορ ἀπηύρα·
ἡ δ' εἴ πέρ τε τύχῃσι μάλα σχεδόν, οὐ δύναταί σφι
χραισμεῖν· αὐτὴν γάρ μιν ὑπὸ τρόμος αἰνὸς ἱκάνει·
καρπαλίμως δ' ἤϊξε διὰ δρυμὰ πυκνὰ καὶ ὕλην
σπεύδουσ' ἱδρώουσα κραταιοῦ θηρὸς ὑφ' ὁρμῆς·
ὣς ἄρα τοῖς οὔ τις δύναιτο χραισμῆσαι ὄλεθρον
Τρώων, ἀλλὰ καὶ αὐτοὶ ὑπ' Ἀργείοισι φέβοντο.

(As a lion easily breaks the tender young of the swift
deer, taking them in his strong teeth, entering the
lair, and takes the tender heart from them. And she,
even if she happens to be very near, cannot help them;
for dread trembling comes upon her and suddenly she
flashes through the thick undergrowth and trees,
sweating and speeding away from the attack of the
strong beast. So there was no Trojan who could save
them from death, but they themselves too were fleeing
before the Argives.)(109)

This simile builds up gradually in typically Homeric

fashion into three main (and theoretically detachable) episodes. But out of traditional materials the poet has constructed a scene of great pathos and drama, underlining the relationship of mother to young(110) and the cruelty and inevitability of nature.

The main task of the simile is, in different ways, to explain, characterise and make more vivid, an action or state in the narrative by means of a comparison. The *raison d'être* of the simile demands that the comparison be taken from the personal experience of the audience(111) and it can form either a reinforcement of, or a contrast with, the action. In the former case, the rushing attack of a hero against the enemy can be described as like that of a lion attacking a sheepfold (of which there are examples too numerous to list); on the other hand the evenness of the battle line is compared to the balanced scales on which a diligent widow weighs her wool, working to keep her children for a pitiful wage - an all too rare glimpse into the life of the contemporary poor.(112)

The simile also constitutes a primitive method of explanation later pre-empted by philosophy (which itself made considerable use of comparisons by simile in its early stages).(113) This is particularly noticeable in attempts by Homer to characterise psychological states and complex human emotion.(114) In 'Iliad', XIV, 16-22, Nestor's mental dilemma is compared to the sea swelling aimlessly before a wind has pushed it in one particular direction; and in 'Odyssey', XX, 25-30, Odysseus' ruminations on the subject of the suitors are compared to the twisting back and forth of a pudding over a fire - both similes containing unusual features which reflect unusual comparisons.(115)

The final source from which the poet takes his inspiration is the society he knew. This appears in fragmented form in the similes, as we have seen. The most extended picture, however, occurs not in the similes, but in the lengthy description, in 'Iliad', XVIII, of the decoration, by Hephaistos the heavenly blacksmith, of the shield he makes for Achilles.(116) Here we have a view of the lively, everyday world of the small, primitive 'polis'. A marriage ceremony, a legal case in the market place, the city under attack, ploughing, reaping, harvesting of grapes, dancing and singing - all these are described with the eye for detail and concern for the most humble of participants which characterise the similes. Just as he shows concern for the inner life of the individual, so the poet of the 'Iliad' and 'Odyssey', composing, doubtless for popular audiences,(117) shows a lively and sympathetic interest in the lives of ordinary people. The existence

of such an attitude in poems which are markedly aristocratic in ethos may seem, at first sight, paradoxical.
However the apparent discrepancy undoubtedly
reflects the divided viewpoint of the poet, whose story,
ostensibly based upon the heroic past, takes a great deal
from his contemporary environment. It is hard to suppose
that this environment was not eighth-century BC Ionia.

The period following the composition of the 'Iliad' and
'Odyssey' is associated with one of the most momentous
events in the history of western civilisation, namely the
introduction, to the Greek world, of the alphabet. The
letters of the Greek alphabet were derived from a variety
of North Semitic current in Phoenicia during the eighth
century BC. The evidence for its introduction into the
Greek world is scanty and its early development only
imperfectly known owing to the relative scarcity of early
inscriptions on stone - the only source preserved from so
early a period.(118) The significance of this for Ionia
will be discussed in the following chapter; here it is
necessary briefly to consider the relationship of writing
to the composition of the Homeric poems. The two events
have often been connected, even if few scholars go as far
as T. Wade-Gery, in suggesting that the alphabet was
developed in order to preserve the Homeric poems.(119)
    There is no Ionian inscriptional evidence earlier than
the seventh century BC and no knowledge of the text of
Homer until the sixth century, when, according to some
authorities, Peisistratos made an attempt to stabilise the
text of Homer for recitation at the Athenian festival of
the Great Panathenaia.(120) The work of Parry and his
successors, strongly suggesting that Homer, as well as his
tradition, made no use of writing, has sharpened the
question of the position of writing in the composition of
the poems.
    Certainty is impossible; yet it does seem as if the
argument that Homer must have been able to write is based
upon certain false assumptions. The large-scale
structural coherence displayed by both the 'Iliad' and
'Odyssey' is thought to be beyond the grasp of an oral
poet. Similarly the quality of the poetry is felt to
presume literacy. Quite apart from the modern prejudice
in favour of letters which this view implies, we have seen
on numerous occasions that the greatest quality arises
naturally out of the oral style itself; Homer's heights
represent not an individual passing beyond the limitations
of traditional style, but a confirmation of it. All the
evidence suggests that Homer would not have considered

tradition a 'limitation'. Similarly, large scale, length
and coherence do not necessarily presuppose written
planning. Illiterates in a variety of circumstances
have phenomenal memories, as anthropologists have
discovered.(121) In any case, the oral poet works not by
memorising a story, but with thematic material which,
skilfully handled, creates the monumental poem by
augmentation, repetition and variation of traditional
themes, none of which necessarily has anything to do with
writing.

A major problem involved in the oral hypothesis
concerns the ultimate writing of the poems. If they were
not written by the poet, when were they committed to
writing and how? Modern experience suggests that the fixed
test - one that has reached a final form and is
subsequently transmitted orally - has little or no place
in the fluidity of an oral tradition, among poets who seem
not to be entirely able to grasp the concept of identity,
as we would understand it, in matters of literature.(122)
It is as well to admit that we are totally in the dark
about this; any suggestion of how the 'Iliad' and
'Odyssey' were trasmitted during the first 150 years or so
after composition is likely to be guesswork. Just after
the beginning of the seventh century BC episodes from the
Trojan cycle became popular in vase-paintings from various
sources, which may suggest, although by no means prove,
the existence of a written text widely distributed. On
the other hand the recension of Peisistratos might equally
well be cited as evidence for the tidying up of oral
traditions which had become diverse and muddled in the
absence of a standard written text. Here the matter must
rest, except to note the absence of any convincing
argument for literacy based upon the internal evidence of
the poems themselves.(123)

Any consideration of an Ionian poetic tradition must take
into account severe limitations. The total quantity of
poetry from Ionia which has survived from the period after
Homer equals rather less than one book of the 'Iliad';
this reflects the fragmentary state of early lyric in
general, where survival usually depends upon the chance
citation of much later writers such as Athenaios, Stobaeus
and Plutarch.

Yet certain facts emerge: the earliest lyric poetry,
which in ethos marked a significant break with Homer,
emerged from the east with Archilochos of Paros and Alkman
of Sparta (who probably came originally from Asia
Minor).(124) The earliest lyric poets, in marked contrast

to Homer, wrote shorter poems suitable either for personal recitation or, in the case of Alkman, for performance by choirs of girls in Spartan religious festivals. The sentiments, even in the choral poems, were personal and topical, the treatment individualistic. The use of complex lyric and iambic metres marked innovation and a conscious turning away from Homer. More especially, the poet's consciousness of his own personality as an individual and his composition as a personal achievement, forms a marked contrast to the anonymity of poets working in the Homeric tradition. This is particularly marked in Archilochos, the first 'personality' in Greek literature; he tells us a great deal about himself and his attitudes, with the consequence that we know a great deal more about him from 100 or so fragments than scholarship has ever managed to find out about Homer. It is possible to see a stimulus for this new poetry in the alphabet which appears (to judge from the variety of alphabetical signs found in early Greek inscriptions) to have spread with remarkable speed and diversity across the Greek world. If the earliest poets wrote (and this remains doubtful), this activity may have done much to promote the idea of the poem as personal property, in sharp distinction from the tradition which preceded it.

As in art, so in literature, Ionia seems to have remained rather isolated from these developments. To the geographical and economic isolation of the early seventh century BC, reflected (as we saw in chapter 3) in artistic stagnation, one might perhaps add the influence of Homer, arguably stronger here than elsewhere. It is probable that in Ionia innovation only slowly made headway against the weight of oral tradition.

D.L. Page, in a study of Archilochos, suggests a possible distinction between poems written in the iambic and trochaic metre, in which there are few traditional elements, and those written in elegiacs where traditional language predominates; he assumes that the former were composed with the help of writing, whereas the latter were still created largely in the milieu of oral composition.(125)

Without assuming the truth of this plausible suggestion and postponing (until chapter 5) the question of what precisely constitutes 'the help of writing' in literary composition, one must admit that it is certainly remarkable that during the innovatory period of the seventh century BC (and, as far as we know, until the second half of the sixth century) Ionia produced only poetry in the elegiac metre. Elegiac metre is a modification of the hexameter which nevertheless still allows, metrically, considerable use of Homeric formulae, advantage of which was, as we shall see, taken.

The earliest lyric poets all wrote elegiacs, and the originator of elegy is not known. The earliest inscribed pentameter comes from a kettle-rim on Samos, and it is possible that it spread from Ionia.(126) Certainly Kallinos of Ephesos has some claim to be the earliest elegist.(127) Only one substantial fragment of his work survives, in which he exhorts his fellow citizens to fight in the face of the enemy (either neighbouring Magnesia or the Kimmerians, (see chapter 2, p.27). There is a great deal that is Homeric: the vocabulary and style is that of oral epic, especially the line endings (the most conservative part of the Homeric hexameter) and many, though not all, of the sentiments would not be out of place in the 'Iliad'.(128) Yet there is a subtle difference which gives the poem individuality. In particular the heroic emphasis has almost imperceptibly changed; the hero is praised more for his ability to defend his city than for valour *per se*. Homeric τιμή (honour) is now put at the service of the city, which is beginning to matter more than the personal ascendancy of the hero. Through Kallinos we catch a brief glimpse of early Ionian struggles with each other and with eastern invaders.

If the concept of a poetic tradition is to be considered valid for Ionia, it must lie in more than conscious reflection or adaptation of Homeric language. In this limited sense, the idea of a tradition may be extended almost indefinitely to Greek archaic literature as a whole. It is necessary to show that Ionian verse, in particular, assimilated something of the Homeric ethos, and transformed it in a particular way. For this, we must turn to Mimnermos, who lived in the second half of the seventh century BC. His birthplace was probably Smyrna and his ancestors among those Kolophonians who captured Smyrna. In his 'Nanno', Mimnermos tells of the capture of 'Aiolian Smyrna',(129) and in verses now lost, he tells of the fighting between the Smyrnaeans and the Lydians as well as composing historical and mythological works on a variety of subjects, including one fragment describing the course of the sun at night back to the east over the ocean.(130)

Most of the extant fragments of Mimnermos, however, concern the pleasures of youth and love and the unpleasantness of old age:

τίς δὲ βίος, τί δὲ τερπνὸν ἄτερ χρυσῆς 'Αφροδίτης;
   τεθναίην ὅτε μοι μηκέτε ταῦτα μέλοι,

κρυπταδίη φιλότης καὶ μείλιχα δῶρα καὶ εὐνή,
   οἷ ἥβης ἄνθεα γίγνεται ἁρπαλέα
ἀνδράσιν ἠδὲ γυναιξίν· ἐπεὶ δ' ὀδυνηρὸν ἐπέλθῃ
   γῆρας, ὅ τ' αἰσχρὸν ὁμῶς καὶ κακὸν ἄνδρα τιθεῖ,
αἰεί μιν φρένας ἀμφὶ κακαὶ τείρουσι μέριμναι,
   οὐδ' αὐγὰς προσορῶν τέρπεται ἠελίου,
ἀλλ' ἐχθρὸς μὲν παισίν, ἀτίμαστος δὲ γυναιξίν,
   οὕτως ἀργαλέον γῆρας ἔθηκε θεός.

(But what life, what joy without golden Aphrodite? May
I die, when these things concern me no longer - secret
love and gentle gifts and the bed - things which are
the flowers of youth, desired by men and women. And
when painful old age comes, which makes a man both
shameful and base, evil cares forever wear away his
heart, nor does he enjoy looking at the rays of the
sun, but to children he is hostile, in the eyes of
women, dishonoured; so painful has god made old
age.)(131)

Again, as with Kallinos, the linguistic dependence on
Homer is almost complete, but in Mimnermos we hear a
characteristic note which originates in Homer, and which
we may register as distinctively Ionian - a tendency
towards voluptuousness and hedonism, an emphasis on youth
and pleasure as the only goals of life. Along with this
goes a basic pessimism, which leads him to adapt the
famous Homeric simile of the leaves on the tree ('Iliad',
VI, 146-9) to his own philosophy of life; whereas Homer
emphasises the cyclic aspect of regeneration of veget-
ation, Mimnermos is concerned with the brevity of spring-
time.(132)
   His poetry exhibits that combination of sensuality
combined with strict formal control which we have already
noted as a characteristic of Ionian sculpture. It is
likely that the elegiac couplet was sung to the
accompaniment of the flute (although not invariably,
according to a recent authority),(133) which may have had
close connections with Phrygia. We may therefore have
here a synthesis (see chapter 1, p.6) in which an alien
element is given purpose and sharper definition by the
Greek. Yet it is more likely that Ionian hedonism was,
whatever later moralists may have supposed, a native
product.(134) Mimnermos' pessimism and sensuality are
qualities which can be traced back to Homer.
   More obvious eastern influence can be detected in the
vocabulary of the sixth-century BC Ephesian poet,
Hipponax. Lydian words and forms reflect strong elements
within the city itself. Hipponax, a writer of satiric

poetry, violent and frequently lewd, was the inventor of
the χωλίαμβος (limping iambic) a metre which became
associated with colloquial invective.

All the elements of the Ionian wit, sensuality and
technical virtuosity come together in the last Ionian
poet, the greatest love poet of archaic Greece, Anakreon
of Teos. The Teians emigrated to Abdera on the north
coast of the Aegean after their city was attacked by the
Persian general, Harpagos c. 540 BC (chapter 2, p.24) and
it is likely that Anakreon went with them. Later he went
to Samos at the invitation of Polykrates, to teach his son
music and poetry, and act as court poet. When Polykrates
was murdered c. 523 BC, Hipparchos, tyrant of Athens, we
are told,(135) sent a fifty-oared galley to fetch Anakreon
to Athens, where he may not have died until much later.
Anakreon lived through the last great flowering of Ionian
culture associated with Miletos, Ephesos and Samos where
the Ionians led the world in architecture, sculpture,
historical and philosophical investigation. His
contribution as a poet fully equalled that of his fellow
citizens in other fields. He brought to the love lyric,
already given intensity and individualism by Sappho of
Lesbos, a perfection of form, a grace and irony
characteristically Ionian:

σφαίρῃ δηῦτε με πορφυρῇ
βάλλων χρυσοκόμης Ἔρως
νῆνι ποικιλοσαμβάλῳ
   συμπαίζειν προκαλεῖται·
ἡ δ', ἐστὶν γὰρ ἀπ' εὐκτίτου
Λέσβου, τὴν μὲν ἐμὴν κόμην,
λευκὴ γάρ, καταμέμφεται
   πρὸς δ' ἄλλην τινὰ χάσκει.

(See, again, golden-haired Love, hitting me with a
bright red ball, summons me forth to play with a maiden
wearing embroidered sandals. But she (for she hails
from well-built Lesbos) blames my hair, for it is
white, and gapes after another girl.)(136)

The poem has great incisiveness and wit which the poet
characteristically turns against himself, as well as the
woman who scorns him. Whereas, for Sappho, love is
serious and jealousy agonising, for Anakreon the rejection
is accepted with wry humour. The virtuosity of style is
apparent in the use of exotic colour imagery and the
deliberate employment of epic language to achieve a mock-
heroic effect.(137) Anakreon's ironic yet committed
attitude to the experience of love finds no parallel in

archaic poetry, and indeed looks forward to the formulation of the paradox in Hellenistic and Roman poets. ἐρέω
τε δηὖτε κοὖκ ἐρέω / καὶ μαίνομαι κοὐ μαίνομαι (I love and
do not love, I am mad and not mad),(138) says Anakreon,
echoed many centuries later in a famous two-line poem of
Catullus.

The meeting of opposites, exotic sensuality with
precision and economy of language and a strong sense of
form, recall irresistibly the chief qualities of the work
of Anakreon's contemporaries in fine art (see above,
chapter 3), summed up by Anakreon himself, in the idea of
χάρις:

ἐμὲ γὰρ λόγων <μελέων> τ' εἵνεκα παῖδες ἂν φιλοῖεν
χαρίεντα μὲν γὰρ ᾄδω, χαρίεντα δ' οἶδα λέξαι.

(For my words and tunes, boys would love me; for I sing
of what is pleasing and I know how to speak pleasing
things.)(139)

The idea of χάρις, so inadequately rendered in English, is
important already in Homer. In the 'Deception of Zeus'
Hera prepares herself to seduce her husband, and her
toilet is described in elaborate detail, summed up by the
words:

χάρις δ'ἀπελάμπετο πολλή.

(Much grace shone around her.)(140)

Yet besides an element of sensuality, later Ionian χάρις
also contains gay mocking humour, beauty of appearance
(which takes us immediately to the near contemporary
maidens at Didyma (chapter 3, p.52)) and a strong sense of
form and intellectual grasp of the emotions. Both are
found in Anakreon, along with daring use of metaphor:

ὦ παῖ παρθένιον βλέπων,
δίζημαί σε, σὺ δ' οὐκ αἴεις
οὐκ εἰδὼς ὅτι τῆς ἐμῆς
ψυχῆς ἡνιοχεύεις.

(Boy with girlish glance, I seek you, but you take no
notice, not knowing that you hold the reins of my
soul.)(141)

Anakreon, it is said,(142) when asked why he did not write
hymns to the gods, but to his boys, replied 'ὅτι οὖτοι
ἡμῶν θεοί εἰσι' (because these are our gods). This

secular deification of passion, even if not entirely
seriously meant, may perhaps be seen as a natural
conclusion of a number of tendencies traceable in the
Ionian poetry of Homer, where the most prominently
displayed qualities of the gods are not majestic but
sensual and pleasure-loving. The following poem of
Anakreon contains little about the gods which would have
been alien to epic:

ὦναξ ᾦ δαμάλης Ἔρως
καὶ Νύμφαι κυανώπιδες
    πορφυρῆ τ' Ἀφροδίτη
συμπαίζουσιν ἐπιστρέφῃ δ'
ὑψήλων ὀρέων κορυφάς,
γουνοῦμαί σε, σὺ δ'εὐμενὴς
ἔλθοις μοι κεχαρισμένης τ'
    εὐχωλῆς ἐπακούων,
Κλεοβούλῳ δ' ἀγαθὸς γενεῦ
σύμβουλος τόν ἐμόν γ' ἔρωτ',
    ὦ Δεόνυσε, δέχεσθαι.

(O Lord, with whom play the subduer Love and dark-eyed
Nymphs and bright Aphrodite, as you haunt the summits
of the high mountains, I beseech you, come to me well
disposed and attentive to my acceptable prayer; be a
good counsellor to Kleoboulos to receive my love,
O Dionysos.)(143)

In the traditional guise of a formal hymn, Anakreon has
created a love poem. Eros, Aphrodite and the nymphs have
striking new epithets largely invented, as far as we know,
by the poet.(144) There is also a pun, impossible to
translate, in the final section, where Dionysos is asked
to be counsellor (σύμβουλος) to Kleoboulos.
The shift towards secular eroticism in Anakreon's
poetry has been related by C.M. Bowra to the change in
circumstances of composition from the writing by aristo-
crats for their peers to what he terms the 'courtly
spirit' of composition under the patronage of tyrants,
where entertainment was the primary consideration; hence
the essential change in spirit from Sappho to
Anakreon.(145) Yet, as we have seen, the elements
brought to perfection by Anakreon, wit, sensuality,
gaiety and perfection of form as well as a 'profane'
religious attitude, were already partially present in his
predecessors. It therefore seems more likely that
Anakreon's poetry is to be explained not as a change of
spirit so much as a final consolidation of all that was
characteristically Ionian.

Anakreon's migration to Athens may be seen as symbolic of the transition between archaic and classical, provincial and Athenian, which marked the progress of Greek culture in the early fifth century BC. Yet it is arguable that certain distinctively Ionian qualities did not travel; classical Athenian culture did not, for all its profundity and style, admit the individuality, urbanity and extravagant sensuality and the careful balance between gaiety and pessimism which marked the Ionian tradition.

5 Myth and reason: the Ionian origin of Greek philosophy

In the year 585 BC the Milesian Thales, according to
Herodotos, foretold an eclipse of the sun which dramatic-
ally turned day into night during a battle between the
Medes and Lydians under their respective kings Kyaxares
and Alyattes, 'setting as the limits of time the course of
that year in which the change actually took place'.(1) The
eclipse, clearly seen by the combatants as a sign from
heaven, effectively led to peace after hostilities lasting
five years. The astronomical nature of the event enables
us to pinpoint the date, with an accuracy quite foreign to
the archaic period, to 28 May. That Thales himself was
capable of such accuracy is, of course, out of the
question. While recent discussions of the subject differ
sharply over the question of how much astronomical
knowledge the Milesians may have had,(2) there is now
general agreement that the real cause of eclipses, and
hence their accurate prediction, could not have been known
to him.(3) Yet there is a tendency among some scholars to
throw out the baby with the bath water and assume that any
kind of prediction was out of the question for Thales. It
is known, however, that the Babylonians, observing
eclipses of the sun and moon for religious purposes, had
built up records of actual occurrences and had evolved a
crude and limited means of prediction by way of a repeated
cycle of 223 lunar months, at the end of which an eclipse
was a possibility, although it did not always occur.(4)
Thales may well have had access to information which
enabled him to foretell the possibility of an eclipse at
roughly the time it occurred. The actual occurrence of
the solar eclipse in 585 BC and its totality over the
region of Asia Minor may be reckoned as a stroke of luck
for the Ionian observer by no means beyond the bounds of
belief.(5) Herodotos appears to choose his words with
care; the accuracy is only to within an ἐνιαυτός (a full

cycle of the year) and the word προηγόρευσε (he announced beforehand) is devoid of the scientific overtones of the modern 'predict'.

More interesting is the question why Thales foretold an eclipse. In the Babylonian empire such events were of profound religious and hence political significance and their occurrences were assiduously observed and recorded by priests for whom these happenings were intimately connected with their guidance of the state. The Greek 'polis', on the other hand, lacking a ruling priestly caste, a developed astrology and a history of mathematical and astronomical expertise, did not supply the motivation for such religious observations (although, as Herodotos tells us, the eclipse did stop the battle). It is reasonable to conclude that Thales' motivation was probably sheer curiosity about the phenomenon itself, or, to put it another way, 'a new commonsense way of looking at the world of things'.(6)

The life and achievements of Thales are largely apocryphal since not one word of his writing - if indeed he did write - has come down to us, or even survived into the classical period. Apart from his prediction of the eclipse, he is credited with a number of mathematical theorems and astronomical discoveries(7) and, most important of all, the theory, in the form Aristotle puts it, that the first principle of existing things is water.(8) Aristotle's formulation is undoubtedly anachronistic, in the sense that Thales could not have expressed himself in this way; yet the idea of water as, in some way, the element from which all things come, is not unlikely to have been created by Thales.

Any degree of scepticism (and scepticism is, as we shall see, more than justified) on the question of how far Aristotle and his Hellenistic successors 'read back' scientific method into the relatively unsophisticated observations of Thales and his successors cannot alter the fact that at this point something entirely new entered human consciousness. The prediction of the solar eclipse sharply defines precisely what this new element was. Thales, like his successors in the Milesian tradition, made his observations on the basis of the accumulated data from centuries of expertise in the mathematical techniques which are implicit in the building of the Egyptian pyramids, the construction of intricate Mesopotamian star-maps, the advanced technology implicit in the smelting of metals, and the geometrical problems connected with land-measurement - all these were the requirements of large, bureaucratic empires with a highly centralised government with great need for specialised skills but none for social

or political change. Archaic Greece could not, and in
this respect did not need to, compare with the older
empires; if we are talking about knowledge in the sense of
technical data, it was not until the Hellenistic age that
Greece 'caught up' with the east. Yet what one seems to
detect in Thales, and what separates him sharply from his
predecessors, is a concern for techniques not as 'rules of
thumb' to be unthinkingly applied in the service of some
centralised government, but as knowledge from which
generalisations could be made. This curiosity and desire
to know about things the Greeks called ἱστορίη (enquiry,
knowledge) and, in its earlier, less specialised sense,
the word can be applied as much to early scientific and
philosophical(9) investigation as to history proper. Both
philosophy and history originate from the same base in
sixth-century BC Ionia. As Aristotle said with at least a
partial degree of truth: 'It is through wonder that men
now, as at first, begin to philosophise.'(10)

This representation of Ionian 'historie' might raise in
the modern mind a vision of disinterested speculation in
an ivory tower far removed from the concerns of everyday
life. The evidence suggests that this would not be a fair
picture. Certainly Plato tells us, in an anecdote, that
Thales, while observing the heavens, fell down a well,
whereupon a witty and attractive Thracian servant girl
cast some doubts upon the value of desiring to know the
things in the sky when he could not even see what was
under his feet.(11) However, this somewhat dubious
testimony to professorial absentmindedness is more than
balanced by a story, recounted by Aristotle, that, by
predicting a bumper crop of olives and buying up and then
hiring out olive-presses, Thales made a handsome
profit.(12) Aristotle draws a moral from this, that 'it
is easy for philosophers to be rich if they wish, but it
is not in this that they are interested.' He tells the
anecdote from a common Greek philosophical point of view
expressed, among others, by Plato, who relegated
practical activities to a third position, well behind
desire for glory and, in the highest place, philosophical
contemplation.(13)

Yet there is no need to project this distaste for
practical activities back on to the small and closely
integrated world of the archaic Ionian city-state. We
have the testimony of Herodotos that Thales, before the
capture of Ionia by the Persians, advised the Ionians to
to federate (see chapter 2, p.24) and that, on an earlier
occasion, he may have used his engineering skill to divide
the river Halys, so that it became fordable by the army of
the Lydian king Croesus.(14) It may be thought that on

the question of the likelihood of philosophers 'rolling their sleeves up', the unphilosophical Herodotos is a better source than Plato or Aristotle. In any case the fact that it was thought possible to combine theoretical and practical activity concedes the major point.

It is not really profitable to sift the meagre evidence for proof one way or the other. Miletos, as we have seen (chapter 2, p.28f.), was an outward looking mercantile city with extensive trading and colonising activities in Egypt and the Black Sea area and numerous contacts with peoples in the interior of Asia Minor. It was also noted (chapter 2, p.30f.) that during the first half of the sixth century BC Miletos went through a period of political turmoil as prolonged and violent as any in the Greek world at this time.(15) There is no evidence, not even anecdotal, to connect the Milesian philosophers with the events described; yet the nature of the early Greek 'polis' makes it very difficult to think of them as living detached, contemplative lives. It is unlikely that Anaximander, as has been suggested,(16) led an expedition to found Apollonia on the Black Sea since, at the most extravagant estimate, the dates do not match.(17) Yet travel, including a visit to Egypt (from which, in ancient times, the wisdom of Greece was supposed to come) is suggested for Thales by later sources. If only apocryphal, it indicates an outward-looking ethos in tune with much of their thought, which covers not merely the development of abstract principles but also the beginnings of anthopology and geography, of which we have evidence in the theories Anaximander is said to have held concerning the origins of man, and his construction of a map of the world. These particular interests were further developed towards the end of the century by Anaximander's fellow citizen, Hekataios (see below, pp.110ff.).

The evidence for all this activity, though mostly late, is cumulative. What does survive implies a great deal more, and leads us in the direction of supposing that Miletos may well have been a central point in the decisive and fruitful meeting of east and west which has much to do with the origins of philosophy (see the conclusion of chapter 6). Yet opportunity for contact was certainly not enough; if it had been, there would have been nothing to stop the Phoenicians, for example, a flourishing mercantile people, from developing philosophy. The fact that they did not, and the Greeks did, requires further investigation.

The experiences of the various 'poleis' in the seventh and sixth centuries BC all represent individual responses to a roughly uniform development which can be related to

the general evolution of the Greek world from the end of
the Mycenaean period. The economic and social pressures
of the late seventh and early sixth centuries led to
violent revolution almost everywhere.(18) In a few cases
we can also detect an informed response to events which
may be regarded as the beginning of man's independent
theorising on subjects such as power and justice, which
forms the beginning of political and moral philosophy.
A.R. Burn, in a lucid analysis of the general development,
points out that Greece was not alone in this; Judaea,
China, India and perhaps also Persia witnessed the beginnings of systematic and questioning moral thought at about
the same time.(19)

The best evidence for this development in Greece comes
from Athens which, paradoxically enough, was at the
beginning of the sixth century BC not yet in the forefront
of the Greek states. Athens' crisis concerned the
increasingly serious state of the smaller peasantry whom
economic pressure had forced into poverty, slavery and, in
some cases, even exile. A potentially serious revolutionary situation, with an outcome such as we have seen at
Miletos, was averted in 594 BC by the appointment of an
arbitrator, Solon. Solon was an aristocrat who had
detached himself from his traditional class alliances to
the extent of joining that section of the aristocracy
which was beginning to engage in trade. Eschewing the
tyranny which elsewhere (as, at about the same time, in
Miletos, see chapter 2, p.30) was the typical, albeit
temporary, outcome of the inevitable political crisis,
Solon attempted, by a series of legal enactments, to
relieve the wretched condition of the poor and set a limit
to the power of the rich. His precise measures are a
matter of controversy which does not directly concern us
here. What is important are the terms in which Solon saw
the crisis and his position within it. He left a
testimony to his activity in a series of poems in elegiac
metre, of which we possess substantial fragments (more
than of any Ionian poet except Anakreon). While his
conception of what was really going on seems, naturally
from our point of view, limited, the poems do reveal that
Solon was able to take a considerably detached and
generalised view of the situation which reflects his
social position within it. His conscious espousal of the
middle way (an idea destined to become canonical in later
Greek political and moral philosophy) involves Solon, in a
concrete image characteristic of archaic thought, standing
between the combatants:

ἔστην δ᾽ ἀμφιβαλὼν κρατερὸν σάκος ἀμφοτέροισι,

νικᾶν δ' οὐκ εἴασ' οὐδετέρους ἀδίκως.

(I stood, with a strong shield thrown before both
[sides], not allowing either to prevail unjustly.)(20)

His attitude is summed up in the concept of εὐνομία
(ordered rule) which reconciles the opposites and saves
the city. The personification recalls the much simpler
use of this device in Homer,(21) but here helps to create
the impression of immediacy and life which the archaic
age appears to have been able to give to ideas. As in
visual art, poets and thinkers of this period reveal the
ability to create the beginnings of a conceptual world
without losing their grip on the vivid and concrete:

οὕτω δημόσιον κακὸν ἔρχεται οἴκαδ' ἑκάστω
    αὔλειοι δ' ἔτ' ἔχειν οὐκ ἐθέλουσι θύραι,
ὑψηλὸν δ' ὑπὲρ ἕρκος ὑπέρθυρεν, εὗρε δὲ πάντως,
    εἰ καί τις φεύγων ἐν μυχῷ ᾖ θαλάμου....
εὐνομία δ' εὔκοσμα καὶ ἄρτια πάντ' ἀποφαίνει,
    καὶ θάμα τοῖς ἀδίκοις ἀμφιτίθησι πέδας·
τραχέα λειαίνει, παύει κόρον, ὕβριν ἀμαυροῖ,
    αὐαίνει δ' ἄτης ἄνθεα φυόμενα
εὐθύνει δὲ δίκας σκολιὰς ὑπερήφανά τ' ἔργα
    πραΰνει, παύει δ' ἔργα διχοστασίης,
παύει δ' ἀργαλέης ἔριδος χόλον, ἔστι δ' ὑπ' αὐτῆς
    πάντα κατ' ἀνθρώπους ἄρτια καὶ πινυτά.

(Thus public evil comes to everyone in their home and
outer doors cannot keep it out any more, but it leaps
over the high fence and finds a man just the same, even
if he flees to a corner of his room.... Good rule
displays all things as well ordered and perfect and
often puts fetters on the evil doers; she smoothes the
rough, checks surfeit, weakens insolence, withers the
blooming flowers of ruin, straightens crooked
judgments and soothes proud actions, stops works of
dissension, halts the anger of bitter strife. By her
are all things among men perfect and wise.)(22)

Drawing to some extent upon the rich heritage of gnomic
poetry in Homer and Hesiod, Solon nevertheless reveals a
concern for general political and moral consequences which
foreshadows the much more penetrating and incisive
expression of the Ionian philosophers, to be investigated
in this and the following chapter.

It is now time to consider three factors which are
intimately connected with Greece's exceptional intellectual development at this time: the spread of literacy, the
development of written law and the introduction into the
Greek world of coined money.

In the course of the seventh century BC the growing use
of writing in the recently introduced alphabet is
illustrated by the earliest inscriptions on stone and
pottery available for observation. The earliest alphabetic writing comes from Athens.(23) No writing as early
as this is recorded in Ionia.(24) Herodotos informs us
that the Ionians (in the broader sense) were taught the
alphabet by the Phoenicians, and called writing material
διφθέραι (skins) - a survival from an earlier period when
papyrus was difficult to obtain, and so they used goat
and sheep skins to write on.(25) L.H. Jeffery sees
valuable evidence that the Asia Minor Ionians were
pioneers in the use of leather in the untidy, hasty
lettering on early Ionian inscriptions which often approx-
imates to a cursive script. She feels that Asiatic Greeks
may have been among the first Greeks to receive the new art,
which originated probably in Al Mina or some other
Levantine entrepôt.(26) Whatever the case, there is no
doubt that the alphabetic script spread very swiftly to
all parts of the Greek world; clear evidence of this comes
from the great diversity of alphabetic signs from the
earliest inscriptions.

The ability to write does not, of course, imply
universal, or even significant literacy. We have no way
of knowing what proportion of the society was literate or
how extensive was the use made of reading or writing by
literate individuals in their everyday life. It is well
known that reliance on memory remained a characteristic of
the Greeks until well after the classical period; writing
and reading a papyrus roll was doubtless a cumbersome and
time-consuming activity with none of the swift accessibil-
ity associated ewith selecting and turning the pages of
the modern book.(27) In considering the earliest period
it is perhaps not without significance that the first
reference to books as such does not come until late in the
fifth century BC; Eupolis, the comic dramatist, refers to a
part of the Athenian market where books can be bought and
Sokrates is represented in Plato's 'Apology' (early fourth
century BC) as referring casually to the book of the
philosopher Anaxagoras as being on sale for a drachma, at
the most, in the 'orchestra'.(28) Before this, we know
nothing about libraries or the book trade. It seems
possible that a great deal of the appreciation of
literature up to, and even including Athenian drama, was

derived, for the great mass of the audience, from the ear rather than the eye. The appreciation of the subtle stylistic parodies of the 'Frogs' of Aristophanes certainly does not, as often maintained, necessarily imply that the bulk of the audience had read the plays in question or even that Aristophanes 'must have depended to some extent on a personal book collection.'(29) These assumptions stem from the modern tendency vastly to underrate the capacity of the aural memory in a society where the spoken word is the primary medium of communication.

The increasing frequency of written legal codes, treaties and dedications all over the Greek world from the late seventh century onwards clearly testifies to the importance of written communication in certain vital areas of activity. Yet, to say that archaic Greek man was able to use writing does not imply that he might always wish to. The transition from the acoustic to the visual is physiologically and psychologically a major step in the development of the child who learns to read, and only accomplished with practice and application. A society, illiterate but highly cultured and skilled in the tech- nique of oral communication, would experience even greater difficulty, to the extent that it might initially be unable to see the advantages presented by so cumbersome a process as reading in all but absolutely utilitarian activities such as trade accounts. The only connection between alphabetic signs and the things they denote is the conventional social value assigned to them by a given group of people. Initially an illiterate might see writing as no more than a complicated code like morse; it is only gradually that he learns the social and literary connotation of language.

Absence of evidence makes all this hypothetical for the Greek archaic perid. However, a prominent medievalist, in a valuable discussion of literacy in the English Middle Ages, emphasises the elementary reading ability of the medieval literate, who still preferred to hear rather than see. When forced to read, he did so audibly and with extreme slowness. H.J. Chaytor, the author of this discussion, suggests, quite incidentally, that his conclusions would doubtless apply *a fortiori* to the ancient world.(30)

The question of the composition of literature is relevant here. The spread of literacy undoubtedly affected poets; the development of poetic signatures or σφρηγεῖς (seals) such as the poet's name or other sign, marked out the composition as his personal property, undoubtedly with the purpose of differentiating it very sharply from the communal and anonymous tradition of oral poetry, and also as a precaution against direct plagiarism. Yet we must be quite clear about the part played by writing. 'Composition with the aid of writing' during the early archaic period was probably confined to the last stages of the process; the poet would commit to writing what he had already composed entire in his head, in order to preserve it for posterity. Again, we are not in the realm of proof; yet it is fascinating to speculate that early Greek poetry would have retained the characteristics of oral composition, as we know it did the circumstances of oral performance.

What, then, is the particular significance of the advent of literacy for the Greeks? Mesopotamia and Egypt had enjoyed the advantages of writing for at least a millennium before it reached the Greeks,(31) and the existence of a literate class in their societies had been the basis both for their extensive achievements in the fields of engineering and technology and also for the survival and maintenance of an extensive body of mythical and religious literature. What was so different about the Greeks?

Clearly, a major factor was not so much the fact of literacy as the purpose for which it was used and the people who used it. In the Near East, writing had been the closely guarded prerogative of a priestly ruling class who used it as a means of perpetuating power. In Greece, there was no such class for whom the ability to read and write could be a source of power. In the fluid and intimate world of the Greek 'polis' it appears that in its official guise the written word merely gave permanence to what had previously been spoken; only gradually did literacy change the character of Greek society.

This fluidity is nowhere better illustrated than in the case of Greek religion. The absence of a written authoritative theology left the field entirely, in the earliest period, to poets. Taking their lead from Homer, the poets of the archaic and even the classical period felt free to interpret the traditional mythical heritage of the Greeks in a personal and idiosyncratic way. The essentially rational and secular atmosphere of much of this theology, despite the disapproval of moralists such as Xenophanes and Pindar, held sway in the Greek world until the time of Plato, and represented a field ripe with potential for intellectual advance.(32)

A very important fact behind all this, and one which until recently has received scant attention, is that literacy came uniquely late to the Greek world. G.S. Kirk remarks, in an interesting discussion of the origins of

Greek philosophy, that Greek culture had many of the
characteristics of a literate society from a very early
period of its development without actually being one.(33)
Consequently the alphabet was introduced into a society
which, in certain vital respects, was already much more
sophisticated than its technically literate neighbours in
the Near East. An outstanding example of this, the poems
of Homer, has already received attention; we have
attempted to show how the Greeks developed traditional
poems of great brilliance and profundity without the aid
of writing. The function of writing when it did come was
not to aid composition but to preserve the poem for
posterity (see above, chapter 4).

A similar example is the field of law. The first
written law-codes in Greece date from the second half of
the seventh century BC, and it is clear that the commit-
ting of law to the permanency of stone or wood was
regarded in itself as a popular act, which preserved the
citizens from the caprice of those who carried the law in
their heads and, could, presumably, alter it to suit
themselves. Hesiod, a peasant farmer from Boiotia, writing
in the epic style in the early seventh century BC, refers
bitterly to the ἄνδρες δωροφάγοι (bribe eaters) who give
crooked judgments.(34) He is undoubtedly referring to a
situation in which no sure permanent record of legal
enactments existed. The Athenian law-giver Drakon was
perhaps the earliest legislator (c. 630 BC). Later
tradition had it that his code seemed to be written in
blood instead of ink, so severe were its penalties.(35)
Yet the severity was perhaps less important than the very
fact that they were permanently on record and so
universally knowable and not subject to arbitrary change.
The existence of the inscription in which this permanence
resided was itself very precious. Many law-codes and
treaties contain a clause stipulating penalties for
changing or defacing the actual lettering; the sixth-
century BC treaty between the Eleans and the Arkadian
Heraians contains a final sentence:

αἰ δέ τιρ τὰ γράφεα ταὶ καδαλέοιτο αὔτε ϝέτας αὔτε
τελεστὰ αὔτε δᾶμος, ἐν τέπιάροι κ' ἐνέχοιτο τοῦ 'νταῦτ'
ἐγραμένοι.

(If anybody defaces these letters, whether private
citizen or official or the state, let him be bound in
the penalty here inscribed [a talent of silver].)(36)

Yet certain elements in early Greek written law point to
its non-literate past. There were, in a number of city-

states, holders of an office whose duties consisted of being recorders of events or decisions in sacred and secular matters, called μνήμονες (remembrancers). In some cases the function seems to have been performed by the αἰσυμνῆται ('judges' or 'arbitrators'),(37) thereby suggesting that the individual who made decisions may also have been the man in whose memory the law reposed. L.H. Jeffery points out that the old name of remembrancer occurs in early inscriptions on a number of occasions and seems not to have been affected by the later practice of writing.(38) We might conclude that the name survived the change in the nature of the office - from 'remembering' enactments to noting them down in writing.

On the other hand, the absence of early evidence for such records of public business such as those erected in the east, and more particularly lists of state officials, priesthoods and the like, leads one to wonder how far, even in the sixth century BC, the influence of the remembrancer pervaded. In the case particularly of Ionia where, it might be supposed, literacy was an early and influential phenomenon, the extant stone fragments of lists of eponymous officials at Miletos date from not earlier than the time of Alexander the Great (late fourth century BC). While earlier lists undoubtedly existed, this does not preclude the possibility that the memories of successive officials may have preserved names for years before it became necessary for them to be permanently committed to writing.(39) We may conclude that the practice of writing spread fairly slowly and selectively to various activities of the Greek city; its availability did not, as it would in modern society, automatically entail its use, as long as other methods were more familiar and seemed, on the face of it, less troublesome.

The emergence of written law-codes had two important consequences for Greece's intellectual development: first, the creation of laws by individuals such as Drakon and Solon took the origins of law out of the hands of the gods and placed them within the grasp of human, albeit legendary legislators, such as Lykourgos at Sparta. Second, the existence of law as a man-made element in society forced men to think more consciously about it instead of accepting without question an ancestral tradition. This progress was speeded up by colonisation, involving as it did the need to pull up the roots of tradition and start afresh, with law as with other social elements, in a new place without the old associations, religious or geographical. In some respects the early 'colonisation' of Ionia represents a prime example of the radical effect of change of habitation; this may have contributed to later intellectual developments.

A further consequence of writing is the tendency to value consistency and eliminate many of the conflicting elements which can exist in a pre-literate society. Curiosity, desire for a clearer definition of rights and obligations and a conviction that law was the servant rather than the master of the state - all these led to the beginnings of a more theoretical approach to justice, wrong-doing and society (cf. the passage from Solon quoted above p. 102), which can already be seen at the beginning of Homer's 'Odyssey', where Zeus, in a statement of unusual generality, makes men responsible for their own misfortunes despite their tendency to blame the gods.(40) The clear separation of conduct and its consequences from the actions and attitudes of the gods did not take place until the age of the Sophists in Athens (second half of the fifth century BC). Yet, a tendency towards critical generalisation undoubtedly formed a suitable background far earlier for the original philosophical formulations of Thales' successor and kinsman Anaximander and the Ephesian philosopher Herakleitos.

The final element which must be mentioned is the introduction into the Greek world of coined money. There is no reason totally to dismiss Herodotos' claim for Lydia as the inventor of coinage as a medium of exchange;(41) however, study of the foundation deposit in the Artemision at Ephesos of electrum coins (now dated c. 600 BC) suggests very strongly that Ionia may well have been the earliest Greek state to manufacture regular coins. The main evidence for this is the existence in the deposit of coins representing the successive stages of development from the simple typeless dump through to the stamped coin. None of these preliminary stages are found in mainland Greek deposits, which suggests that they are probably derivative.(42)

During recent times the significance of the advent of coined money in the economy of the ancient world has been well appreciated. It has recently been suggested that the small denominations and limited circulation of the earliest coins makes it more likely that they were invented to serve the needs of government rather than trade;(43) nevertheless its swift adoption by commerce can hardly be doubted. It led to a completely new relationship between traders, farmers, government and the means of production which helped to precipitate the political crises of the sixth century BC. At the same time it facilitated the enormous economic expansion of cities involved in colonisation.

Yet it also indirectly acted as a stimulus for the

development of abstract thought. Money introduced what
has been termed the 'universal equivalent' - a common
standard by which the value of goods could be judged; this,
in its turn, aided the evolution of the concept of a
unified principle in terms of which the multiplicity and
diversity of things in the world could be explained. That
philosophers were themselves aware of this is clear from a
fragment of Herakleitos:

πυρός τε ἀνταμοιβὴ τὰ πάντα καὶ πῦρ ἁπάντων ὅκωσπερ
χρυσοῦ χρήματα καὶ χρημάτων χρυσός.

(For fire all things are an equal exchange and fire for
all things, just as goods for gold and gold for
goods.)(44)

Amid all the uncertainties associated with the study of
archaic Greece, one point stands out very firmly: the
discovery of an intellectual or scientific outlook on the
world was the achievement of the Ionians. It was their
greatest gift to Hellenism, and indeed the only gift from
Ionia ever genuinely acknowledged by the recipients. The
Ionians set themselves against an accumulated weight of
myth and tradition in order to go behind man's immediate
experience and explain it. In this they were wholly
original.

So much for basic considerations. It is now necessary to
focus more closely on the Ionian achievement in sixth-
century BC Miletos. Any attempt to get to grips with the
nature of early philosophical speculation involves
consideration of the nature of the sources. The original
words of the Milesians are very few and most of our
knowledge of their achievement comes to us in the language
and, inevitably, the thought forms of later times.
Central to the whole question is Aristotle, whose
presentation of the earliest Presocratics (as thinkers
before the Socratic schools of the early fourth century BC
are conventionally called) deeply influenced all later
ancient historians of thought.(45) Aristotle saw his
predecessors from the point of view of his own developed
theory of causation; they all participated, as he saw it,
in the quasi-dialectical progression towards himself
ὥσπερ ὑπ' αὐτῆς τῆς ἀληθείας ἀναγκασθέντες (as if
compelled by truth itself). This essentially teleo-
logical approach tends to obscure or ignore those elements
in the Presocratics which did not fit into Aristotle's
system. Attempts which have been made to rescue

Aristotle as a historian of thought from the severe
strictures of H. Cherniss,(46) by asserting undoubted
proofs of his factual accuracy(47) do not really answer
the basic criticism, formulated by Cherniss forty years
ago: 'Merely to say that Aristotle had the habit of
"putting things in his own way regardless of historical
considerations"... does not help us much in restoring them
to their original shape, for while the matter may be
historically correct and only the form Aristotelian, the
form reshapes the matter and the two elements in the unit
cannot be separated by instinct.'(48)

The question of philosophical anachronism is a wide-
ranging one which, in the case of the Milesians, takes a
very acute form, owing to the absence of original material
to counteract unhistorical reconstruction.(49) One of the
most obvious losses is a clear indication of the range and
relative importance of the various aspects of the world
covered by the Milesians. Aristotle and his followers,
quite apart from the considerations just mentioned, were
concerned with the degree to which the Milesians had
anticipated their metaphysical principles; accordingly this
question takes the central place in their reconstruction
of the Milesians. However, we learn from extremely
fragmentary sources that these men were also concerned
with meteorology, ethnography, biology, geography,
astronomy (see above, pp.99ff.) and politics. Such
questions as the origins of wind, thunder and lightning,
the heavenly bodies, the measurement of time as well as
anthropocentric questions such as the origin of man and
animals, the shape of the world and the nature of its
contents, were all grist to their mill.

Their later fellow-citizen Hekataios had a range of
interests which indicates more clearly the general nature
of Ionian activity. Fragments from a lost work on
genealogies suggests that he was attempting to tidy up the
mass of Greek tradition on rational principles:

Ἑκαταῖος Μιλήσιος ὧδε μυθεῖται· τάδε γράφω, ὥς μοι
δοκεῖ ἀληθέα εἶναι· οἱ γὰρ Ἑλλήνων λόγοι πολλοί τε καὶ
γελοῖοι, ὡς ἐμοὶ φαίνονται, εἰσίν.

(Hekataios the Milesian speaks thus: I write these
things as they seem true to me; for the stories of the
Greeks are many and laughable, as it seems to me.)

Though the content of this work does not quite live up
to this proud declaration, its spirit is clear.(50) The
systematising of myth was one of the activities promoted
by a growing reliance upon the written word. That

Hekataios is one of the earliest prose-writers whose words
survive is not coincidental (see below, p. 130). Hekataios,
like Anaximander, is credited with the construction of a
map; this certainly would seem to follow from his other
great work, already mentioned earlier, the περιήγησις τῆς
γῆς (geographical guide of the world).(51) Hekataios'
great geographical knowledge may have been the basis of
his pessimism concerning the ability of the Ionians to
take on the Persian Empire at the outset of the Ionian
Revolt.(52) Herodotos also tells us that Aristagoras, the
Ionian leader, took a χάλκεον πίνακα ἐν τῷ τῆς γῆς ἁπάσης
περίοδος ἐνετέτμητο καὶ θάλασσά τε πᾶσα καὶ ποταμοὶ
πάντες (a bronze tablet on which was engraved a map of the
whole earth, all the sea and all the rivers).(53) This
may have been the map of either Anaximander or Hekataios,
or the latter's revisions of the former.

The bias of our sources makes it likely that the
ethnographical achievement of the Ionians is underestimated. A recent authority concludes that, in the
perennial controversy over how far Herodotos' manifest
prejudice against his predecessor Hekataios is justified,
the latter must be given his due for giving the Father of
History (as Herodotos has rightly been called) a valuable
basis in chronology, geography and cartography.(54) The
proximity of the Ionians to foreign lands encouraged in
them an interest in and a sympathy for alien habits and
customs which, later on the mainland, does not appear to
have survived Herodotos.(55) In considering the most
original abstract speculations of the Ionians, this
background in the more practical and outward-looking
aspects of thought must not be forgotten. Indeed, just as
no real distinction can be made between the men as
practical citizens and as speculative thinkers, so the
more conceptual side of their achievement will be seen to
be inseparable from the concrete and social.

So far we have been concerned with the question of why
Greek philosophy originated in Ionia in the sixth century
BC. It is now necessary to consider where it came from
and what made it take the form it did.

Thales' emphasis on the importance of water derives, as
Aristotle (to give him his due) perceptively realised,
from older mythical speculation, such as that of Homer,
who, in isolated passages, refers to Ocean as the γένεσις
πάντεσσι (source of all things).(56) This idea does not
form part of Homer's basic world view, which is notably
free of cosmological speculation; it seems to derive from
Eastern theological poems concerned with the birth of the

gods, in which water plays a fundamental part, reflecting
without doubt, the importance of this element in the
river-based civilisations of Mesopotamia and Egypt. This
element of continuity in early Greek thought, however
superficial it may seem, nevertheless illustrates a
general tendency in the Milesians to utilise, rather than
reject, their heritage.

We have already had occasion to consider the Akkadian
version of Gilgamesh in the context of Homer (see above,
chapter 4, pp. 75ff.). Another important Akkadian poem
which originated in Babylonia is the famous 'Enuma Elish'
or 'Hymn of Creation' (as it is conventionally called in
English).(57) Although no extant text of this poem ante-
dates the first millennium BC, internal evidence would,
according to the majority of experts, date the poem as
early as the early part of the second millennium.(58)   The
poem was chanted on the fourth day of the Babylonian New
Year festival which took place at the spring equinox; the
hymn and the ritual surrounding the whole festival were
closely connected with the annual conflict of the powers
of order and chaos which was an intrinsic part of the life
of an agrarian river-based people. In this poem, as in
other Near Eastern theogonies, speculation about the
origins of the world is intimately connected with an
understanding of the means by which a world-order is
maintained; the annual victory, in ritual and hymn, of the
power of order, is a celebration of an original
victory.(59)

As in theogonies generally, the origins of the world in
the 'Enuma Elish' are genealogical; pairs of deities
produce children, and they all represent the gradual
emergence of the known features of the universe from an
original watery chaos.(60)

The word 'represent' does not imply that the creators
of the hymn were 'dressing-up' already abstract
formulations in an anthropomorphic guise; the relation of
individuals to the universe was immediate and personal.
The powers of the world, sun, sky, earth, wind, storm and
flood, were all gods of varying degrees of strength,
arranged hierarchically; man's relationship with them was
largely a direct and immediate confrontation.(61)

In general terms the social order is reflected in the
order of the universe. The idea of personal confrontation
outlined in the previous paragraph must, however, be
treated with some caution (the word 'largely' in the last
sentence but one was chosen advisedly). Although it
usefully contrasts in very general terms two distinct ways
of looking at the world, namely the scientific or philosophical with the personal and anthropomorphic, it must be

appreciated that the Babylonians were by no means
primitive in the sense that this word might be applied to
West African tribal societies, for example. Furthermore,
there is evidence, in the opening section of the 'Enuma
Elish', of an element which is more important even than
the apparent cosmological references, namely simplicity of
conception and consistency of pattern (the emergence of
the earliest generations of gods by twos) which considerably modifies the personal element implied in the sexual
generation of anthropomorphic gods.

A key factor in early creation myths is conflict, which
normally takes the shape of a battle or duel, an element
which appears almost universal in the myth and ritual of a
variety of peoples.(62) In the 'Enuma Elish' there is a
conflict between the older and younger generations of gods
which eventually threatens the existence of the latter.
Then Ea (the god of wisdom) begets Marduk, who emerges as
a champion who agrees to face Tiamat, the great adversary,
on condition that he receives the kingship of the gods
with full authority. He kills Tiamat and her supporters,
divides her carcass into two and with each half creates
heaven and earth. The last section of the hymn (more than
one third of the whole) tells of Marduk's ordinances. He
creates stations for the gods, sets up constellations and
fashions men from the blood of one of the defeated
gods.(63)

Certain features of the 'Hymn' are significant in the
present context. Despite the pattern mentioned above, the
action takes place on a very personal level. In the
battle between the young champion, Marduk, and the
primeval monster of the sea, Tiamat, we can easily recognise the conflict between order and chaos which formed a
recognisable and vital fight for human existence. Such
matters as these were part of the state religion,
controlled by priests who ordered the cycle of the seasons
and the livelihood of the people. The emergence of a
victor in the duel and his personal organisation of the
world both justified for humans the existing world-order
and guaranteed its stability.

It has long been recognised that Hesiod's account of
the birth of the gods in his 'Theogony' owes a great deal
to the Babylonian and other Near Eastern creation myths(64)
to the extent that direct influence is a probability.(65)
Yet, in comparing Hesiod with his predecessors, we meet a
contrast in circumstances of composition not dissimilar to
that encountered in the previous chapter between
'Gilgamesh' and Homer. Hesiod was a peasant farmer in
early Iron Age Boiotia composing a poem not as part of an
official state festival but in the oral epic tradition of

Homeric bardic improvisation.

His 'Theogony' contains an account of the origins of the world:

ἤτοι μὲν πρώτιστα Χάος γένετ᾽· αὐτὰρ ἔπειτα
Γαῖ᾽ εὐρύστερνος, πάντων ἕδος ἀσφαλὲς αἰεί
ἀθανάτων οἳ ἔχουσι κάρη νιφόεντος Ὀλύμπου,
Τάρταρά τ᾽ ἠερόεντα μυχῷ χθονὸς εὐρυοδείης,
ἠδ᾽ Ἔρος, ὃς κάλλιστος ἐν ἀθανάτοισι θεοῖσι,   120
λυσιμελής, πάντων τε θεῶν πάντων τ᾽ ἀνθρώπων
δάμναται ἐν στήθεσσι νόον καὶ ἐπίφρονα βουλήν.
ἐκ Χάεος δ᾽ Ἔρεβός τε μέλαινά τε Νὺξ ἐγένοντο·
Νυκτὸς δ᾽ αὖτ᾽ Αἰθήρ τε καὶ Ἡμέρη ἐξεγένοντο,
οὓς τέκε κυσαμένη Ἐρέβει φιλότητι μιγεῖσα.   125
Γαῖα δέ τοι πρῶτον μὲν ἐγείνατο ἶσον ἑωυτῇ
Οὐρανὸν ἀστερόενθ᾽, ἵνα μιν περὶ πάντα καλύπτοι,
ὄφρ᾽ εἴη μακάρεσσι θεοῖς ἕδος ἀσφαλὲς αἰεί.

(Now, at the very first Chaos came to be; but then broad-breasted Earth, safe seat for ever of all the immortals who hold the peaks of snowy Olympos, and murky Tartaros in the recesses of Earth of the broad ways, and Eros, who is fairest among the immortal gods, looser of limbs; she overcomes the mind and wise counsel in the breasts of all gods and all men. From Chaos Erebos and black Night came to be; from Night came forth Aither and Day, whom she bore after conceiving from Erebos, joining in love with him. And Earth first brought forth starry Heaven equal to herself to cover her all over so that he might be a safe seat for ever for the blessed gods.)(66)

Earth goes on to bear the sea, hills, etc. (in which capacity she is clearly cosmological). She also bears Kronos who, with the help of his mother, castrates his father, Ouranos, with a jagged sickle, and usurps him. Kronos marries his sister Rhea and swallows all their children. This fate awaits all except Zeus whom Rhea, on the advice of her parents, allows to be reared in Crete. She presents Kronos with a stone wrapped in swaddling-clothes which he swallows. In the course of time, Zeus grows up, defeats his father aided by Earth, and overcomes a number of other opponents whom he imprisons, along with his father Kronos, in Tartaros under the Earth. Zeus concludes by marrying a number of goddesses including Themis, Eunomia, Diké and Eirené, all of whose names reveal their social, ethical and political connections.

Hesiod's poem is traditional, and as such contains material on a number of different levels, making logical consistency in the details of the story not always easy to find.(67) The thinly veiled cosmogony of the initial section, quoted above, may be constrasted with the personal conflict of generations, including the castration motif. Creation by sexual reproduction, the emergence of a champion and a final ordering of the world are all elements which we have already met in the 'Enuma Elish', and the details of the myth as a whole probably reflect a number of versions of the basic story current in the eastern Aegean area at the beginning of the first millennium BC.

Yet certain details in the initial section distinguish Hesiod's version from earlier ones. There is a much greater degree of abstraction; Chaos simply came to be(68) as did Earth, Tartaros and Eros.(69) Night and Erebos generate their opposites; Earth, apparently without sexual intercourse, bears her future husband Ouranos (heaven) whose description (equal to herself to cover her all over...) clearly reflects an early world view of the Greeks, in which the heaven was a dome which fitted, like a cover, on the flat earth. Chaos has been the subject of some controversy; it is likely that the word signifies not modern, or what we understand by Biblical, chaos but a 'gap' between Earth and Heaven which occurs inconsistently in the poem before the separation of Heaven and Earth at 126-7.(70) The first stage in the cosmogony is therefore the creation of a gap, as in many other creation myths.(71)

Hesiod's work is to some extent one of collecting together a number of different traditions about the beginning of the world. He was not a proto-philosopher and his treatment, almost as much as that of the creators of the 'Enuma Elish', was concrete and mythical, and his explanations of happenings were in terms of personal motivation.

Yet, like his great predecessor Homer and in sharp contrast to the Near Eastern poets, Hesiod looks at the world from a human standpoint. At the beginning of the 'Theogony', Hesiod relates how the Muses of Olympos, daughters of aegis-bearing Zeus, spoke to him as he was shepherding his lambs under holy Helikon, saying:

'ποιμένες ἄγραυλοι, κάκ' ἐλέγχεα, γαστέρες οἶον,
ἴδμεν ψεύδεα πολλὰ λέγειν ἐτύμοισιν ὁμοῖα,
ἴδμεν δ' εὖτ' ἐθέλωμεν, ἀληθέα γηρύσασθαι.'

(Field-dwelling shepherds, wretched creatures of shame, mere bellies, we know how to speak many false things as though true, but we know, when we wish, how to sing truth.)(72)

The familiar tone of abuse and banter here recalls the close relationship Homeric heroes sometimes enjoyed with their gods (see chapter 4, pp.83-4). Despite his basic pessimism based upon a peasant's realistic assessment of the shortcomings of others, Hesiod's human standpoint shows up more clearly in the 'Works and Days', his other major poem. It is hardly accidental that one of the major stories told by Hesiod in this entertaining and instruct-ive account of peasant life in the hard lonely years of the early city-states, should be the famous myth of Prometheus, the god who stole fire from Zeus to give to mortals.

The origins of speculative thought took the form, in Greece, of a transition from myth to reason: that is, from a view that the world was created and organised by the personal impulses of powerful deities towards an attitude which saw the universe as the product of impersonal forces working in a predictable manner, from μυθολεγεῖν (= basically 'to tell stories') to φιλοσοφεῖν (discuss philosophically).(73) The general achievement of the Greeks in this field is well expressed in the following summary:

> The birth of philosophy in Europe ... consisted in the abandonment, at the level of conscious thought, of mythological solutions to problems concerning the origin and nature of the universe and the processes that go on within it. For religious faith there is substituted the faith that was and remains the basis of scientific thought with all its triumphs and all its limitations: that is, the faith that the visible world conceals a rational and intelligible order, that the causes of the natural world are to be sought within its boundaries, and that autonomous human reason is our sole and sufficient instrument for the search.

Written in 1962, the above passage, from a history of Greek philosophy destined probably to remain the standard work on the subject for the foreseeable future,(74) represents a careful and sensitive mediation between the extremes of nineteenth-century scientific positivism and the equally strong reaction from the early twentieth-century Cambridge anthropological school.(75) Its author, W.K.C. Guthrie, demonstrates what few would deny, that whatever reservations one may have about the details, the aims of the Greek intellectual revolution, seen in retro-spect, do contain an undoubted striving towards reason.

Yet what such formulations require is further explanation. Guthrie assumes almost without argument that the line between myth and reason is to be drawn between Homer and Hesiod on the one hand and the Presocratics on the other.(76) Yet, as Kirk has recently pointed out, if one is to postulate intelligible order as a criterion of reason, Homer already exhibits many of the elements which distinguish philosophy from myth.(77) Compared with the myths of other cultures, Greek myths already exhibit a consistency and internal coherence which make them unusual examples of the type. In particular the extensive use of myth in Homer and the lyric poets as a paradigm (story-with-a-moral) to justify or recommend a course of action or attitude, displays an element of detachment which is already half-way towards reason. Furthermore the 'personal confrontation' of Homer's individuals with their gods must be modified to the extent that one acknowledges that, in their frequent personification of War, Love, Sleep, Fear, Terror, etc., the characters of Homer were not creating allegories or flights of fancy but feeling their way towards a more rational approach, finally realised in the 'powers' of Presocratic cosmology.(78)

Kirk places the real transition from myth to reason much earlier - in fact in the period before the Greeks even emerged into the light of history. By the time of the earliest extant literature, society is basing its behaviour upon a rational, if largely traditional code of conduct which, as we have seen, allows reasoned departure from the norm (cf. Achilles in 'Iliad', IX, chapter 4, p. 77).   This goes hand in hand with the humanistic ethos of Homer, in which myths are largely reduced to literary form and play an aesthetic or otherwise supportive role. Philosophy, Kirk concludes, when it emerged, represented not a violent break with tradition, but the natural conclusion of a process which had been long in gestation. By the sixth century BC the scene had already been set.

Kirk's analysis of the situation is undoubtedly the most original and acute to emerge for many years, and he has clearly shown the degree to which an apparently personal and immediate relationship between man and god was penetrated by speculative and rational elements. It is, of course, Homeric man's possession of a full person-ality which makes the heroic situation emotionally relevant to us; his ability not only to feel but also to think gives Homer a value for us which, as we have seen, separates him decisively from his predecessors.

Yet the coin has a reverse side. If reason had an effect on myth, what about the effect of myth on reason?

Paradoxically enough, it was the very intellectual vitality
of the Greek myth and its adaptability which ensured its
survival as the vehicle of serious thought long after the
advent of the formal philosophical argument presented an
alternative method of procedure. It is a remarkable fact
that in Greece the intellectualising of myth (which, as we
have seen, was already happening in Homer) did not lead,
at least until the Hellenistic period, to trivialisation,
sustained allegory and antiquarianism. The Greeks rarely
discarded myths in the face of reason and scepticism but
adapted and refined them to suit a changing and developing
consciousness. Already in early choral lyric from Alkman
and Stesichoros to Pindar the myth as paradigm occupied a
traditional place in the poetic narrative. Within certain
limits of propriety individual poets had the liberty to
treat Greek myth and legend in a personal way. This
applies *a fortiori* to fifth-century BC tragedy. For
example, Hesiod's Prometheus, the crafty demi-god and
supreme trickster,(79) attains in Aeschylus' 'Prometheus'
high moral dignity and revolutionary status as the ally of
man against the tyranny of Zeus. Homer's account of the
murder of Agamemnon by his wife Klytemnestra is narrated
on several occasions and looked upon with disapproval as a
radical violation of accepted standards of behaviour; the
revenge of Orestes in killing his mother is held up to
Odysseus' growing son, Telemachos, as an ideal of conduct,
just as Penelope, Odysseus' faithful wife, is contrasted
with the faithless Klytemnestra.(80) Essentially the same
story is used by the three Greek tragedians, Aeschylus,
Sophocles and Euripides in sharply contrasted ways to
explore the profound theological, social and moral
dilemmas which, as they and presumably their audience saw
it, arose from the events - conflicts such as Homer had
never dreamed of! Even Euripides' tendency to oppose myth
and legend with reality in his plays, influenced, without
doubt, by the intellectual movements of his time, did not
involve the reduction of the myths to allegory or
convention. The audience, even while they are invited to
approach the traditional stories in a critical spirit, are
not expected to discard the whole mythical apparatus as
such; Aphrodite in the 'Hippolytos' or Dionysos in the
'Bacchae' are far more than abstractions or psychological
projections. As individuals they are intended to survive
the tragedian's moral censure, and any greater understanding of reality takes place within the framework of the
traditional stories.(81)
   The important point about the Greek myths and legends
is that, in a swiftly changing and intellectually radical
society, they not only retained their vitality but

largely remained the basic vehicle for the expression of
the most profound contemporary truths. In the absence of
a received body of sacred literature - Homer was the only
'bible' - poetry, and especially drama, still regarded
itself as competent to consider religious and philosophical questions as the province of a poetic imagination and
a dramatic form. The authority to consider these
questions was, in the fourth century BC, largely pre-
empted by the philosophers. Despite Plato's allegorical
use of myth, or perhaps partly because of it, the stories
lost their power, ending as the quarry of erudite Hellenistic court poets composing for private, informed enjoy-
ment.

The position of archaic Ionia in this development is an
interesting one. Despite the claims of Hekataios (see
above, p. 110) and the sharp criticism of existing
mythology on moral and intellectual grounds by Xenophanes
of Kolophon (see below, chapter 6), the vitality of the
concrete, personal element in myth is clearly visible in
the radical world-view of the philosophers. The attendant
circumstances we have touched on, social, economic and
cultural, resulted in a meeting of myth and reason quite
unique in the development of western thought. It is to
this synthesis we now turn, and to the central figure,
Anaximander of Miletos.

The remains consist of only one sentence which is beyond
question the thinker's original words. The remainder has
to be reconstructed from paraphrases in which Anaximander's
original ideas are expressed in updated phraseology
through which we obtain the occasional glimpse of the
original. This highly unsatisfactory situation has to be
endured since Anaximander is the most important figure in
the earliest period (pre-480 BC) of Presocratic philosophy.(82)

Anaximander of Miletos is credited with an explanation
of the world not in terms of the personal motivation and
conflict of the gods of myth, but as a natural process.
For whatever reason - and the evidence only allows us to
speculate on his motivation - he introduced something
which he called τὸ ἄπειρον (the boundless). As soon as we
ask what the 'apeiron' (as it is normally called) is, we
run into difficulties inherent in attempting to understand a mind far removed in outlook from our own.
Aristotle, clearly almost as perplexed as we are, concluded that Anaximander was trying to construct a material
principle of existence, and somehow neglecting everything
else.(83) Yet we also learn, and from Aristotle too, that

the 'apeiron' was ἀθάνατον ... καὶ ἀνώλεθρον, ὥσπερ φησὶν ὁ ᾿Αναξίμανδρος καὶ οἱ πλεῖστοι τῶν φυσιολόγων (immortal and deathless, as Anaximander and most of the enquirers into nature say)(84) and that it περιέχειν ἅπαντα καὶ πάντα κυβερνᾶν (surrounds all things and steers all things).(85)

One of our main problems is connected with the linguistic form of the words τὸ ἄπειρον. The second word, preceded by its definite article, is an adjective whose ending presupposes a neuter noun which does not, in Greek, require direct expression. It is this, as much as the inherent difficulty of the concept, which causes difficulty to modern intellects. 'The boundless thing' we might say (although the abstraction presupposed by the word 'boundless' in English does not go very happily with 'thing'). At the outset we meet the recurring difficulty associated with these early thinkers - the limited resources of one language to express the ideas of another. It has been well remarked (of Herakleitos, though the point has a general application): 'to translate is some-times to have taken sides already in a disputed question of interpretation.'(86)

The 'apeiron' seems to have acted as a source from which the world as we know it comes. The question, often posed, whether it lacked external or internal boundaries, is not strictly relevant since the term ἄπειρον probably embraced both.(87) As an undifferentiated source the 'apeiron' recalls the primeval state of myth, the 'waters commingling as a single body',(88) and as an unlimited one it would be capable of controlling all things (as Anaximander seems to have said, see above). Our difficulty, which was obviously shared by later Greek thinkers also, involves understanding an idea of such generality which nevertheless demonstrates a firm grasp on the concrete. It is clear that with this idea Anaximander is at one step disposing of the anthropo-morphism of creation myths to create something recognis-able as an impersonal principle. There clarity ends. Controversy has raged over the precise nature of the 'apeiron', ranging from Burnet's belief, not imcomprehens-ible from the standpoint of one who saw the Milesians as early scientists, that the 'apeiron' was a material plenum,(89) to a more recent view that Anaximander was responsible for presenting the world with its first metaphysical idea.(90) In the last analysis later classical commentators do not provide us with any decisive evidence, for the reason, one suspects, that they were basically as much in the dark as we are.

Over the operation of the 'apeiron' we have more

information. The origin of the world is described by a
later commentator in a book of physical extracts falsely
attributed to Plutarch. Despite the lateness of this
source, the language and style betray features which
suggest some degree of fidelity to an archaic original:

φησὶ δὲ τὸ ἐκ τοῦ ἀιδίου γόνιμον θερμοῦ τε καὶ ψυχροῦ
κατὰ τὴν γένεσιν τοῦδε τοῦ κόσμου ἀποκριθῆναι καί τινα
ἐκ τούτου φλογὸς σφαῖραν περιφυῆναι τῷ περὶ τὴν γῆν
ἀέρι ὡς τῷ δένδρῳ φλοιόν· ἧστινος ἀπορραγείσης καὶ εἴς
τινὰς ἀποκλεισθείσης κύκλους ὑποστῆναι τὸν ἥλιον καὶ
τὴν σελήνην καὶ τοὺς ἀστέρας.

(He says that which gave birth from the eternal to the
hot and the cold at the birth of this world was
separated off, and a kind of sphere of flame from this
grew around the air surrounding the earth, like the
bark around a tree. When this was broken off and shut
off in certain circles the sun and the moon and the
stars were formed.)(91)

This account can be supplemented by the second-century AD
Hippolytus:

τὰ δὲ ἄστρα γίνεσθαι κύκλον πυρός, ἀποκριθέντα τοῦ κατὰ
τὸν κόσμον πυρός, περιληφθέντα δ᾽ ὑπὸ ἀέρος. ἐκπνοὰς δ᾽
ὑπάρξαι πόρους τινὰς αὐλώδεις, καθ᾽ οὓς φαίνεται τὰ
ἄστρα· διὸ καὶ ἐπιφρασσομένων τῶν ἐκπνοῶν τὰς ἐκλαίψεις
γίνεσθαι.

(The stars came into being as a circle of fire,
separated off from the fire in the world, and
surrounded by air. Breathing holes exist, certain
pipe-like passages, through which the stars show themselves; accordingly when the breathing holes are
blocked, eclipses happen.)(92)

This description, no doubt rather quaint to us, represents
a remarkable first step on the road to a developed
cosmology. Notable is the economy and consistency with
which Anaximander uses the basic hypothesis of opposites
separating off from the 'apeiron'(probably to be identified with the 'eternal' here) to explain the subsequent
emergence of the heavenly bodies ('stars' includes the sun
and moon). The 'sphere of flame' and 'air surrounding the
earth' are doubtless to be identified, in the first
extract, with 'the hot' and 'the cold'. The remarkable
idea of rings of air filled with fire showing at small
holes to explain the appearance of the heavenly bodies and

the occurrence of eclipses shows both remarkable powers of
observation and, more important, the imagination to construct a radical but coherent hypothesis to explain
appearances - to 'go behind the phenomena' - a procedure
which scientists have attempted to follow ever since. It
is this power of grasping something in its totality and
presenting an impersonal yet vividly concrete picture
which links Anaximander both with his mythical forbears
and with the subsequent Greek tradition of abstract
thought.

Certain features in the above extracts demonstrate
Anaximander's unique position between these two worlds -
the mythical and the conceptual (to describe them roughly).
'Gonimon' is, *pace* Kirk and Raven,(93) not metaphorical
but a word which demonstrates that Anaximander still saw
cosmology in terms of sexual generation (a point that was
recognised, and possibly over-emphasised, by Cornford).(94)
'Hot' and 'cold', although appearing here without a
definite article, clearly recall the linguistic form of τὸ
ἄπειρον. They are not seen as merely qualities but
'things', belonging to a period before a clear distinction
had been made between quality and the substance in which
the quality inheres (Cornford's 'quality-things' is rather
unsatisfactory, but nobody has improved on it.)(95)
Their concreteness is emphasised by their transformation,
later in the first extract, into 'fire' and 'air'.
Clearly no anomaly in description was felt.

The prevailing sexual aspect makes it unnecessary to
ask, as Aristotle did, how the opposites pre-existed in the
'apeiron',(96) any more than modern man feels the need to
enquire how children pre-exist in their parents. The
separation of two opposites from the parent 'apeiron'
(this seems to be a reasonable interpretation of what the
source of the first extract is saying) recalls inevitably
the first stages of a theogony, which, as we noted in the
case of Hesiod, proceeded in opposite pairs (see above,
p.114), 'Theogony', 123-8). It is perhaps significant in
this context to note that the author of the first extract
describes the process as 'separating off', whereas
Aristotle, clearly seeing the 'apeiron' as some kind of
mechanical mixture, says ἐκκρίνεσθαι (separating out);(97)
the use of the former term may(98) demonstrate the
author's partial independence of Aristotle and his
reliance upon an older tradition in which 'separating off'
describes much better what Anaximander had in mind.

Biological models are clearly apparent in the
description of the behaviour of fire, both in the botan-
ical 'grow around' and the homely simile 'like a bark
around a tree'. Such comparisons recall the Homeric

simile (see chapter 4, pp.85ff.) and illustrate the need of
the early philosopher and his audience for visual aid in
the familiar and everyday. This is apparent in the second
extract, where the homely musical comparison brings home
strikingly what Anaximander has in mind. To be quite
certain his audience understands this strange idea, he
gives another comparison, and tells us that the sun is a
circle twenty-eight times the size of the earth:

> ἀρματείῳ τροχῷ παραπλήσιον, τὴν ἀψῖδα
> ἔχοντα κοίλην, πλήρη πυρός, κατά τι μέρος
> ἐκφαίνουσαν διὰ στομίου τὸ πῦρ ὥσπερ διὰ
> πρηστῆρος αὐλοῦ.

(like a chariot-wheel with its felloe hollow, full of
fire, showing the fire at a certain point through a
hole just as through the nozzle of a bellows.)(99)

He has this to say about the earth: it is 'cylindrical in
shape, and it has a depth equal to one third of its width;
its shape is curved, round, similar to the drum of a
column; of its flat surfaces we walk on one and the other
is on the opposite side. The earth is in mid-air,
confined by nothing, but remaining on account of its
similar distance from all things.'(100)

Through the later and more impersonal syntax of the
commentators we can hear distinctly the authentic archaic
tone: the simple comparison, the pictorial imagery and the
essentially sexual genealogical conception derived from
the world of myth. Anaximander's universe is living and
immediately experienced. Yet, at the same time, he had
made the essential break with the personal motivation of a
mythical deity and his world is simple, economically
organised and comprehensively explained. The mere falsity
of the details does not really matter by the side of the
power of the conception.

A further point of the greatest importance may be
observed: the traditional does not exercise a repressive
influence on the radical but gives it strength. While, in
retrospect, we are at liberty to see Anaximander as a
thinker who had not yet liberated himself from the chains
of myth, this is not a historical picture. Anaximander
represents a unique balance in the history of thought -
the point at which daring abstractions could still be
conceived without eliminating or rejecting the immediacy
and personal world of the poet. Thus the concept of
ὁμοιότης (equilibrium), although expressed by Aristotle in
language that Anaximander would hardly have used,(101)
demonstrates Anaximander's feel for abstract argument

based upon symmetry of design, while the world which
possesses this harmony is alive, concrete and
'primitive'.(102)

Further elucidation of these points is afforded by the
one original fragment of Anaximander, which is preserved
by the sixth-century AD Neoplatonist, Simplicius, quoting
from Theophrastos' 'Opinions of the Physicists':

ἐξ ὧν δὲ ἡ γένεσίς ἐστι τοῖς οὖσι καὶ τὴν φθορὰν εἰς
ταῦτα γίνεσθαι κατὰ τὸ χρεών· διδόναι γὰρ αὐτὰ δίκην καὶ
τίσιν ἀλλήλοις τῆς ἀδικίας κατὰ τὴν τοῦ χρόνου τάξιν.

(Those things from which there is birth for existing
things - into those there is also destruction according
to necessity; for they pay the penalty and retribution
to each other for injustice according to the ordinance
of time.)(103)

Few words in the Greek language have occasioned so much
speculation, interpretation and comment; consequently,
only the immediately relevant questions will be raised
here.(104)   The fragment is embedded in a context which is
clearly post-Aristotelian in its aims and expression, from
which the original words can only be extracted with the
greatest difficulty, especially since the whole is in
indirect speech.(105)   The matter is further complicated
by the suspicion that the expression of at least the first
clause of the above extract may be Aristotelian and the
relationship between the two clauses problematic.(106)

The genuineness of the second clause (whatever the
status of the γάρ (for)) is not disputed, and is clinched
by Simplicius' own comment immediately after it:
ποιητικωτέροις οὕτως ὀνόμασιν αὐτὰ λέγων (expressing
himself thus in rather poetic words).   In any case the
style and content is not Aristotelian.   The things which
pay the penalty to each other are probably opposites of
some kind, two of which were mentioned in the Pseudo-
Plutarch quotation (on p.121 above).   The precise number
of opposites or their nature (i.e. whether they were 'the
hot', 'the cold', etc. or substances such as 'fire', 'air',
etc.) is not known.   We have no extant reference to a
canonical four opposites before Herakleitos,(107) although
their appearance as apparently well-established
traditional elements in Empedokles (first half of the
fifth century BC) suggests that they may go back to
Anaximander.   The opposites are aggressors who encroach
upon each other and pay a penalty for the encroachment, as
in a court of law.   There is therefore a cycle of mutual
injustice, mutually repaid through the infliction of

punishment on the wrongdoer by the wronged which is itself
in turn an injustice, which brings a corresponding reaction
against the former aggressor. Hence the 'assessment of
time'.(108) Anaximander's failure to fit this more
schematic account of the workings of the world into the
more detailed cosmology should not be taken too seriously.
The absence of clear detailed logical links between
different aspects of their thought is a general characteristic of early thinkers, and reflects the disjointed
apophthegmatic nature of their utterances.

This fragment of Anaximander has some claim to be
considered as the world's earliest philosophical statement;
as such it contains a number of features of the greatest
interest. In abandoning the personal disposition of Zeus,
Anaximander inherited and faced squarely the mythical
problem of conflict. His answer to a mythical escalation
of injustice, which, at the moment of greatest peril, is
redeemed by the final conqueror - Zeus or Marduk - was to
construct a self-regulating system whereby the aggression
was not arbitrarily crushed but regulated in a dynamic
equilibrium.(109) Perhaps one of the most significant
presuppositions of this position, and one which is responsible for a great deal of its strangeness for us, is that
the world had, of itself, life and movement. It was only
at the beginning of the fifth century BC that philosophers
gradually began to make a distinction between living and
inert matter. For the earlier, 'hylozoist' thinkers, of
which Anaximander was one, there was no need to posit a
source of life and motion since the world had within
itself the power of change. This is inherited from the
pre-philosophical world. The opposites which enter into
the conflict are not abstract entities but things -
concrete aggressors with their own power of movement.
Anaximander's conceptual vision was matched by the vividness and dynamism of his material.

The choice of a legal image for conflict is not, of
course, an arbitrary one. It has long been remarked that
the dynamic equilibrium of opposites bears a remarkable
resemblance to a recurring feature of the social organisation of primitive societies, and countless examples can
be quoted of social coherence which appears to depend upon
the deliberate antagonism, often in a ritual context, of
opposed groups.(110) In Anaximander's cosmology, the
process by which order is maintained is that of law in
which two litigants give and receive justice, with Time
standing by as an assessor. The phrase κατὰ τὴν τοῦ
χρόνου τάξιν (according to the ordinance of time) has
frequently reminded observers of Solon's claim to be
vindicated ἐν δίκῃ χρόνου (in the judgment of time) by the

witness of Earth, from whose land he removed mortgage
posts.(111)   Yet the legal metaphor (which merely
indicates Solon's belief that he will eventually be proved
to have acted justly) becomes in Anaximander an integral
part of his system and an indication that he believes not
in arbitrary justice but in a legal conflict which is fair,
unbiased and a continual, reversible process.

In reading the last paragraph, a doubt may be felt over
whether Anaximander is talking about the cosmos, society
or both. Yet it is clear that he inherits certain aspects
of the pre-philosophical world-view in which the cosmological order was a moral and social order, presided over by
Marduk or Zeus.(112)   Hence Anaximander's cosmological
solution may be seen as an implicit comment on society.
As such it is much more compelling and far-sighted than
either Solon's attempts at reconciliation or Phokylides'
middle way. Anaximander solves the problem of conflict
not by eliminating it but by admitting, regulating and
perpetuating it.

Attempts to find a precise political context for
Anaximander have not been conspicuously successful;
G. Vlastos refers Anaximander's conception of the alternate
power of opposites to the political idea of the rotation
of office, typical of Greek democracy;(113) this, besides
being historically anachronistic (democracy was not a
sixth-century phenomenon) ignores the fact that the
essence of democratic ideology was reconciliation of
opposites, not their mutual antagonism. A more explicit
formulation, such as that of George Thomson - that the
struggle is an escalating one between rich and poor - is
not only incompatible with the most likely interpretation
of Anaximander's words (see above, p.125 and n.108) but
also fails to come to terms with the equality of the
opposites.(114)

Similar objections can be made to Vlastos' model in
Hippocratic medicine, again on historical grounds, and
because the prevailing fifth-century medical model of
'powers' in the human body lays emphasis upon their κρᾶσις
(blending) or ἰσονομία τῶν δυνάμεων (equilibrium or
balance of powers) according to the earliest
authority,(115) but not on the element of dynamism present
in Anaximander. The crux of the objections to the so-
called 'models' on the basis of which Anaximander,
consciously or unconsciously, may have been working, is
that Anaximander's formulation stands very much alone,
historically, as the earliest expression of a dynamic
world view which involved the conflict, and yet the interdependence, of opposites. It was Anaximander's achievement to have introduced into Greek thought an idea which

guided the thinking of such later thinkers as Herakleitos
(see chapter 6), Empedokles and the dramatist Aeschylus.
The abandonment of the dynamic model in favour of a static
world of the intellect, in which the world as it appears
to the senses is to be (in varying degrees) rejected, was
foreshadowed by Parmenides at the beginning of the fifth
century BC and found its overwhelming advocate in Plato.

We have seen that Anaximander's increasing conceptual
clarity is matched by the concreteness with which he
expresses the insight. In order to proceed further with
this, we must look at the language of the fragment.
Simplicius' comment (see above, p.124) clearly indicates
that he feels the language to be more elevated. The
problem is - than what? It has usually been assumed that
the comparison is between this fragment and the rest of
Anaximander's lost discourse, which C.H. Kahn supposes to
be in the language of sixth-century BC spoken Ionic.(116)
The doxographical tradition clearly imagined that
Anaximander was illustrating metaphorically a view of the
universe conceived in less emotive, poetic terms.
W. Jaeger supposes that, 'moved involuntarily by the
profundity of his conception', Anaximander's composition
took on a poetic quality.(117) The problem with this is
that we have no evidence that Anaximander used a less
poetic style elsewhere, or any contemporary evidence
against which to measure our one extant fragment.

Stylistic comments on the Presocratics are rare since,
on the whole, Aristotle and his successors were concerned
to extract what their predecessors were saying from the
context without concerning themselves much about the
medium through which they said it. The only remark on
Anaximander which gets near to being a stylistic comment
(apart from the comment on the fragment itself in
Simplicius, see above, p.124), is by Aristotle; in the
'Physics' he is clearly aware of the σεμνότης (solemnity)
with which Anaximander describes the 'apeiron'; this
corresponds with the words used to describe it (see above,
p.120). Certainty is, of course, impossible, but the
weight of evidence suggests that Anaximander's language
may have been both syntactically simple and rich in
elements we normally associate with poetry. Consequently
the extant fragment may not have represented a move into
poetic language, either involuntary or controlled, but the
natural way in which the philosopher expressed his ideas.
Just as his conception of the world retained much of the
immediacy and dynamism of earlier poetic writers such as
Hesiod and Homer, so his language may have retained many
of the characteristics of poetic composition. Simplicius,
in characterising the fragment as expressed 'in rather

poetic words' may have been applying the standard not of
the remainder of Anaximander nor even of sixth-century
prose, but of the less emotive, more sophisticated and
specialised philosophical style of the fifth and later
centuries BC. This hypothesis becomes more cogent if one
takes a pessimistic view (see below, chapter 7) of the
amount of Anaximander available in the fourth century. If
all Theophrastos (Simplicius' source) had to go on was
this and other isolated fragments, his ability to make
valid stylistic judgments on Anaximander is seriously
impaired.

This has important consequences. The word 'metaphor',
which is normally used to describe Anaximander's fragment,
implies a conscious transference of ideas, i.e. the
metaphor is used to express something else. But since we
know nothing of Anaximander's linguistic expression
outside this one fragment, we have no means of telling how
he would otherwise have expressed himself on the subject
which he supposedly treats in 'metaphorical terms'. It
follows from this that we have no grounds upon which to
make a radical distinction between the language of the
fragment and a 'prose style' in which the remainder of
Anaximander's philosophy was supposedly expressed.

If the legal 'metaphor' in the extant fragment is not
a metaphor at all, it must represent the way in which
Anaximander saw the world. The opposites were living
aggressors and litigants at the bar of justice.
Anaximander's reaction to a poetic cosmological tradition
was to remove the personal and arbitrary element without
losing the poetic outlook.

Talk of 'poetry' must be carefully qualified, since the
distinction usually made between poetry and prose and
their respective areas of application cannot here be taken
for granted. For the greater part of the archaic period,
verse was the only medium of expression. The introduction
of prose was a comparatively late phenomenon usually attributed to the Milesians and seen as reflecting their
new impersonal and 'scientific' outlook on the world.
Furthermore, this medium is usually contrasted with the
somewhat later verse-medium of the Italian school of
Parmenides and Empedokles (with, behind them, the shadowy
figure of Pythagoras) which is thought to serve a more
reflective, inward and mystical train of thought.

The latter hypothesis is not easy to maintain.
Empedokles was certainly concerned with religious
purification in his Καθαρμού (Purifications) but the
purely cosmological parts of the poems (he also wrote a
Περὶ Φύσεως (On Nature)) betray as much 'scientific'
interest in the fundamental workings of the world as

Anaximander and go into considerably more detail (as far
as we can tell) concerning the minutiae of meteorological
phenomena.(118) Empedokles, whose work survives in
greater bulk than any other Presocratic, uses the Homeric
hexameter and exhibits many of the characteristics of a
poetic style, for example, 'ornamental' epithets and
metaphor.(119) If we wish to ask how Anaximander could
have expressed his ideas in poetic terms, Empedokles
provides a possible answer. Moreover there is no evidence
that Empedokles 'chose' his medium in preference to an
already existing developed philosophical prose style,
unless we can find concrete evidence for the latter in the
early fifth century BC.(120) Parmenides, an earlier
thinker (c. 510-460 BC), brings the argument to a point.
Concerned, as he was, with pursuing a rigorous logical
argument which involved the denial of the world of the
senses in favour of a world of 'Being', he nevertheless
used the Homeric hexameter, maintained a high percentage
of Homeric vocabulary and syntax and also composed a
prelude, normally taken (I think, mistakenly) allegorically, in which the poet is seen as an initiate passing
from the region of night to the light in a chariot drawn
by horses.(121) The evidence of Empedokles and Parmenides
makes it unlikely that the verse medium was chosen by
these thinkers for merely extraneous or technical
reasons.(122)
    But where does this leave prose? If we attempt to list
the fragments of Greek prose which undoubtedly antedate
the fifth century, the find is meagre. Besides Thales
and Anaximander, there is one fragment of Anaximenes (the
third and last of the Milesian philosophers), but even
this has come under suspicion as a Peripatetic
reformulation.(123)
    If we pass outside the immediate context of Milesian
philosophy, there are two sixth-century BC prose-writers
who, in contrasted ways, present us with valuable
evidence - Pherekydes of Syros and Hekataios. Pherekydes,
who lived roughly contemporary with Anaximander, composed
a work which stands on the borderline between myth and
philosophy, in which the traditional creation stories are
gradually giving way to a more rational approach.(124)
The only fragment of any length demonstrates this. It is
an account of the wedding of Zeus and Χθονίη (Earth) in
which Zeus presents his bride with a large cloth on which
he has decorated Γῆ (Earth) and Ὠγηνός (Ocean) and the
halls of Ocean (the cosmological significance of this as a
creation motif is clear):

αὐτῷ ποιοῦσιν τὰ οἰκία πολλά τε καὶ μεγάλα. ἐπεὶ δὲ ταῦτα

ἐξετέλεσαν πάντα καὶ χρήματα καὶ θεράποντας καὶ θεραπαί-
νας καὶ τἆλλα ὅσα δεῖ πάντα, ἐπεὶ δὴ πάντα ἑτοῖμα γίγνεται, τὸν γάμον ποιεῦσιν, κἀπειδὴ τρίτη ἡμέρη γίγνεται
τῷ γάμῳ, τότε Ζὰς ποιεῖ φᾶρος μέγα τε καὶ καλὸν καὶ ἐν
αὐτῷ ποικίλλει Γῆν καὶ 'Ωγηνὸν καὶ τὰ 'Ωγηνοῦ δώματα....

(For him they make the houses, many and great. And when
they had finished all these things and the furniture
and the man-servants and the maid-servants and all the
other things that were necessary, when all things are
ready, they hold the wedding. And when the third day
of the wedding comes, then Zas (Zeus) makes a cloth,
great and beautiful and on it he decorates Earth and
Ogenos and the halls of Ogenos.)(125)

The style is simple, paratactic and repetitive, resembling
in some ways a formulaic 'genre' scene in Homer. In
neither conception nor execution does it offer any useful
comparison with Anaximander, but does in many ways
anticipate the narrative style of the λέξις εἱρομένη
('running-on' style) of Herodotos. Hekataios, whom we
have already met (see above, p.110) survives in enough
detail to make it clear that his style was dry, pedestrian
in expression and clearly serviceable for its purpose –
the setting out of information as simply and precisely as
possible.
    Prose has its origins in the practical, everyday world
of inscriptions recording treaties, laws, dedications,
etc., where writing gradually took over from the human
memory in the recording and preservation of information
(see above, pp.103-8). The earliest inscriptions (see the
example on p.106) are composed in a simple but nevertheless balanced and rhythmic style to which clarity lends
its own dignity. Hekataios, the 'first prose-writer' we
are told (for what the information is worth) by the
Suda,(126) clearly follows in this tradition, judging from
the extant fragments and later stylistic comments.(127)
    The term 'pedestrian', in the last but one paragraph,
was advisedly chosen. Greek prose was regarded as a πεζὸς
λόγος (lit. discourse on foot) as opposed to the winged
metre of poetry. Yet we must beware of making this
distinction too early. Reference to prose in the above
terms belongs, as far as our extant sources allow us to
judge, to the later period of the literary critics (first
century BC and later); the word πεζός refers, in the only
extant examples from the fifth century BC, to something
rather different – verses without musical accompaniment.(128)   The linguistic evidence supports what we
should suppose anyway on other grounds – that during the

sixth century BC there was no sharp and conscious
distinction between subjects suitable for one medium or
the other, yet it must be remembered that poetry was the
norm; the task of prose was, slowly and often without
great distinction, to mark off its own territory.

We cannot, however, ignore evidence of yet another
aspect of early prose, of which Anaximander's fragment
seems to be almost the sole remaining example - its
poetical colouring (on Herakleitos, see below, chapter 6).
That early prose 'imitated' poetry is suggested by
Strabo;(129) its breadth of style recalls epic and even
Plato, not the most sympathetic of Presocratic commentators, in the 'Sophist' recognises in the 'Ιάδες Μοῦσαι a
tendency to create ideas within a semi-personalised world
as opposed to his own more conceptual approach.(130)
Anaximander had at his disposal the riches of a poetic
tradition of great elegance and fluency, already fully
equipped to express ideas of considerable complexity. It
seems hard to resist the conclusion that, even if
Anaximander did not compose in verse (and the universal
ancient tradition is that he did not) he made extensive
use of poetic style and vocabulary both as the automatic
and presumed vehicle for ideas of any importance and as a
natural reflection of his outlook on the world which (as
we have seen) shared much with his predecessors.

The ancient evidence further suggests that the development of a prose-style capable of expressing philosophical
ideas was a gradual process. The development of a common
and agreed vocabulary for the expression of complex philosophical ideas began to take place during the fifth
century BC, and the increasing complexity of Greek prose-
style is reflected in the emergence of extended logical
arguments in the writings of e.g. Zeno and Melissos (see
below, chapter 7). Paradoxically enough, it was the
'poet' Parmenides who contributed most to the origins of
this latter development.

This is, of course, not simply a question of style or
tradition. Just as the organised structure of Plato
reflects the complexity and interdependence of the
different aspects of his thought, so the absence of these
qualities in the early Ionians is reflected in the style;
as J.D. Denniston remarks: 'They expounded truth in
oracles rather than proceed to it by the ordered march of
logic. Hence their writing gives the effect of stiffly
piled-up masses; it is static, not dynamic.'(131) The
early Greek world-view began not with careful argument but
with commanding, splendid intuitions expressed in terms
which, while puzzling and exasperating their successors,
often strike a familiar note today. This characteristic

will occupy us extensively in the following chapter, to the end of which a general summary of Ionian philosophy is postponed.

6 Xenophanes and Herakleitos: the interaction of language and thought

καὶ ποτέ στυφελιζομένου σκύλακος παριόντα
    φασὶν ἐποικτῖραι καὶ τόδε φάσθαι ἔπος·
'παῦσαι μηδὲ ῥάπιζ', ἐπεὶ ἦ φίλου ἀνέρος ἐστίν
    ψυχή, τὴν ἔγνων φθεγξαμένης ἀίων'.

(And once, they say, passing by while a puppy was being
beaten, he pitied it and spoke as follows: 'Stop, don't
beat it, for it is the soul of a man who was my friend,
which I recognised when I heard it crying out.')(1)

In relating this amusing anecdote about the philosopher
and religious teacher Pythagoras, Xenophanes of Kolophon
appears to be satirising the doctrine of the transmig-
ration of souls - the idea that the human (and animal) soul
was separable from its body and, after death, could return
inside another. He does this by reducing the idea to the
absurdity of supposing that the soul of a friend was still
recognisable through the barking of the beaten dog.
    Ironically enough, Xenophanes' dismissal constitutes
the earliest authentic evidence for a doctrine which
assumed such great importance in later centuries; the
elegiac metre and archaic language in which the fragment
is composed make it difficult to suspect its authenticity
(a problem we encountered frequently in the previous
chapter) and Xenophanes' familiar tone suggests that the
idea was not new in the later sixth century BC.(2)
    The connection of Xenophanes with Pythagoras is
historically an interesting one. Pythagoras, the son of a
gem-engraver from Samos, emigrated westward c. 530 BC,
apparently out of dislike for the tyranny of Polykrates,
who ruled the island at that time.(3) He settled at
Kroton in southern Italy and founded a society which
wielded great philosophical and political influence in
that area and contributed a great deal to the inward,

133

mystical character of Italian Presocratic thought.(4)

Like Pythagoras, Xenophanes went into voluntary exile from his birthplace and spent by far the greater part of his long life wandering:

ἤδη δ' ἑπτά τ' ἔασι καὶ ἑξήκοντ' ἐνιαυτοὶ
βληστρίζοντες ἐμὴν φροντίδ' ἀν' 'Ελλάδα γῆν·
ἐκ γενετῆς δὲ τότ' ἦσαν ἐείκοσι πέντε τε πρὸς τοῖς,
εἴπερ ἐγὼ περὶ τῶδ' οἶδα λέγειν ἐτύμως.

(Now there have been seven and sixty years tossing my thought up and down the land of Greece; from my birth till then there were twenty-five to be added to these if indeed I know how to speak truly about these things.)(5)

It is usually assumed that 'then' in ℓ.3 refers to the 'coming of the Mede' (see DK B.22,5), i.e. the Persian capture of Kolophon (546-545 BC),(6) although attempts to date the extant fragments to periods of Xenophanes' long life have not been conspicuously successful. Diogenes Laertius says that Xenophanes went west to Elea in southern Italy,(7) but, in view of the later tradition which attempted to make Xenophanes the founder of Eleatic thought (see below, p.139) this evidence is suspect. In fact we know nothing at all about the geographical location of his prolonged wanderings. As we have seen (chapter 2, pp.23f.) the Persian conquest of Ionia led to exile for whole communities as well as individuals, who were either forced out or preferred to make their lives elsewhere. Pythagoras and Xenophanes were distinguished examples of a general movement which reached its peak, demographically as well as artistically speaking, after the fall of Ionia in the early fifth century BC (see below, chapter 7).

Here the similarity between the two thinkers ends. Pythagoras can be called Ionian only in a purely technical sense; Xenophanes occupied a more equivocal position, which the violently contrasted judgments of later generations have done little to clarify. In marked contrast to the Pythagoreans in the west and the earlier Milesians in Ionia, Xenophanes and his later contemporary, Herakleitos, appear as isolated figures. Later comment-ators, despite their zeal to construct 'schools of thought' and fit all known philosophers into them, were able to suggest only that Xenophanes was a teacher of the distinguished Parmenides, and as such, founder of the Eleatic School.(8) In point of fact, the surviving fragments of Xenophanes point to a much more ambivalent

relationship between Ionia and the west. Along with the
ironic, witty self-assurance and lively interest in the
external world that we nave already associated with Ionia,
there are two elements which are new: first, the development of a more explicit, and at the same time, all-
embracing conception of god in sharp and deliberate
contrast to Greek religious tradition; second, an insist-
ence on the limits of human knowledge and, in particular,
a distinction between knowledge and belief that, to a
limited extent, foreshadows Plato.(9)

     In contrast with the anonymity of the members of the
Milesian school, Xenophanes emerges as a quite distinct
personality. His contempt for the luxury and arrogance of
the Kolophonians (see above, p. 22) who were often so
drunk that they saw the sun neither rise nor set,(10) is
part of a much broader social criticism of the lack of
respect shown to ἡμετέρη σοφίη (my wisdom) which is of
greater worth than the much prized achievements of athletes
and contributes more to the good government (εὐνομίη) of
the city.(11) This consciousness of the status of the
thinker is perhaps reflected in the ἐμὴν φροντίδ' (my
thought) of fr.8,2 (if our interpretation of the words be
correct, see above, n.6) and anticipates the prophetic
tone of Herakleitos (see below, p.145ff.)

     Social criticism by individuals we have met before;
Solon of Athens was concerned with the morality of class-
struggle (see above, chapter 5, p.102) and Theognis of
Megara, an embittered, reactionary aristocrat, bewailed
the dissolution of his own privilege, without the faintest
understanding of why it was happening. Yet Xenophanes
goes well beyond either of these in his intellectual grasp
of the basis of individual and civic morality.

     πάντα θεοῖσ' ἀνέθηκαν "Ομηρος θ' 'Ησιοδός τε,
     ὅσσα παρ' ἀνθρώποισιν ὀνείδεα καὶ φόγος ἐστίν,
     κλέπτειν μοιχεύειν τε καὶ ἀλλήλους ἀπατεύειν.

     (Homer and Hesiod have ascribed to the gods all the
     things which among mortals are a reproach and a
     disgrace: stealing, debauchery and mutual
     deception.)(12)

     This fragment is taken from the 'Silloi' (poems of
mockery or parody, although the title may be later than
Xenophanes). The moral grounds on which Xenophanes
objects to Homer have already become clear in fr.1,22-3,
where edifying stories should accompany a feast and not
πλάσματα τῶν προτέρων... τοῖσ' οὐδὲν χρηστὸν ἔνεστι
(fictions of our ancestors ... in which there is nothing

useful,(13)) and men should hymn the gods:

εὐφήμοις μύθοις καὶ καθαροῖσι λόγοις·

(with pious stories and pure words).(14)

This startling anticipation of Plato comes, at first
sight, rather oddly from the lips of an Ionian;
Xenophanes' criticism seems to have more in common with
that of Pindar, who, in 'Olympian Odes', I,42, refuses to
accept the picture of the gods implied by the story of
Tantalos. (Indeed it is possible to see the development
of criticism of traditional stories on moral grounds as a
natural consequence of the paradeigmatic nature of early
lyric, see chapter 5 above, p.117.)   In Xenophanes, on
the other hand, we miss the worldly acceptance of
'immoral' stories displayed by Anakreon, for example. Yet
Xenophanes goes further, to show himself no mere
moraliser:

αλλ' εἰ χεῖρας ἔχον βόες <ὕπποι> ἠὲ λέοντες
ἢ γράψαι χείρεσσι καὶ ἔργα τελεῖν ἅπερ ἄνδρες,
ὕπποι μέν θ' ὕπποισι βόες δέ τε βουσὶν ὁμοίας
καὶ <κε> θεῶν ἰδέας ἔγραφον καὶ σώματ' ἐποίουν
τοιαῦθ' οἷόν περ καυτοὶ δέμας εἶχον <ἕκαστοι>.

(But if oxen and horses and lions had hands, or could
draw with their hands and do the works that men do,
horses would draw the forms of the gods like horses,
oxen like oxen and they would make the bodies such a
shape as they themselves each had.)(15)

It is difficult to exaggerate the impact of this idea.
Not content with moral objections, Xenophanes explodes
intellectually the basis of Greek anthropomorphic
religion - the assumption that gods take the shape of men.
As with the Pythagorean anecdote with which this chapter
began, Xenophanes makes the comparison witty and
ridiculous - the idea of an animal kingdom with animal
deities - yet, at the same time, intellectually
suggestive.

He develops the idea a little further:

Αἰθίοπές τε <θεοὺς σφετέρους> σιμοὺς μέλανάς τε
Θρῆκες τε γλαυκοὺς καὶ πυρρούς <φασι πέλεσθαι>.

(Ethiopians say that their gods are snub-nosed and
black, the Thracians that theirs are blue-eyed and

red-haired.)(16)

The validity of Greek anthropomorphic religion is attacked
by applying the argument of relativity not only between
the images constructed by men and animals but even between
those of different human racial types. It seems not too
fanciful to see here the effects of Ionian ethnography on
human thinking. In the following century, Herodotos
observed with great interest the radical differences in
the customs and beliefs of the peoples he studied - an
interest which reflected the fifth-century awareness of
the relativity of custom incorporated in the basic
distinction between νόμος (custom, law) and φύσις (nature,
i.e. that which does not depend upon arbitrary differences
between races). It seems likely that this awareness of
relativity has its origin in sixth-century Ionia where a
familiarity with 'barbarians' and a much greater absence
of condescension towards them, may well have provoked
intellectual advance, even if, as here, appearance rather
than 'habits' is under consideration (see chapter 1,
pp.1ff.).
   In Xenophanes it can be said that the Ionian intellectual movement which originated in Miletos found a successor
who turned his attention away from cosmology towards
criticism of institutions and beliefs. Yet the revelation
of the anthropomorphic fallacy in Greek religion - that
men project their own particular image onto the divine
(as Xenophanes explicitly says in B.14) - was only the
negative side of his thought.
   In a work 'On Nature'(17) Xenophanes proceeds to the
more revolutionary part of his contribution:

εἷς θεός, ἔν τε θεοῖσι καὶ ἀνθρώποισι μέγιστος,
οὔτι δέμας θνητοῖσιν ὁμοίιος οὐδὲ νόημα.

(One god, the greatest among gods and men, in no way
like mortals either in body or in mind.)(18)

οὖλος ὁρᾷ, οὖλος δὲ νοεῖ, οὖλος δέ τ' ἀκούει.

(He sees as a whole, thinks as a whole, hears as a
whole.)(19)

ἀλλ' ἀπάνευθε πόνοιο νόου φρενὶ πάντα κραδαίνει.

(But without toil he shakes all things with the thought
of his mind.)(20)

αἰεὶ δ' ἐν ταὐτῷ μίμνει κινούμενος οὐδέν

οὐδὲ μετέρχεσθαι μιν ἐπιπρέπει ἄλλοτε ἄλλῃ.

(Always he remains in the same place, not moving at
all, nor is it fitting for him to go to different
places at different times.)(21)

These four fragments, although from diverse sources,
may legitimately be taken together as expressing
Xenophanes' central idea. As with Anaximander, the
problems of interpretation are immense; we are faced with
the great problem of understanding an intellect very
remote (and not just historically) from our own. Part of
the difficulty also lies in the fact that early thinkers
like Xenophanes (and later, Parmenides) were faced with
the problem of expressing ideas for which a suitable
language had yet to be developed. Hence, language and
thought at this time have a specially close relationship;
the form of Xenophanes' sayings and the content are
inextricably related.

     First, the problem of the form. The examples quoted
from the elegiac section of fragments, and even the
hexametric 'Silloi' (see above, pp.135-7), display an
elegance and clarity of expression which match the poet's
wit and vigour. The fragments which express Xenophanes'
conception of god (quoted immediately above) display the
same qualities: yet one cannot help feeling that the
medium of the Homeric hexameter is inadequate to the task
of expressing a profoundly new and, apparently, more
abstract idea. Why, to put it in a nutshell, did
Xenophanes choose (if he did choose) to write in verse,
when, as we saw in the previous chapter, a number of his
fellow Ionians were pioneering prose? And why, of the
verse forms available, did he choose the hexameter?

     The first point to make is a purely historical one:
the impossibility of knowing when, during the long period
of his adult life (possibly 550-480 BC) Xenophanes
composed his poems, makes it difficult to place him in any
kind of relationship to a developing prose-style. More
fundamentally, the choice of the hexameter may have been
motivated by its traditional poetic role as a vehicle for
the most serious religious and philosophical ideas; the
elegiac metre may have been thought unsuitable because of
its associations with, on the one hand, erotic poetry,
and, on the other, social rather than abstract philosophical matters. On the other hand, the persistence of
the hexameter as the verse-form of both Parmenides and
Empedokles and the success of its adaptation to the
expression of ideas of great complexity and logical
rigour, especially in Parmenides, suggests that, for

Xenophanes, the choice was not dictated merely by the force of tradition.

Diogenes Laertius informs us that Xenophanes ἐρραψῴδει τὰ ἑαυτοῦ (recited his own [poems]).(22) While there is no need to equate Xenophanes with a professional Homeric rhapsode (and, indeed, his attitude to Homer would completely rule this out) his wandering life and certain details of the fragments, such as his presence at drinking parties, suggests that his circumstances would lend themselves to oral recitation of his poems.(23) It is hard to suppose, however, that this would apply to the verses immediately under discussion, unless Xenophanes' audience was a very exceptional one!(24)

There is a tension, still latent in Xenophanes, between the form and content of the fragments. There is a certain irony in the choice of the Homeric metre to express ideas which constitute a radical denial of the Homeric theology both on a moral and intellectual plane. The emphatic denial of polytheism at the beginning of B.23 (see above, p.137) is immediately, on the face of it, contradicted by the formulaic phrase 'greatest among Gods and men', where the illogicality is merely the result of a traditional language; the only way that Xenophanes can express the overwhelming superiority of his god is by means of a phrase which happens to contradict what he is trying to say. It is unlikely, however, that the illogicality would have worried any of his contemporaries.(25) In B.25 (see above, p.137) 'the thought of his mind' recalls Homer.(26) And, when attempting to describe the power of this god to initiate movement, Xenophanes describes him as 'shaking all things'. Homer describes Zeus, in 'Iliad', I, 530 as 'causing great Olympos to shake' - an idea that Xenophanes probably had in his mind. Hence anthropomorphic Zeus provides the model for at least some aspects of Xenophanes' god. At the same time, we meet the unexpected juxtaposition of abstract and concrete: κραδαίνω ('agitate' or 'tremble'; hardly ever used metaphorically, according to LSJ) describes the (to us) mental processes of a god!

The content of the fragments is difficult for reasons which are connected with the language (see immediately above) and the history of thought. It has proved difficult to estimate how far Xenophanes is anticipating the later Eleatic position which his theology undoubtedly resembles, and how far this position has been imposed upon him by later commentators.(27) The somewhat conservative position of Kirk - that Xenophanes' god was probably imagined in very little more detail than is available in the existing fragments(28) may be contrasted with that of

Guthrie who, while rejecting the Eleatic implications of
later tradition, nevertheless argues strongly for the view
that Xenophanes imagined his god as of spherical shape.(29)
His argument – that Xenophanes must have given his god
some shape – is tempting, and the conclusion – that 'for
Xenophanes the cosmos was a spherical body, living,
conscious and divine, the cause of its own internal
movements and change'(30) – seems a reasonable interpet-
ation of Xenophanes' own words. Our problem is to know
how far Xenophanes' words may be taken to imply later,
more familiar ideas. B.26 describes the god's immobility;
the very difficult B.24 (see p.137) has been interpreted
as implying the identity of god with the cosmos (i.e. a
body which sees, thinks and hears as a whole). Yet the
extensive help this idea requires from later commentators
in order to father it on Xenophanes does not inspire
confidence.(31)   The sheer difficulty of language (e.g.
what does οὖλος in B.24 mean precisely?) is illustrated in
the opening words of B.23, εἷς θεός. A translation of
these words as 'One god', 'there is one god' or 'god is
one' (all are possible) radically affects the preconceptions with which one attempts to interpret the
fragments.(32)

   The evidence of the later tradition is not
conclusive;(33) the fragments themselves are ambiguous.
The modern investigator is wise, at this point, to enter
a discreet *non liquet*. We may confess ourselves beaten,
not only by the absence of evidence but also by our own
inability to enter the archaic mind.

   Yet certain conclusions may be tentatively offered,
which link Xenophanes with the Milesians. The unity of
common origin emphasised by Anaximander in his 'apeiron'
has become a unity by virtue of a single divine being who
has will and intelligence. Yet, like Anaximander,
Xenophanes is searching for a new explanation of the world
without entirely leaving behind the living, concrete
anthropomorphic world of his predecessors. This is
responsible for both the difficulty of Xenophanes' ideas
and also for the tendency to define his god negatively,
that is, to say much more clearly what he felt it was not
than what it was. It was left to later generations of
Eleatics to articulate the details more precisely.

   In contrast, Xenophanes' attitude towards knowledge
points decisively forward:

κeven τὸ μὲν οὖν σαφὲς οὔτις ἀνὴρ ἴδεν οὐδέ τις ἔσται
εἰδὼς ἀμφὶ θεῶν τε καὶ ἄσσα λέγω περὶ πάντων·
εἰ γὰρ καὶ τὰ μάλιστα τύχοι τετελεσμένον εἰπών,
αὐτὸς ὅμως οὐκ οἶδε· δόκος δ' ἐπὶ πᾶσι τέτυκται.

(As for the truth, no man has seen it, nor will there
be a man who knows about the gods and about all the
things I speak of. For if he should succeed fully in
saying what is true, he himself nevertheless does not
know it; but seeming is built over all things.)(34)

Again, care must be taken not to make Xenophanes
anticipate either Plato or Scepticism. Xenophanes was
neither denying entirely the possibility of knowledge nor
making a clear distinction between two types of understanding, one of which led to objects of certain knowledge
and another only of opinion. Yet, there is no doubt that
his statement above was the beginning of a move away from
the naïveté of the automatic presumption that the evidence
of the senses presented what was true - a move which
ultimately dealt the death-blow to Ionian philosophy. In
the place of moral and physical limitations separating
mortals from gods in the traditional picture, Xenophanes
has, for the first time, substituted a barrier which later
generations would call epistemological.(35)   Yet B.34 must
be read in conjunction with B.18:

οὔτοι ἀπ' ἀρχῆς πάντα θεοὶ θνητοῖσ' ὑπέδειξαν,
ἀλλὰ χρόνῳ ζητοῦντες ἐφευρίσκουσιν ἄμεινον.

(Indeed, the gods(36) have not revealed to mortals all
things from the beginning, but in time they find out
better by seeking.)

Here we can see the beginnings of a view of history as a
progress based upon man's increasing knowledge of both his
environment and himself, and especially the awareness of
his innate capacities displayed in every facet of an
expanding sixth-century BC world, rich in opportunity for
enterprise and adventure - a view which was very
influential (see below, chapter 7). This attitude became
prominent in marked contrast to the older view of history
as a decline, implicit in Homer and explicit in Hesiod's
five ages of man in the 'Works and Days' (110-201). That
this progressive view of human evolution, with its
emphasis upon human initiative, was Ionian seems to be
indicated by the evidence of Anaximander that man
'ascended' from earlier forms of life. He seems to have
believed that men were born inside fish-like creatures who
nurtured them until they were capable of independent
existence.(37) Lacking the scientific basis of Darwin,
this was nevertheless a brilliant conjecture which
reflected the outward-looking trend of Milesian thought.
Xenophanes, characteristically, expanded the idea to

include man's own initiative, tempering it with an
awareness of his intellectual limitations.

Xenophanes' own contribution to Ionian science is a
notable one, and constitutes one of the most remarkable
scientifice deductions of the Presocratic period. He
observed a number of fossil impressions on dry land at a
variety of places and saw this as an indication that they
had been made when the earth's surface was covered with
mud or slime (an idea which already had currency among the
Milesians). What Xenophanes did was to relate his
observations to a general theory of the cyclic alternation
in the world, over long periods of time, of earth and
water. As he himself said:

ἐκ γαίης γὰρ πάντα καὶ εἰς γῆν πάντα τελευτᾷ,

(For all things come from earth and all things return
at last to earth.)(38)

The theory, and the deductions from it, stand out
notably from the remainder of his physical theories which
are not impressive, as far as the extant evidence allows
us to judge.(39)

Despite his exile and reputedly close connection with
Elea, Xenophanes' intellectual links are with his homeland.
His severe moral criticism of Homer, it is true, does not
strike the detached and perhaps even permissive Ionian
note; moreover, it is a long way from Anakreon's love and
wine in the Samian court (see chapter 4, pp. 93-6) to
Xenophanes' more decorous symposium in B.1 (see above,
p.136), where:

οὐχ ὕβρις πίνειν ὁπόσον κεν ἔχων ἀφίκοιο
    οἴκαδ' ἄνευ προπόλου μὴ πάνυ γηραλέος.

(It is not an outrage to drink so much that you might
be able to reach home without a guide, be you not very
aged.)

Yet he also reveals himself as a witty, sceptical
rationalist who, like his contemporary, Hekataios of
Miletos (and, as far as we can see, with much greater
justification) believed that his fellow Hellenes enter-
tained 'ridiculous ideas'.(40) Both these aspects, a keen
critical intelligence and an acute moral indignation
verging on the satirical, are united with a much profound-
er intellect in the last great archaic thinker - and
arguably the greatest of the Presocratics - Herakleitos of
Ephesos.

Uniquely among his fellow Ionians, Herakleitos has
possessed over the last 150 years an importance beyond the
merely historical. His aristocratic exclusiveness, his
epigrammatic style and, above all, his apparent anticipation of some elements in modern historical dialectic made
a great impression upon German philosophers of the
nineteenth century AD, especially Hegel and Nietzsche; for
the latter Herakleitos represented one of the pinnacles of
Greek thought.(41) While few today would uphold
Nietzsche's view of archaic thought and his somewhat
eccentric under-valuation of Greek philosophy from Sokrates
onwards, it is true that in modern times Herakleitos has
come to have a peculiar relevance for those who, in the
pursuit of truth and self-fulfilment, have begun to search
for an alternative to logic and scientific discovery and
have found inspiration in what they feel to be his
intuitive perception of reality. Such popularity has its
dangers. Oracular but obscure, incisive but disjointed,
Herakleitos' utterances have provided a mirror to reflect
countless faiths, cults and movements. Illumination of
the source, however, has not been great. One is forced to
concur with the low estimation of Herakleitos'devotees
and even many of his scholars held by the author of the
most sober and detailed modern study, G.S. Kirk.(42)

The great posthumous fame and notoriety that
Herakleitos - ὁ σκοτεινός (the obscure one)(43) - has
enjoyed from the time of Plato to the present day may tend
to obscure his contemporary significance as an Ionian
thinker who, standing in lonely eminence on the edge of
the archaic world, both summed up its main characteristics
and also contributed to its passing. It is in this
context that he will be considered here, stripped, as far
as possible, of the assimilations, Platonic, Stoic,
Christian or Hegelian, to which his thought has, at
various times, been subject.

Herakleitos, unlike Xenophanes, was no wanderer; he was
and remained a citizen of Ephesos. This city, as we
remarked earlier, can be sharply contrasted with Miletos
in character and outlook (chapter 2, p.19). After early
struggles against Lydian invasion, Ephesos did not feature
much in early Ionian history. Non-Greek influence was
strong from a very early stage and especially marked in
Anatolian features of the superficially Greek cult of
Artemis (chapter 2, loc.cit.). In later times, when
Miletos was degenerating into a swamp-infested village,
Ephesos blossomed into a major city as a Roman metropolis
and a Byzantine episcopal seat. It owed much to its
geographical situation but also something perhaps to its
religious tradition. St Paul's 'Diana of the Ephesians',

whose prestige was threatened by the Christian God (see chapter 2, p.19) was directly descended from the famous cult of Artemis which was itself an offshoot of a pre-Greek cult taken over by the first Ionian settlers.

Ephesos sent out no colonies and took no recorded part in the Ionian revolt beyond the 'accidental' slaughter of the remains of the Chian contingent after the battle of Lade when the Ephesians were under the impression that the Chians were brigands intending to carry off their women, who were holding a festival in honour of Demeter.(44) Despite earlier heroic struggles recorded by Kallinos (see chapter 4, p.91), the city enjoyed close relations with the Lydians (Sardis was no more than fifty miles distant) and may well have accepted Persian control more or less willingly (as it did much later in 411 BC). Despite a degree of separation from the rest of the Ionian cities, including exclusion, with Kolophon, from the common festival of the Apatouria, (see chapter 2, p.19), Ephesos always enjoyed great prestige, partly from her status as the original seat of the Ionian kingdom (see chapter 2, p.15) partly from her political stability in which oligarchical rule rested upon a largely agricultural economy – a system which the Lydians and, later, the Persians, may have found useful to counterbalance the democratic and independent tendencies of Miletos and Chios.

The significance of Ephesos in the early history of Ionian Greek sculpture (see chapter 3, pp. 46-9), architecture (p.54) and coinage (see chapter 5, p.108) is matched by the obvious signs of orientalisation. This may have increased after the setting up of a tyranny (c. 600 BC) with close Lydian connections. At about this date it is probable that the population underwent a large expansion from outside, leading to the subordination of the traditional Ionian tribes to an organisation in 'chiliastyes' (thousands), a development also recorded elsewhere in Ionia.(45) At all events, the absence of Lydian influence in the elegy of Kallinos (for what this argument is worth) may be compared to its presence in the sixth-century Hipponax, whose language is permeated by Lydian vocabulary.(46)

This excursus has been attempted in the belief that the background information, scanty as it is, is not entirely irrelevant to the life and work of Herakleitos. He flourished rather later (c. 500 BC) and probably lived to see Ionia pass from Persian into mainland Greek hands after the battle of Mykale in 479 BC. It is doubtful if this liberation made much difference to Ephesos or Herakleitos, whose enthusiasm for democratic movements is

not marked, in contrast to his trenchant manner of
expressing himself:

ἄξιον 'Εφεσίοις ἡβηδὸν ἀπάγξασθαι πᾶσι καὶ τοῖς
ἀνήβοις τὴν πόλιν καταλιπεῖν, οἵτινες 'Ερμόδωρον
ἄνδρα ἑωυτῶν ὀνήστον ἐξέβαλον φάντες· ἡμέων μηδὲ
εἷς ὀνήστος ἔστω, εἰ δὲ μή, ἄλλη τε καὶ μετ' ἄλλων.

(All Ephesian men would do well to hang themselves and
leave the city to the boys, since they have expelled
Hermodoros,(47) the best man among them, saying: 'Let no
individual among us be the most valuable, or if there
be one, let it be elsewhere and among others.')(48)

There is little reliable information about his life,
though Diogenes Laertius, the third-century AD
biographer, abhoring a vacuum, gives an anecdotal 'life
and habits' in which the Stoic distortion of doctrine is
matched by the banality of the prosopographical detail –
the latter largely culled from unintelligent deductions
from the fragments themselves.(49) However, we have no
reason to doubt the information that Herakleitos was a
direct descendant of the royal Ephesian house; out of
arrogance he surrendered to his brother the title of king
(to which, according to Strabo, the descendants were still
entitled) and the attendant privileges: a front seat at
the games, the right to wear royal purple and the organisation of the religious rites of Eleusinian Demeter.(50)
Herakleitos' exclusiveness has an almost Homeric ring:

αἱρεῦνται γὰρ ἓν ἀντὶ ἀπάντων οἵ ἄριστοι, κλέος
ἀέναον θνητῶν· οἱ δὲ πολλοὶ κεκόρηνται ὅκωσπερ
κτήνεα.

(For the best men choose one thing instead of all:
everlasting fame among mortals; but the majority glut
themselves like cattle.)(51)

Yet the aristocratic basis for κλέος (renown) and the
corresponding contempt for the masses is not merely
political exclusiveness but a mirror of his philosophical
views. Herakleitos shares Xenophanes' critical spirit and
awareness of his own isolation, but takes it further. Men
are worthless because they fail to see the truth.
Herakleitos expounds this in his longest surviving
fragment:

τοῦ δὲ λόγου τοῦδ' ἐόντος ἀεὶ ἀξύνετοι γίνονται
ἄνθρωποι καὶ πρόσθεν ἢ ἀκοῦσαι καὶ ἀκούσαντες τὸ

πρῶτον· γινομένων γὰρ πάντων κατὰ τὸν λόγον τόνδε
ἀπείροισιν ἐοίκασι, πειρώμενοι καὶ ἐπέων καὶ ἔργων
τοιούτων, ὁκοίων ἐγώ διηγεῦμαι κατὰ φύσιν διαιρέων
ἕκαστον καὶ φράζων ὅκως ἔχει· τοὺς δὲ ἄλλους ἀνθρώπους
λανθάνει ὁκόσα ἐγερθέντες ποιοῦσιν, ὅκωσπερ ὁκόσα
εὕδοντες ἐπιλανθάνονται.

(Although this Logos exists always, men are unable to
understand both before they have heard it and when once
they have heard it. For, while all things come to pass
according to this Logos, they seem like men of no
experience, experiencing such words and deeds as I set
forth, distinguishing each thing according to its
nature and telling how it is. But as for the majority
of mankind - they are unaware of what they do when
awake, just as they forget what they do while
asleep.)(52)

As one of the earliest prose fragments of any length,
this is worthy of the closest attention. It has an
elaborate antithetical structure which is not merely
stylistic artifice; it reflects an antithesis between
Herakleitos' principle of existence, the Logos, and the
ignorance of most men.(53) The idea of men's ignorance is
made deliberately paradoxical: men are as ignorant when
they have heard as before they have heard; they are also
inexperienced, when they experience (the repetition of the
word in the translation is intended to reproduce the
paradoxical effect of the original) the truth. Furthermore men act in their waking state much as they do when
asleep - mere exposure to the truth is not enough:

Τοῦ λόγου δ' ἐόντος ξυνοῦ ζώουσιν οἱ πολλοὶ ὡς ἰδίαν
ἔχοντες φρόνησιν.

(The Logos being common, most men live as if having
their own understanding.)(54)

ἀξύνετοι ἀκούσαντες κωφοῖσιν ἐοίκασι· φάτις αὐτοῖσιν
μαρτυρεῖ παρεόντας ἀπεῖναι.

(Those failing to understand when they have heard are
like the deaf; the saying bears them witness: 'present,
they are absent.')(55)

Possession of senses, and even the full use of them,
does not of itself lead to understanding, although it may
lead to an accumulation of knowledge:

πολυμαθίη νόον ἔχειν οὐ διδάσκει· Ἡσίοδον γὰρ ἂν
ἐδίδαξε καὶ Πυθαγόρην αὖτίς τε Ξενοφάνεά τε καὶ
Ἑκαταῖον.

(Much learning does not teach intelligence; for otherwise it would have taught Hesiod and Pythagoras, and
again Xenophanes and Hekataios.)(56)

Herakleitos does not mention Anaximander in the extant
fragments, though it is hardly likely that he was unaware
of the teaching of his great predecessor. Silence from
Herakleitos is possibly the highest complement!

Even without the above personal references, we would be
aware that Herakleitos' whole approach separates him
decisively from the outward-looking, genial and essentially
'inquisitive' character of Ionian enquiry. His devotion
is not to facts or theories, but to reality.

Before we pass on to consider in what this truth lay,
it is important to consider certain preliminary questions
concerning Herakleitos' language.

First, the style. It must be pointed out to readers
without Greek that English translation inevitably expands
and blunts the edge of many of Herakleitos' sayings owing
to the greater resources of the older language for
compression - omission of the verb 'to be', significant
use of word inflexion, word order, etc. Yet Greekless
readers need not feel alone in their exclusion. Aristotle
expresses his perplexity over the exact reference of ἀεί
(always) in B.1 (above, p.145 and n.53).(57) It is clear
that Herakleitos' style was strange to later generations
of commentators. Diogenes Laertius, with his usual lack
of acumen, informs us that he wrote ἀσαφέστερον (rather
obscurely) 'so that those of status should alone have
access to it and so that it should not be easily held in
contempt by the people.)(58) Sokrates, rather more to the
point, pokes gentle fun at Herakleitos; when asked
(improbably!) by Euripides what he thought of Herakleitos'
book, he was said to have replied: 'What I understood was
fine, and what I didn't understand also, I expect, except
that it needs a Delian diver to get to the bottom of
it.'(59) Plato, again humorously, at least in part,
pictures contemporary Herakleiteans supporting the theory
of Universal Flux (see below, p.158) by aiming oracular
aphorisms at their opponents in place of reasoned
argument.(60)

These comments are all at one in assuming that the
style is to be seen clearly as either affectation or
ornament - something largely foreign to and separate from
the content of what Herakleitos was trying to say. Enough

has been said already about style and content in archaic
literature to make this hypothesis unlikely. But we must
go further and try to establish what Herakleitos' style
was and what it was doing.

Herakleitos' use of language differs markedly from the
plain unadorned style of Hekataios in that it eschews
simple and flowing prose rhythms for the more jerky,
highly wrought effects of declamation, oracle and epigram
with strong emphasis upon rhythm, phonetic patterns and
antithetical structure (what the Germans call 'Satzparal-
lelismus'). Herakleitos owes a great deal to the 'gnomic'
style of the elegists but departs radically from the
Homeric rhythms and vocabulary that the elegists tended to
preserve (see chapter 4, pp. 91f.). The compression and
finish of his style resembles some fragments of Anakreon
(see chapter 4, pp. 93ff.) – although there, one must
hasten to add, the resemblance ends; χάρις (grace) was the
last quality Herakleitos wished to bring to his words.

In B.1 (quoted above, p.145), the flowing balance of
clauses, reminiscent of Pherekydes (see chapter 5, pp.129-
30), is tauter and much more carefully controlled.
Herakleitos does not relinquish the paratactic style (see
chapter 4, p. 80) and, indeed, uses it for his own
purposes. (See above, p.146 for the apparently clumsy,
but, in reality, deliberate repetition of ἀπείροισι/πειρώ-
μενοι ('to men of no experience'/'experiencing')) to
unfold his message. We shall see later that Herakleitos
uses this apparently primitive method of repetition with
deadly effect. On other occasions, he prefers concrete
images to logical exposition:

ὁ θεὸς ἡμέρη εὐφρόνη, χειμὼν θέρος, πόλεμος εἰρήνη,
κόρος λιμός· ἀλλοιοῦται   δὲ ὅκωσπερ <πῦρ>, ὁπόταν
συμμιγῇ θυώμασιν, ὀνομάζεται καθ᾽ ἡδονὴν ἑκάστου.

(God day night, winter summer, war peace, satiety
hunger; he changes in the way that fire, when it is
mixed with spices, is named according to the scent of
each.)(61)

Connected with a preference for the concrete and
imagistic is Herakleitos' use of puns and riddles. For
example, B.48:

τῷ οὖν τόξῳ   ὄνομα βίος, ἔργον δὲ θάνατος.

(Of the bow the name is life, but the work, death.)

This is an answer to a possible riddle which contains

a pun (impossible to translate) on the similarity of the
words βίος (life) and βιός (bow) which also contains a
paradox - the similarity of name conceals a polarity of
function. On a lighter note, Herakleitos tells of a
riddle which, he says, deceived even Homer 'the wisest of
all Greeks'. Some boys while killing lice told him that
'what we saw and caught, those we leave behind; what we
did not see or catch, those we bring with us.'(62)

These examples may seem trivial; puns and riddles were
elements of an underlying popular culture which only
occasionally surfaced in more formal literary contexts.
Yet they were not despised, but appear in a much more
formal guise in oracular responses. These, though hardly
popular in the strict sense of the word, were the product
of an institution which had its roots deep in Greek social
and religious life. Although our early sources for these
oracles tend to be literary, we are familiar enough with
oracular responses in Herodotos, Tragedy, etc. to know
that they were delivered in verse in a manner which
frequently disguised the truth or was actively misleading.(63) For example, in response to Croesus' enquiry
whether he should march against the Persians, the Delphic
oracle replied Κροῖσος Ἅλυν διαβὰς μεγάλην ἀρχὴν καταλύ-
σει (Croesus, crossing the Halys [river] will destroy a
great empire).(64) For another example, we need go no
further than the riddle of the Sphinx to the Thebans,
solved by Oidipous, which, although not oracular, exhibits
similar features.(65) More to the point was the oracle to
Oidipous' father Laios which was fulfilled against all
probable expectation.(66)

The connection of oracular pronouncements with his own
thought was explicitly recognised by Herakleitos in B.93:

ὁ ἄναξ, οὗ τὸ μαντεῖόν ἐστι τὸ ἐν Δελφοῖς, οὔτε λέγει,
οὔτε κρύπτει ἀλλὰ σημαίνει.

(The lord, whose oracle is that at Delphi, neither
speaks nor hides but signifies.)

So, Herakleitos in his utterance signifies reality for
those who understand.

Another thing that Herakleitos has in common with
oracles is an affinity with oral culture. The circumstances of oracular response presupposed a verbal answer
from the priest of Apollo. There are also elements in
Herakleitos which point to oral composition. The surviving fragments display a finish and internal coherence
which has led some scholars to suspect that they are
isolated utterances rather than quotations from a longer,

more discursive work.(67)   The ascription by Aristotle and
later commentators to Herakleitos of a book does not, in
the absence of earlier testimony, constitute weighty
evidence.(68)   The story, retailed by Diogenes Laertius,
that Herakleitos deposited his book in the Ephesian
Artemision, may be, as Kirk remarks, (69) a story invented
to explain its absence after the famous fire which
occurred there in 353 BC. While the question cannot be
settled finally, it may be conjectured that we have here a
situation not dissimilar to that of early lyric poetic
composition (see above, chapter 5, p.105) where writing
may be used in the preservation rather than the composition. As E.A. Havelock pertinently remarks: 'the clues
to the philosopher's [Herakleitos'] own situation are to
be sought ... not in the existence of the book, but in the
verbal form in which he originally cast his doctrine.'(70)

A further argument against the existence of a book,
from which the existing fragments are a selection, is as
follows. If the concise, epigrammatic sentences are
merely survivals and much explanatory and connecting
material has perished, it is clear that such 'lost'
information was already unavailable to the Peripatetic
School since, if it had been available, it would surely
have been used as an aid to the interpretation of a
thinker whose way of expressing himself was in many
respects so alien to the fourth and later centuries.(71)
As it is, Diogenes, reporting Theophrastos, complains
that Herakleitos was defective as a source, but clearly
has nothing of any value with which to supplement him.(72)

Herakleitos' reputation for obscurity (his nickmane
was, revealingly, αἰνυκτής (riddler)) was a direct result
of a process of thought which puzzled his successors. It
is now time to see just what this process was.

As we have observed, Herakleitos saw reality contained
in something called the Logos. The common meaning is
'word' or 'account', with a usage which puts the word into
an antithesis with μῦθος (story or word) to imply 'true' or
'reasoned' account.(73) Clearly, for Herakleitos, the
Logos is in some sense the principle according to which
the world is organised (since one of the basic meanings of
the root from which it is derived is 'gathering' or
'choosing', from which comes the idea of 'measure' or
'orderly relationship') and at the same time the word is
associated(74) with the discourse of Herakleitos (since
another basic meaning of the root is 'account' or
'narration'). Scholarly dispute over the question whether
the Logos is to be identified with the discourse of
Herakleitos (see n.74) reveals the general failure of
modern commentators to appreciate the close connection

between Herakleitos' 'word' and the objective truth of
what he reveals, and indeed the unlikelihood of his
audience making a clear distinction between the two.(75)
    What is there, then, which gives us the clue to the
Logos? Scholars who have tended to play down the literal
meaning of the word in favour of the 'measure' idea
contained in it,(76) have, perhaps, put too little
emphasis upon the style of the fragments. It is perhaps
not without significance that the paradox in which pun or
word-play is employed tends to be found in fragments in
which Herakleitos wishes to describe the attitude of the
majority of men to his Logos. Two of these we have
already encountered in B.1 and 34 (pp.145-6 and 146).(77)
For Herakleitos the truth is something which is encountered, but not recognised for what it is. The clues are
there, accessible to all, but only the intelligent or
those with insight will penetrate the appearance and reach
the reality. The remainder are like 'men asleep'.(78)
Herakleitos takes full advantage of the opportunities for
serious and significant punning afforded by the Greek
language:

δοκέοντα γὰρ ὁ δοκιμώτατος γινώσκει, φυλάσσει.

(For the man most in repute knows, guards that which is
reputed(79).(80)

Here the paradox (reinforced by a superlative, δοκιμώτατος)
is obtained by the use of different forms of the same word
to convey potential opposites: high status and knowledge
only of what seems to be true. For Herakleitos, social
status and reputation may well go hand in hand with superficial understanding. A different idea illustrates the
same principle:

ἐὰν μὴ ἔλπηται, ἀνέλπιστον οὐκ ἐξευρήσει, ἀνεξερεύνητον
ἐὸν καὶ ἄπορον.

(If one does not hope, one will not find the unhoped-
for, since it is not to be searched out and hard to
discover.)(81)

This illustrates admirably the difficulty of translation,
since the paradox of hoping for the hopeless is sharpened
if one punctuates after, rather than before ἀνέλπιστον
(unhoped-for).

    A difficult fragment is B.15:

εἰ μὴ γὰρ Διονύσῳ πομπὴν ἐποιοῦντο καὶ ὕμνεον ᾆσμα
αἰδοίοισιν, ἀναιδέστατα εἴργαστ᾽ ἄν· ὡυτὸς δὲ ᾽Αίδης
καὶ Διόνυσος, ὅτεῳ μαίνονται καὶ ληναΐζουσιν.

If it were not for Dionysos that they made the
procession and sang the hymn to the private parts, they
would be acting most shamelessly. But Hades and
Dionysos are the same, for whom they rave and
celebrate Bacchic rites.)

The meaning of the fragment is difficult and obscure, and
no simple interpretation fully convinces.(82) One obvious
element, however, is a full exploitation of the polar
associations of αἰδώς, which indicates both 'shame' or
'respect' and also 'that which is shameful'. The identity
or close association of the sacred and profane in religious
belief is a widely attested phenomenon, especially in
anthropological contexts.(83) The polar ambiguity of
αἰδώς was noted by Euripides 'Hippolytos', 385ff.) as an
instance of a lack of precision inherent in language. For
Herakleitos, however, the linguistic association of
opposites shows that the sanctity of shameless rites is
not an absurd contradiction arising from the erroneous
belief of mortals, but a paradox which has objective
truth.(84)
    The impossibility of reproducing, in translation, the
variety of relationships exposed in this fragment (there
may be a further punning link with ᾽Αίδης (Hades)) is the
result of the compression of utterance possible in a
linguistic milieu in which puns and word-plays could be
regarded not as artifice but as in themselves revealing
a serious philosophic truth. As with the bow (βιός) and
life (βίος), so with other puns; the ability, as
Herakleitos saw it, of language to reveal such polar
tendencies, concealed in the very nature of language but
evident for all to see confirmed him in his belief that
opposites in the world, taken as a whole, coincided. Just
as men fail to look below the surface of linguistic
coincidence (and Herakleitos, in common with his archaic
contemporaries, believed that there was no such thing) the
uninitiated fail to penetrate the surface of nature to
reach reality. As Herakleitos says, 'nature loves to
hide' and 'a hidden harmony is stronger than an apparent
one.'(85)
    In Xenophanes, as we saw, the interaction of language
and thought is to be seen in terms of style and tradition
in which antithetical expression often, even against
logic, remains his only recourse (see p.139). Antithetical
style, the use of parallel clauses and polarity in the

expression of ideas is a commonplace of Greek literary
style from Homer onwards which, as Eduard Norden was the
first to show, has close connections with liturgy.(86)   In
a later work Norden briefly notes Herakleitos' use of
antithesis as an early anticipation of the highly wrought,
dialectical style of the later fifth-century BC rhetoric-
ian and philosopher, Gorgias of Leontini, in Sicily, who
came to Athens on an embassy during the Peloponnesian War
and dazzled the citizens with his display of verbal
virtuosity.(87)   Yet, if, with Norden, we are to see
Herakleitos' language as a 'Kunstsprache', we ought also
to be quite clear on the difference between him and
Gorgias.

The use of contradiction and paradox as a dialectical
or rhetorical weapon belonged properly to the period of
the Sophists, and had its most elaborate formulation in
the 'Dissoi Logoi' (Double Arguments)(88) which, as its
title implies, was a rhetorical exercise in arguing
opposite sides of a given argument.   This anonymous
sophistical essay, written after the Peloponnesian War,
is one of a number of attempts to exploit the ambiguities
of a developing logic - ambiguities parodied with such
deadly humour by Aristophanes in the 'Clouds'(89) and
reflected in the charge against Sokrates in the 'Apology'
of making the lesser argument the stronger.(90)

In 'De Sophisticis Elenchis' (On Sophistic Refutations),
Aristotle treated contradiction, paradox and ambiguity
exclusively from a logical and dialectical standpoint.   In
his discussion on fallacies common in argument he
distinguished a number of different methods of producing
an illusion of validity, and demonstrated, with examples,
how ambiguity or flat contradiction might result.(91)
Aristotle's belief that ambiguity and paradox were
perversions of logic led him to the conclusion that
examples of such figures were either unintentional, and so
the result of incompetence, or deliberate, and so employed
for purposes of equivocation.(92)   As his discussion makes
clear, he was aware of the distinction between names,
which are finite in number, and their corresponding
objects, which are infinite.   The same expression must
therefore necessarily signify a number of different
things, with the consequence that the ignorant are
deceived by the resulting ambiguities, and the clever are
able to use them to their own advantage.(93)

In this respect, Herakleitos was inhabiting a totally
different world.   His language was highly wrought and
paradoxical not because he was clever, stupid or (as
Diogenes would have us believe) arrogant, but because for
him, as for other archaic thinkers, language was a direct

reflection of objective reality. Hence revelation of the
identity of opposites in language was a clear indication
of a harmony of opposites in the world.

The idea of the unity, harmony or (occasionally) the
identity of opposites, normally regarded as Herakleitos'
most important discovery, had much influence upon ways of
thinking in Greek archaic and classical thought. The
tension and regulation of warring opposites (already seen
as a central doctrine of Anaximander (chapter 5, pp. 124))
was applied equally to the balance of opposite powers in
the human body to produce health, or to a reconciliation
of political or ethical opposites in the mean (an idea
which became canonical in fourth-century philosophical
ideas).(94) Herakleitos' position in the historical
development of the idea of the ἁρμονία (harmony) of
opposites was a striking one; he asserted that the harmony
of opposites consisted not in their reconciliation with
each other, but in mutual strife. Homer deserved to be
thrown out of the games and beaten, said Herakleitos,
because he expressed the wish that strife should perish
from among Gods and men.(95) On the contrary it is the
existence of strife which guarantees the stability of the
world. He demonstrates this startling announcement not by
argument but by concrete, almost pictorial examples:

οὐ ξυνιᾶσιν ὅκως διαφερόμενον ἑωυτῷ ὁμολογέει· παλίν-
τροπος ἁρμονίη ὅκωσπερ τόξου καὶ λύρης.

(They do not understand how that which is at variance
agrees with itself; a backwarding-turning(96) harmony,
as in a bow or lyre.)(97)

A bow or a stringed lyre appears to be at rest, whereas
really it is a war of opposites, the inward pull of the
string against the outward pull of the wood.

Some more examples will help to clarify Herakleitos'
discovery:

ὁδὸς ἄνω κάτω μία καὶ ὠυτή

(Road up down one and the same.)(98)

θάλασσά ὕδωρ καθαρώτατον καὶ μιαρώτατον, ἰχθύσι μὲν
πότιμον καὶ σωτήριον, ἀνθρώποις δὲ ἄποτον καὶ ὀλέθριον.

(Sea - water most pure and most foul, for fishes
drinkable and salutary, but for men undrinkable and
deadly.)(99)

Herakleitos adds substance to his criticism of Hesiod in
B.40 (see above, p.147).

δυδάσκαλος δὲ πλείστων 'Ησίοδος· τοῦτον ἐπίστανται
πλεῖστα εἰδέναι, ὅστις ἡμέρην καὶ εὐφρόνην οὐκ
ἐγίνωσκεν· ἔστι γὰρ ἕν.

(Teacher of most men Hesiod; this man they are sure
knew very many things, who did not recognise day and
night; for it is one.)(100)

On a religious practice:

καθαίρονται δ' ἄλλῳ αἵματι μιαινόμενοι οἷον εἰ τις εἰς
πηλὸν ἐμβὰς πηλῷ ἀπονίζοιτο. μαίνεσθαι δ' ἂν δοκοίη, εἴ
τις αὐτὸν ἀνθρώπων ἐπιφράσαιτο οὕτω ποιέοντα.

(They purify themselves, staining themselves with
other blood, as if one were to wash off mud by stepping
into mud. A man would be presumed mad if any of his
fellow men were to catch sight of him acting like
this.)(101)

It was probably the diversity and commonplace nature of
the examples which impressed Herakleitos; everywhere he
looked, it seemed, apparent diversity and separation
concealed coincidence or identity.
     Unfortunately, it is these very qualities which
bewilder the modern observer. The diversity and haphazard
nature of Herakleitos' observations may lead a reader
versed in elementary logic to put in a few points here:
first, Herakleitos conflates (the critic may, if he is
sufficiently out of sympathy with the object of his study,
say 'confuses') examples from a variety of different
sources. Second, in expressing himself in pictorial
rather than abstract terms, he fails to adduce a coherent
principle to which the examples may clearly be related.
All they have in common is an apparently polar relationship which, by a manipulation of predication, may be shown
as paradoxical. More specifically, we might be inclined
to assert that some of his opposites are not really
opposites at all, and even of those that are, it can
never be sensibly asserted that they are identical. His
examples are either trivial (e.g. the way up and the way
down on a road are not really opposed) or explicable in
different terms (e.g. day and night are one in the sense
of forming a continuum; sea-water exhibits different
aspects to different observers).
     All these points have been made, either in criticism or

mitigation of Herakleitos.(102) Yet, they all contain the
shortcoming, from the historical point of view, that they
make distinctions of which Herakleitos would have been
unaware. To try to explain his thought in terms of any of
them would be to introduce anachronism. In a sense, to
assert that the way up and the way down are one and the
same is to voice a truism which is on the point of
banality;(103) it seems self-evident that 'up down' are to
be identified by virtue of their physical identity in the
road. Yet, for Herakleitos, it is the coincidence of the
opposites and not the resolution on a logical level which
is important. Again, with the sea-water of B.61,
Herakleitos is not asserting the relativity of sensations,
but the objective existence, in the sea-water, of
opposites - 'the most pure and the most foul' which the
observers, humans and fish, discover.(104) The union of
day and night in B.57 (see above, p.155) is, on the face
of it, a scientific fact, in which the more rigorous
Herakleitos was correcting his predecessor. Yet, an
element of paradox would not have been entirely lost upon
a contemporary audience, for which day and night were also
powerfully symbolic, as representatives of opposing and
often antagonistic elements in Greek religious practice.
    A similar intention informs B.58:

οἱ γοῦν ἰατροί, ἐπαιτέονται μηδὲν ἄξιοι μισθὸν
λαμβάνειν, ταὐτὰ ἐργαζόμενοι.

(For instance, doctors demand, though in no way
deserving, a fee, producing the same [pains as the
disease].)(105)

A paradox exists by virtue of the good and evil elements
in surgery, where pain is inflicted to effect a cure. Men
experience the pain, or they inflict it, but do not fully
understand the mystery of the coincidence of opposites,
'pain curing pain', which they experience. Sickness and
health is also the subject of B.111:

νοῦσος ὑγιείην ἐποίησεν ἡδὺ καὶ ἀγαθόν, λιμὸς κόρον,
κάματος ἀνάπαυσιν.

(Sickness makes health sweet and good, hunger satiety,
toil rest.)

    Herakleitos comments on a phenomenon that none of us
has failed to experience at some time or other. However,
it is unlikely that he wished to state the obvious. For
Herakleitos, the obvious conceals something else which

men find much harder to recognise; it is not man, but
sickness which has the capacity to produce an effect with
which, one would suppose, it is normally in conflict.(106)
Herakleitos enjoyed, with his Ionian predecessors, a
direct confrontation with the world, in which logical
transformation was only just beginning to make itself felt.
Moreover, the identity of opposites and the consequent
paradox were not primarily the result of reflection upon
the various ways in which opposites were related, but the
explanations, if supplied at all, were of facts which had
already been grasped intuitively. The absence of
explanations clarifies another point - the lack of a clear
distinction between the enunciation of Herakleitos'
principle and examples of it. For Herakleitos, as for
archaic sculptors, abstract and concrete were not yet
wholly distinct (see above, chapter 3, p.50). He was
enabled to conduct a rigorous enquiry into the nature of
reality without relinquishing his hold on the vivid,
dynamic world of the senses. Principle and example were
one.

So far, we have confined our attention fairly strictly
to the opposites. But Herakleitos was not merely content
to observe a principle. His search went wider. As we
have already seen (p.148) in B.67 the opposites are
identified with God, which seems to be similar to the
Logos:

οὐκ ἐμοῦ, ἀλλὰ τοῦ λόγου ἀκούσαντας ὁμολογεῖν σοφόν
ἐστιν ἓν πάντα εἶναι.

(Having listened not to me but to the Logos, it is wise
to agree (107) that all things are one.)(108)

The unity of all things is an idea which had great
influence both in mystery religion and in the development
of more formal modes of thought. In Herakleitos it
occupies a transitional position. We have already seen,
in Xenophanes, that One God may have been identified with
the world (see above, p.140). Later, in Parmenides, the
unity and immobility of reality is sharply contrasted with
the illusion of diversity and movement. However,
Herakleitos has not yet banished diversity from his world:
in a most important fragment, he makes it clear that the
Logos does not transcend or reconcile the opposites in any
'higher' peace:

εἰδέναι δὲ χρὴ τὸν πόλεμον ἐόντα ξυνόν, καὶ δίκην ἔριν,
καὶ γινόμενα πάντα κατ' ἔριν καὶ χρέων.

(It is necessary to know that war is common and justice
strife, and all things come to be through strife and
necessity.)(109)

It is not difficult to suppose Herakleitos was here
correcting his distinguished predecessor Anaximander, who
saw the strife of opposites as injustice (above, chapter
5, p.124) For Herakleitos, strife is justice (or justice,
strife - the ambiguity may be deliberate to give point to
the identity). War is said to be common (like the Logos
in B.2, see above, p.146 and so, by implication,
associated with it). Since for the Greeks, it was
precisely the absence of ἔρις (strife) which suggested
conditions favourable for δίκη (justice), the expression
of their identity is paradoxical in the extreme, and
reveals the sharp originality of Herakleitos' conception.
War is, in an unequivocal sense, peace. The identity of
these two opposites in particular assumes a position of
central importance in Herakleitos' thought, since it
characterises the relationship between individual
opposites, the hidden workings of objects such as the bow
and the lyre, and the strife which ensures the continual
existence of the Universe. If opposites are continually
in strife, one might legitimately ask how all things are
one. Herakleitos is also thought to have asserted that
everything was in a perpetual motion - πάντα ῥεῖ (all
things flow), although it is problematic whether or not he
actually said this.(110) I would follow Guthrie in
thinking that the idea of flux is presupposed by not only
individual fragments but the whole tenor of Herakleitos'
thought.(111) If there is stability other than the
equilibrium of opposite tensions, it is hard to see how it
could be reconciled with the remainder of Herakleitos'
thought.
    At the same time, he asserted that the world was a fire:

κόσμον τόνδε, τὸν αὐτὸν ἀπάντων, οὔτε τις θεῶν οὔτε
ἀνθρώπων ἐποίησεν, ἀλλ' ἦν ἀεὶ καὶ ἔστιν καὶ ἔσται πῦρ
ἀείζωον, ἀπτόμενον μέτρα καὶ ἀποσβεννύμενον μέτρα.

(This world, the same for all, no god or man made, but
it was ever and is and will be an ever-living fire,
kindled in measures and quenched in measures.)(112)

Later commentators tended to suppose that Herakleitos'
fire was the basic element from which the world was made,
like Thales' water, Anaximenes' air, etc. However it has
long been accepted that fire is not a substratum or ἀρχή
(first principle) in the Aristotelian sense,(113) since it

seems to possess not only the ability to transform itself,
but also to direct; as Herakleitos himself says:

τὰ δὲ πάντα οἰακίζει κεραυνός

(The thunderbolt steers all things.)(114)

Fire is also ever-living;(115) in a polar expression which
reminds us of Xenophanes B.23 (see above, p.137),
Herakleitos emphasises this in B.30 (above). We learn
elsewhere that there is a cosmological cycle in which fire,
sea and earth undergo mutual transformation. The idea of
exchange (see also B.90, quoted in chapter 5, p.109, in
which fire is compared with gold in its relationship to
other elements) is, at least partly, linked with the
tension of opposites and also with the idea of all things
being one. The link is provided by B.10:

συνάψιες ὅλα καὶ οὐχ ὅλα, συμφερόμενον διαφερόμενον,
συνᾷδον διᾷδον, καὶ ἐκ πάντων ἓν καὶ ἐξ ἑνὸς πάντα.

(Joints whole and not whole, that which is in agreement
differs, and that which is in tune is out of tune and
from all things one and from one all.)

This difficult fragment seems to describe the different
ways in which the elements of the world are related.(116)
One one side, a tendency towards unity is stated, and, on
the other, a tendency away from it. All things are
unified by fire(117) but are at the same time also diverse
and at war with each other. Thus, at the most general
level, Herakleitos maintains the paradox of the coincidence, or identity of opposites.(118)
    One's interpretation of Herakleitos depends to a large
extent on the relative emphasis placed upon the various
disjointed elements in what remains of his thought: it
could be argued that here too little has been made of his
cosmology and the relationship of fire to his meteorological doctrines. One can only argue that attempts to
'relate' these elements necessarily rely upon a great deal
of guesswork which rarely convinces;(119) moreover, we
possess important evidence from antiquity that, for
Herakleitos, descriptions of natural phenomena were
essentially subordinate to a preoccupation with man and
his relationship with the underlying principles which
govern his existence.(120) For example, the Logos is by
no means merely cosmological:

ξύν νόῳ λέγοντας ἰσχυρίζεσθαι χρὴ τῷ ξυνῷ πάντων,

ὅκωσπερ νόμῳ πόλις, καὶ πολὺ ἰσχυροτέρως. τρέφονται γὰρ
πάντες οἱ ἀνθρώπειοι νόμοι ὑπὸ ἑνὸς τοῦ θείου· κρατεῖ
γὰρ τοσοῦτον ὁκόσον ἐθέλει καὶ περιγίνεται.

(Those who speak with intelligence have to rely on that
which is common to all,(121) just as a city on its law,
and much more strongly. For all human laws are
nourished by one, the divine; for it has as much power
as it wishes and suffices for all and is left
over.)(122)

Just as the Logos governs men as external law, so it is
also connected with their internal life:

ψυχῆς πείρατα ἰὼν οὐκ ἂν ἐξεύροιο, πᾶσαν ἐπιπορευόμενος
ὁδόν· οὕτω βαθὺν λόγον ἔχει.

(You could not, in your journey, discover the boundaries of the soul, travelling every road; it has so
deep a Logos.)(123)

We have already seen, from Xenophanes' ironic dismissal
(above pp.133) that there existed in the sixth century BC
a view of the soul different from the Homeric, in which it
is seen in material terms as something which leaves the
body at death and departs to an ineffective and unenviable
life in Hades. The Pythagoreans emphasised the independence of the soul from the body, and Anaximenes, the last
of the Milesians, appears to have connected his basic
substance, air, with soul, which was responsible for
organising the Universe and the individual human body.(124)
Herakleitos appears to be taking the idea a stage further
in suggesting the intellectual and emotional possibilities
of the soul as man's inner self. The enquirer after truth
apprehends it with the soul, explicitly contrasted with
the senses, as Herakleitos seems to imply when he says
that 'eyes and ears are bad witnesses for men if they have
barbarian souls.'(125)
    Yet we must beware of assuming that the 'soul' of
Herakleitos can be opposed to any materialistic conception;
it is also closely connected with the cycle of elements in
his cosmology:

ψυχῆσιν θάνατος ὕδωρ γενέσθαι, ὕδατι δὲ θάνατος γῆν
γενέσθαι, ἐκ γῆς δὲ ὕδωρ γίνεται, ἐξ ὕδατος δὲ ψυχή.

(For souls it is death to become water, for water,
death to become earth; from earth comes water, from
water, soul.)(126)

The unexpected substitution of ψυχή for πῦρ in the cycle
emphasises the closeness of the connection between cosmic
fire and the life of man; soul is best (and wisest) when
dry (and, presumably, nearest to fire).(127)
    We are prevented from taking this theory much further
by the absence of connections in the text itself (the
methodological dangers of trying to invent these were
emphasised earlier) and, more fundamentally, by the
difficulty of putting ourselves into the position of a
thinker for whom the cosmological, physical, epistemological, social and psychological worlds were one.
Herakleitos' thought is like a circle, of which he
himself says 'the beginning and the end are common.'(128)
Fire, the Logos, the identity of opposites, the law are
all manifestations of the basic dynamic flow of the
universe, the continual motion which contradicts the
assumptions of the many, who think in terms of a superficially ordered, static world. Moreover, the immediate
means of initiation is speech - not the subtle dialectic
of a later age, but words which reveal their close
association with reality through their own formal
characteristics and arrangement.
    It is this possibility of immediately apprehending the
world, regarded by later thinkers, quite understandably,
as naïve, which separates the archaic Ionian thinkers from
their successors. Herakleitos' younger contemporary,
Parmenides,(129) represents the beginning of the
separation of αἰσθητά (perceptibles) from νοητά (what can
be known). The Ionians, from Thales to Herakleitos, while
emphasising the reality which lay behind appearances,
clearly regarded the world as it presented itself to the
senses as the starting-point in any investigation.
Indeed, this is the basis of the more practical aspect of
the Ionian achievement, as well as the more 'philosophical'
side.

In this chapter and the previous one, two main aspects of
this outlook have been emphasised; first, the heritage of
myth, which represented less a regressive mode of thought
than a chrysalis from which early philosophy and science
could emerge and from which it partly drew its unique
quality. Second, the medium of expression which, far from
being a question of minor importance, both reflects the
philosophers' debt to the imaginative world of the Ionian
epic poets and early Greek lyric, and reinforces the
direct link between language and reality, in which lies
the key to the immediacy with which the Ionians viewed the
world. It is scarcely coincidence that two of Parmenides'

most acute problems, in severing the link between
perception and reality, were the question of his
relationship to a world of myth(130) and the enormous
difficulty, linguistically, of expressing what he wished
to say. Parmenides' poem represents the beginnings of the
realisation of language as something quite separate from
the world as it immediately presents itself and even, in
his own case, a medium for a logical argument which denies
the validity of this world altogether.

In reviewing the meagre evidence for this vitally
important period in the history of thought, it is
necessary to recall a methodological problem encountered
in chapter 3 (p.37), in which it remained doubtful if
certain Ionian works of art represented examples of a
tradition or unique products of an otherwise fairly
mediocre genre. In the case of the Ionian ἱστορίη
(enquiry) it is much easier to be positive; the remains
are scanty but, as we have seen, highly suggestive; they
represent the visible peaks of an extensive mountain range.
This is clear not only from the vast extent of the later
tradition (where we would expect the survival of original
material to be tenuous(131)) but also from the clear
existence, in the fifth century BC, of an Ionian
'tradition' which traced its origins back to the sixth
century.(132)
    Moreover, it is clear historically that during the
sixth century this activity was almost exclusively Ionian.
C.H. Kahn has demonstrated philosophically what seems
probable on other grounds - that the Italian contribution
to Presocratic philosophy was essentially an offshoot of
Ionian thought rather than a rival. The basic idea of the
universe as an ordered and rational phenomenon was taken
over by the Eleatics from sixth-century Miletos.(133)
Moreover, the detailed cosmologies of Parmenides and
Empedokles, while separated from the Ionians by a definite
conceptual gap, still operate with cosmological opposites
derived from their Ionian predecessors. It is perhaps
significant that when we move from theories of matter to
the more mundane questions of meteorology and astronomy,
the gap between the earlier and later Presocratics seems
much narrower.
    Finally, it has been suggested that Ionia owed this
revolution partly to her unique position between the
worlds of mainland Greece and the older civilisations of
the east, and some of the detailed advantages of this
situation were enumerated in chapter 5. The question
inevitably arises: how far did Ionian philosophy derive

its substance from the east? In a recent book, 'Early
Greek Philosophy and the Orient', M.L. West seeks to
relate the main ideas of early Ionian thought directly to
Babylonian, Hittite and, later, Persian originals. West's
argument involves detailed correspondences between Greek
and Near Eastern ideas, some of which seem convincing,
others less so, and the author is often involved, prior to
his attempts at comparison, in fairly speculative and
controversial reconstructions of Greek thought which have
already been mentioned on several occasions (above, notes
49, 74 and 118). However, even if the most optimistic
view is taken (and it can hardly be denied that eastern
religious and quasi-philosophical ideas would have been
available to the Greeks, especially after the Persian
conquest of Ionia) one is continually conscious, in
reading West, first, of the tenuous evidence for the early
date of some of his eastern evidence (e.g. p.175) and,
second, of the enormous gap, which he seems to minimise,
between the personalised, often semi-mystical expression
of ideas in e.g. Iranian and Indian philosophies
contemporary with Anaximander and Herakleitos and the more
secular, humanistic atmosphere of sixth-century Miletos.
It is significant that the most convincing correspondence
shown by West is between eastern thought and Pherekydes, a
figure who, as we have seen (chapter 5, p.129) represents
a transitional stage between the old and the new. It
seems fair to conclude that, as we discovered in the case
of visual art in chapter 3, the East may have provided the
spice, but not the substance of early Ionian thought.(134)

7 The aftermath: the Ionian legacy to Hellenism

The Persian victory at the battle of Lade in 494 BC marked
the end of the political and cultural independence of the
eastern Greeks. As we have already seen (chapter 2,pp.32-5)
this independence had been gradually diminishing for a
long time as the Persians slowly took a tighter grip on
Ionia's political institutions and the Athenians and
others began to take over traditional Ionian commercial
interests, notably in Egypt and the Black Sea.

Ionian solidarity did not even outlast the battle. Of
those cities which furnished contingents (and, as we have
seen, a number were conspicuous by their absence) the
Chians, forewarned of disaster, according to Herodotos, by
a number of unpleasant incidents in their island,(1)
fought bravely, losing most of their ships, only to be
massacred in their retreat by the Ephesians who mistook
them for robbers.(2) Dionysios of Phokaia, the much
resented commander of the battle fleet, seeing all was
lost, made good his escape and took up piracy in the
western Mediterranean.(3) The Samians, whose case
Herodotos pleads with great plausibility, accepted, before
the battle began, a proposal put to them by the pro-Persian
Aiakes (who had been expelled as tyrant from Samos by
Aristagoras at the beginning of the revolt in the general
deposition of tyrants (chapter 2, p.33)) that they
should withdraw from the league. The historian gives as
their motives the idleness and discontent of the Ionian
force and the size of the Persian fleet - thereby
demonstrating that, for Herodotos, two excuses might be
thought better than one.(4) Eleven ships remained,
manned, doubtless, by aristocratic anti-Persian forces.
Herodotos leaves us in no doubt, however, that the
defection of the Samians caused a general disintegration
of the Ionian fleet. After the battle Samos alone escaped
sack and burning by the conquerors.(5) The city was

164

depleted by the migration of a detachment of their
citizens, joined by Milesian stragglers, to Sicily, in
order to escape from the pro-Persian elements in their own
island.(6)   The ringleaders, Aristagoras (ψυχὴν οὐκ ἄκρος -
poor spirited(7)) and Histiaios, when things did not work
out satisfactorily, looked around for means of escape and
were killed, the former by the Thracians after he had fled
to Thrace, the latter while still trying to reingratiate
himself with the Persians.(8)   Thus, the end of the
authors of the revolt, whom Herodotos never sees as more
than unprincipled agitators.

Once they had reduced Ionia to submission, the Persians
acted with surprising leniency; Herodotos tells us that
the Persian general, Mardonios, ejected despots from all
the Ionian cities and set up democratic institutions.(9)
It may be wondered if this is precisely what happened.(10)
At all events, Ionia clearly needed much more than a
change of government.   The material poverty of the Ionian
cities throughout the fifth century BC is attested from
the almost total lack of evidence for extensive rebuilding
after the collapse or for architectural undertakings
remotely resembling the achievements of the later sixth
century.(11)   Sculpture virtually disappeared and vase
painting tailed off (in common with other non-Athenian
styles) with the late Ionian Black-Figure style associated
with the series of sarcophagi from Klazomenai (see chapter
3, p.59 and n.108).

The most cogent evidence for decline comes from the
tribute assessment made by the Athenians when they
incorporated the Ionians, along with others, into the
Delian League, and later the Athenian Empire; for Ionia
this is remarkably low, Miletos never paying more than ten
talents, and no other Ionian city paying as much.(12)   The
Ionian mainland and islands were among the least prosperous districts of the Athenian Empire, as inscriptional
evidence from Miletos shows.(13)

The precise reasons for the severity of this decline
are hard to determine.   Gradual and long-term depopulation,
the burden of tribute to the Persians and failure in
economic competition have already been mentioned (chapter
2, pp.32-3).   Herodotos (for whom the suddenness of the
Ionian fall is an essential element in his dramatic
structure and, as such, historically suspect)(14) tells us
that after the Ionian Revolt Artaphernes, the Persian
governor of Sardis, fixed the tribute payable to the
Persians at a figure which remained unaltered up to his
(Herodotos') own time, and the amount was much the same
as it had previously been.(15)   The implications of this
statement have caused controversy; it has been suggested

that the Ionians may have been forced to pay both the
Persians and the Athenians during the period of Athenian
supremacy or that there may have been a fluid situation in
which certain powerful individuals paid either or both
sides to protect their position. The view has also been
put forward that the Athenians took over Artaphernes'
method of taxation when they incorporated the Ionians into
the league or, alternatively, that the Persian king may
have ignored the reality of the situation and still (in
Herodotos' day) laid claim to tribute he was no longer
receiving. There has been no definitive solution to this
difficult historical problem, nor can we proceed any
further in attributing Ionian poverty to exactions of
tribute.(16)

The permanence of the Ionian collapse undoubtedly owes
most to the emergence of Athens as the dominating power
and the subsequent decline of Ionia into provincial status.
The relationship between Athens and her Ionian 'allies' is
revealed in a limited but unusually detailed manner in a
series of inscriptions recording political interventions
and settlements made by the Athenians in various cities
during the mid-century; these show that the Ionians were
in a peculiarly sensitive position and suffered considerable internal disruption from the conflicting pressures of
the Persian and Athenian empires. From at least the
middle of the century the Athenians intervened frequently
and often permanently in the internal government of the
cities and forcibly suppressed revolts. For example, an
inscription from Erythrai (c. 453-452 BC) tells us in
detail how, in the wake of Athenian intervention to expel
a small faction supporting the Persians, the Athenians
supervised the setting up of a democratic council on the
Athenian model whose ultimate stability depended on the
φρούραρχος (garrison commander); it is clear that, from
this point on, the city, which may previously have
revolted, enjoyed little political freedom.(17) A series
of political expulsions from Miletos (the exact chronology
of which is difficult to disentangle),(18) probably the
result of temporary withdrawal of the city from the league
under the guidance of a medising faction, left the city
economically weakened and politically impotent. Intervening shortly afterwards in a dispute between Samos and
Miletos over Priene, the Athenians under Perikles forcibly
installed a democratic government in Samos; further revolt
resulted in a full-scale attack followed by a blockade;
the Samians surrendered after eight months and were
required to demolish their walls, surrender their fleet
and repay the cost of the war.(19) Amid the detail it is
possible to detect a gradually hardening attitude on the

part of the Athenians towards their fellow Ionians
illustrated by the earlier references to an 'alliance'
(χσυνμαχία (Regulations for Erythrai, ℓ.31, Meiggs and
Lewis, 90)) which later changes to references to 'cities
ruled by the Athenians'. While arguments tracing the
exact course of this domination tend either to be circular
(i.e. the inscriptions are dated from a presumed situation
which itself rests on very little other evidence) or
weakened by the difficulties of dating various ortho-
graphic developments,(20) the general picture clearly
shows the progressive domination and increasing economic
demands of Athens.(21)

The ostensible basis of this oppressive patronage lay
in Athens' presumed role as founding city of its 'colony'
Ionia, during the Dark Ages, which served as a suitable
pretext for protection after the Persian Wars. To some
extent the Ionians were hoisted with their own petard.
Aristagoras, attempting to persuade the Athenians to send
help at the beginning of the Ionian Revolt, used, among
other arguments, the point that the Milesians were
colonists (ἄποικοι) of the Athenians, making it only
natural that the latter should use their great power to
help the Ionians in a time of trouble.(22) It is possible
that Herodotos, composing his history in the second half
of the fifth century, was anachronistically putting words
into Aristagoras' mouth; yet the appeal is a plausible one
and we have already seen that the special position of
Athens, if not as clear-cut as Aristagoras made it, was
nevertheless not a fifth-century invention, but extended
back to the migrations (see chapter 2, pp.13ff).(23)
After the Persian Wars, the close ties in religion and
sentiment which traditionally existed in ancient Greece
between a colony and its mother city provided a convenient
weapon for Athens in her role as champion of the Ionians.
In the council on Samos after the battle of Mykale in
which the Greeks freed Ionia from the Persians, helped by
the Ionians, the Peloponnesians advocated resettling the
Ionians in the territory of the mainland Greeks who had
supported the Persians during the wars. The Athenians
disagreed, and felt that the Peloponnesians had no right
to deliberate about their colonists (περὶ τῶν σφετέρων
ἀποικιέων).(24) Shortly afterwards, Thukydides tells us,
the Ionians, resenting the arrogance of the Spartan
admiral, Pausanias, begged the Athenians, as their own
kinsmen, to protect them, which the Athenians gladly
did.(25)

Thus, right from the beginning, Athenian protection of
Ionia was based upon their presumed historical relationship. Moreover, the choice of the island of Delos, the

ancient religious centre of the Ionian Greeks, as the
treasury of the league against Persia, showed how far the
Athenian alliance was based upon her traditional role.
Later in the century when the league had turned into an
empire, this role became a powerful weapon of propaganda
which the Athenians fully appreciated; for example it may
have been on these grounds that the Athenians were
prepared to tolerate briefly, in the late 450s BC, an
oligarchy in Miletos in which the Neleids, descendants of
the Milesian founders, had some share.(26)

The general status of Ionia in fifth-century Greek
estimation is not just a matter of historical interest; it
affects the perspective through which the Athenians, and
hence later ages, viewed the Ionians in their heyday and,
as such, is of vital importance in the present context.
The change in Athenian attitudes may be reflected in an
interesting way in contemporary sources. Sympathy for the
Ionians in the immediate aftermath of the fall of Miletos
is clearly indicated by the famous incidents surrounding
the staging of Phrynichos' play the 'Capture of Miletos';
the audience burst into tears and the author was fined
1,000 drachmas for reminding them of their 'domestic ills'
(οἰκήϊα κάκα).(27) Later, in the period after the Persian
Wars, the ignominy suffered by the Ionians under the
Persians and especially their shame at being forced to
fight against their own race at the sea battle of Salamis
as part of the Persian fleet, are delicately and subtly
conveyed by the Athenian playwright Aeschylus in his play
'The Persians' (472 BC). The name 'Ionian' which,
according to Herodotos, was disliked by all Ionians
outside the twelve cities of the league,(28) is used
ambiguously to associate the Ionians with the heroic Greek
victory of Salamis, where they had in fact fought on the
other side: for example ℓ.1025 where the Chorus says:

'Ιάνων λαὸς οὐ φυγαίχμας

(the Ionian people do not desert)

the Greeks in general are denoted,(29) but this way of
naming them, unique to 'The Persians' and emphasised
several times,(30) is clearly a way of expressing sympathy
and solidarity with the Ionians in the aftermath of their
liberation from the Persian yoke. Elsewhere in the play
Aeschylus' references to the Ionians are tactful and
indirect: for example ℓℓ.770f., where a nice distinction
is made between the Lydians and Phrygians whom Cyrus
'acquired' (ἐκτήσατο - hardly a fair summary of the
subjugation of the Lydians, at least according to

Herodotos I, 79ff.!) and the Ionians whom 'he subdued by
force' (ἤλασεν βίᾳ), thereby emphasising a distinction
between the Asia Minor Greeks and her neighbours to the
east which became increasingly blurred as time went on.
Thirty or so years later, Herodotos' account of the Ionians
At Artemision reveals less delicacy; while some Ionians
were distressed at the Athenians' plight, others, he says,
welcomed the opportunity to fight as well as possible for
the Great King.(31) Later, despite a message from
Themistokles, cut on the rocks where the Ionians would
collect drinking-water, urging them either to remain
neutral or defect since they were of the same blood and
the original cause of the Greek quarrel with Persia, the
majority fought hard at Salamis and earned commendation
from Xerxes.(32)

By the time of Herodotos, tact was no longer necessary,
since Greek solidarity in a prospective war of revenge
against the Persian Empire had turned into an Athenian
empire kept together by force. It is arguable that it was
Herodotos who, in his history, set the seal upon the
traditional picture of the Ionian archaic age in terms of
weakness, irresolution and inferiority. Herodotos
disliked and despised the Ionians (although, individually,
he discriminated, showing a notable bias towards the
Samians, from whom he may have obtained much of his
information). This was possibly from racial antipathy,
although Halikarnassos, a Dorian foundation and Herodotos'
birthplace, enjoyed a predominantly Ionian culture; it had
been expelled early from the Dorian hexapolis of South
Asia Minor and the earliest known inscriptions are already
in Ionic. It is highly ironic that not only did Herodotos
write his history in Ionic but also owed a great deal in
style and outlook to his much-despised Ionian forebears
(chapter 5, p.111).

The destruction of Ionian civilisation, Herodotos felt,
was an inevitable result of its failure to achieve
freedom.(33) Weakness was demonstrated by the Ionians'
inability to combine in the face of common danger; whether
the Greek mainland had a creditable record in this respect
he does not say. The Ionian Revolt is for Herodotos, as
we have seen, a personal piece of mischief which brought
great general suffering. After his account of the capture
of Miletos, Herodotos reinforces his conviction that
Miletos' destruction was retributive justice by quoting a
Delphic Oracle to the Argives which contained an additional
passage recounting the fate of Miletos 'κακῶν ἐπιμήχανε
ἔργων' (contriver of evil deeds).(34) The offence may
have been an earlier proposed confiscation of the
treasures at the Milesian oracular shrine at Didyma to pay

for the war.(35)   If so, then the punishment, as so often
in the drama of Greek history, far outweighed the crime.
Herodotos also emphasises the Ionians' untrustworthiness
and 'slave mentality'.   In an episode during Dareios'
Skythian expedition, the Skythians, tricked by the Ionians
left by the king to guard the bridge over the Hellespont,
deliver their verdict that 'the Ionians, considered as
free men, are the basest and most cowardly of all men; but
reckoning them as slaves, none would be more loving to
their captors or have less desire to escape.'(36)

   Ionia's almost universal association with effeminacy
and lewdness had, as we have seen, some support in the
archaic period in such sources as Xenophanes and Anakreon.
In the late fifth century, Aristophanes, in his
'Ecclesiazusae' refers to μελύδριον ... τι τῶν 'Ιωνικῶν
(some Ionian ditty)(37) where something lewd is obviously
intended; then and later, lewd verses were universally
known as 'Ιωνικά.(38)   Ionia's dedication to luxury,
inebriation, voluptuousness, effeminacy and addiction to
flamboyant clothing is catalogued conveniently by
Athenaios.(39)   By this stage the image is quite clearly a
stereotype, no doubt at times well-earned.   There is
little doubt that this, combined with the pseudo-scientific
theory of the Hippocratic author of 'Airs, Waters, Places'
(see chapter 1, pp.1f.) which implied that the Ionian lack
of distinction could be attributed to the climate, sealed
her fate.   The last word is given by Herodotos to Cyrus
the Great; in reply to a suggestion that the Persians
should migrate to a less barren land, he is said to have
replied: 'from soft countries come soft men; it is not the
way of any one land to produce fine crops and good
fighters too.'(40)

   A reason for the lack of distinction in the cultural
life of fifth-century Ionia may have been the migration of
the majority of her more remarkable citizens to Athens.
One of the most remarkable was Aspasia, a courtesan from
Miletos who became the second wife of the Athenian leader
Perikles, and bore him a son.   Aspasia combined beauty
with intellect and, quite exceptionally for a woman in
classical Greece, associated with the philosophical and
literary circle which grew up around Perikles.   Her
influence upon political developments was considerable
(even if we discount Plutarch's suggestion that Perikles
proceeded against the Samians in 440 BC (see above, p.166)
to gratify his Milesian wife)(41) and contemporary comedy,
slandering her profession, saw her as Hera to Perikles'
Olympian Zeus; and Aristophanes himself suggests, in
parody, that the Megarian decrees which led up to the
Peloponnesian War were caused by Perikles' anger at the

theft of two of Aspasia's prostitutes.(42)

An immigrant of a different kind was Ion of Chios, a
poet and philosopher of whose works very little survives.
Sent by his father to Athens as a youth, he completed his
education in the household of the moderate Athenian
statesman, Kimon. His admiration for Kimon and his
policies probably explains his dislike of later Athenian
imperialism associated with Perikles. He wrote a number
of plays and appears to have studied philosophy,
especially under the influence of Pythagorean ideas. He
also wrote a work, probably in prose, on the founding of
Chios. While it is probably premature to base Ionian
intellect on what we know of Ion, his position as an
admirer and supporter of Athenian patronage, at least in
its early stage, may have been typical of a number of his
fellow citizens. Ion died c. 421 BC, and was thus spared
the desperate struggle which marked Ionia's late fifth-
century BC history.(43)

More significant than all the philosophers and poets,
at least for the later history of the ancient 'polis', was
the Milesian Hippodamos, who gained great fame as the
presumed inventor of a new method of regular city planning
known as the 'gridiron' - the arrangement of all buildings,
public and private, into regular, aligned blocks. That
Hippodamos was not the inventor of this method is clear
from the anticipations of 'gridiron' in seventh-century BC
Smyrna (chapter 3, p.53) and the sixth-century BC layout
of the Black Sea Milesian colony of Olbia.(44) Yet, the
Ionians may well have pioneered this design, so well
demonstrated in Hellenistic Priene, Pergamon and Miletos
itself. Hippodamos is credited, impossibly, with the
rebuilding of Miletos before his emigration to Athens, the
designing of the Piraeus, the harbour of Athens, and the
planning, in 408 BC, of the new city of Rhodes.(45)
Hippodamos, in best Ionian tradition, was not merely a
town-planner but developed theories concerning the ideal
size, social organisation and legal procedure of the
city.(46) Aristotle's personal remarks are revealing: 'In
his general life too, he was led into eccentricity by a
desire to attract attention; and this made a number of
people feel that he lived in too studied and artificial a
manner. He wore his hair long and expensively adorned; he
had flowing robes, richly decorated, made from a cheap but
warm material, which he wore in summer-time as well as in
winter; and he aspired to be learned about nature
generally.'(47)

The existence of a number of figures who are little
more than names, Oinipodes of Chios, an astronomer and
mathematician who estimated the length of the solar year,

Hippokrates of Samos, a mathematician, and Hippon, also of
Samos, a philosopher, shows the debt Athens owed to the
scientists of Ionia. Of other Ionian philosophers, much
more is known; Anaxagoras, from Klazomenai, came to Athens
and enjoyed the friendship of Perikles; Melissos of Samos,
an Eleatic follower of Parmenides, commanded the fleet
which defeated the Athenians in 441 BC and relieved the
blockade on the island, a philosophical occupation firmly
in the tradition of Thales and Hekataios! Archelaos of
Miletos was an early teacher of Sokrates; Protagoras, the
famous and important early Sophist, and Demokritos, the
creator of ancient atomic theory, both came to Athens from
Abdera, descendants of sixth-century Ionic immigrants from
Teos (see chapter 2, p.24).

It is significant that, with the single exception of
Melissos (about whose life little is known), all the
distinguished Ionians about whom we have any information,
migrated to Athens. In this they are distinct from their
western counterparts; Sicily and Magna Graecia enjoyed
much greater political independence; while welcomed as a
visitor, Zeno of Elea, a distinguished philosopher and
author of the famous paradoxes, stayed loyal to his home
town 'preferring it to the arrogance of Athens whither he
refused to emigrate'.(48)

The idea that Ionian cosmology was generally seen in
Athens as subversive and atheistic is given some weight
from the prosecution of Anaxagoras for impiety, in
particular for teaching about meteorological phenomena.
However, as in the more celebrated prosecution of Sokrates
in 399 BC, the actual charge had little to do with the
real motives behind the prosecution, which was probably an
oblique attack on Perikles through his association with
the philosophers (Aspasia also suffered prosecution for
impiety, doubtless because of her association with
Perikles.(49)) The satirical picture of Sokrates in
Aristophanes' 'Clouds' (423 BC) in which certain physical
and meteorological doctrines are parodied, does not
confine itself to cosmology; it is more likely that
Aristophanes wished to expose intellectualism generally,
but it does not therefore follow even from this that his
audience seriously agreed with him.(50)

The traditional view of Athenian humanism taking the
place of Ionian science is, as W.K.C. Guthrie has clearly
demonstrated, a false historical picture.(51) In fact,
the speculations of the last great Ionian thinkers, such
as Anaxagoras and the Atomists, were either contemporary
with, or even post-dated the Sophists. Moreover the
parody of Ionian thought as concerned merely with τὰ
μετέωρα (things in the heaven above) is borne out by our

knowledge of the achievements of neither the Milesians nor their fifth-century successors. Theories which embraced the origins of man and life, the idea of 'nature' and the tradition of rational enquiry all had their origins in sixth-century Ionia. It is here that humanism, strictly speaking, began. But, in the fifth century, we do see the beginnings of the integration of different elements of the somewhat disjointed Ionian world picture into a whole which links nature and society. Hence the wide-ranging antithesis of 'nature' and 'convention' to include not only theories of social and political behaviour but also distinctions between 'conventional' qualities and 'real' atoms and void in Demokritos' atomic theory. It is this application of philosophical ideas to the whole range of human activity and the urgent relevance of these ideas to everyday conduct that distinguishes the later from the earlier modes of thought. Ionian speculation had been modified not only by the enormous intellectual advances of the Eleatic school in the west, which changed completely the nature of the perception of reality, but also by the needs and pressures of a thriving democracy. Hence, the ideas were no longer 'Ionian', in the sense that we have hitherto understood the term.

A good example of this is the most distinguished of the later Ionian philosophers, and the man possibly respons- ible for bringing Ionian cosmology to Athens, Anaxagoras. Underlying an apparently traditional cosmology, involving the separation of opposites from an initially undifferentiated state, was a much more sophisticated attitude towards the nature of matter, involving ideas of its infinite divisibility which owed a great deal to the doctrines of the Eleatics, Zeno and Melissos, to whom the Parmenidean denial of motion and change bequeathed a number of problems. Anaxagoras' restoration of cosmology in the face of the categorical Eleatic denial of the reality of the world of the senses was only achieved by the assertion that every portion of matter, however small, contains everything; as he says: ἐν παντὶ παντὸς μοῖρα ἔνεστι... (in everything there is a portion of every- thing).(52) This had the general effect of removing the emphasis of cosmology away from large-scale organisation and towards a theory of the constitution of matter. Anaxagoras' other innovation was the creation of a force apart from matter, Mind (νοῦς). The fact that, as Aristotle complains, having created Mind, Anaxagoras made it responsible only for the initial movement of the universe,(53) is less important than the confirmation that, in the creation of a moving cause apart from matter, the old Ionian world, in which matter had automatically

possessed life and the power of self-movement, had passed
away.

Other philosophers turned for inspiration to the
theories of the sixth-century Ionians, but revealed at the
same time the vital difference between this world and the
earlier one. Diogenes of Apollonia harked back to the
Milesian Anaximenes in making air the basis of his
physical theory. For Anaximenes, air had been the basic
substance from which, by rarefaction and condensation, the
world was made. It also probably(54) contained the power
to direct and organise both the human body and the world.
For Diogenes, the choice of an underlying substance
constituted an answer to Eleatic problems of change and
the directive quality of Anaximenes' air enabled him to
explain the origin of motion and intelligence. His
detailed physical doctrines, fully in the Ionian tradition,
are extremely important; his cosmology is an eclectic
combination of the Milesians and Anaxagoras.(55) The
little we know of Archelaos of Miletos (or Athens)(56)
suggests that he instructed his pupil Sokrates in
doctrines very similar to those of Anaxagoras and
Diogenes.

In the face of this situation the simple and 'naive'
world of the early cosmologists was transformed; opposites
were reduced from dynamic elemental forces into subsidiary
features of other, more analytic theories of cosmology,
epistemology and ethics, not to mention anthropology and
medicine. The medium of expression changed also; the
direct, poetically inspired prose of Anaximander and the
oracular utterance of Herakleitos was replaced, on the one
hand by a less emotive prose style in which the emphasis
lay on clarity of expression and coherence of argument,
and on the other by the highly wrought rhetorical
'Kunstprosa' of Gorgias of Leontini. The change was not
abrupt; Herakleitos in his opening fragment (see above,
chapter 6, pp.145-6) foreshadows the simple and paratactic,
yet coherent argumentative style of Anaxagoras and, at the
same time, the antithetical prose of Gorgias. The transformation of the medium of expression is of fundamental
significance in reflecting a radical change of attitude in
Greek thinkers - a process of further secularisation which
placed the emphasis even more strongly upon man and away
from the gods. The famous dictum of Protagoras may be
taken as typical of the later fifth century:

πάντων χρημάτων μέτρον ἔστιν ἄνθρωπος, τῶν μὲν ὄντων ὡς
ἔστιν, τῶν δὲ οὐκ ὄντων ὡς οὐκ ἔστιν.

(Of all things the measure is man, of things that are,
that they are, and of things that are not, that they

are not.)(57)

Man replaced the gods as the centre of attention and
argument replaced insight and revelation as the method of
communication.

It seems to follow that the early Ionians *per se* would
have had little relevance for Athens, since, strictly
speaking, their world was out of date. As models for
later theories they had, as we have seen, some currency.
Yet it would be rash to suppose that the words of
Anaximander or his fellow Milesians were actually available in writing during this period. As we know to our
cost, the life of words committed to papyrus was short;
recopying was continually necessary, but would only have
been performed in the case of works of current interest.
Herakleitos may have been preserved by his followers, the
Herakleiteans, whom Plato refers to as existing in his
day;(58) yet the conclusion is inescapable, and is borne
out by the absence of personal citation, that the scanty
nature of original evidence for the early Ionians owed a
great deal to this early neglect and that the Peripatetic
School may, in this respect, have been in a position
little better than our own.

The various cities of Ionia come into prominence in the
last pages of Thukydides as the centre of conflict in the
closing stages of the Peloponnesian War. The general
revolt of Ionian cities from the Athenian Empire at the
instigation of Sparta and the Persian satrap Tissaphernes
heralded the final downfall of Athens. Once more the
inherent instability of Ionia's position was revealed, as
warring factions within the cities struggled to gain power
through the support of either side. The struggle was a
three-cornered one, with the Persians supporting the
Peloponnesians in the hope of eventually receiving the
tribute denied them by the Athenian exactions.(59) At the
end of the war Samos was the only ally remaining faithful
to Athens; this trust was rewarded by formal acknowledg-
ments at Athens both in 405 BC and in 403, after the
restoration of Athenian democracy (although by this stage
the Samian democrats were in exile).(60)

During the early fourth century the Ionian cities
existed in a state of transition. Ceded to Persian rule
by the King's Peace of 386 BC, they came increasingly
under the influence of Karia, where a dynasty of despots
gradually brought the Greek towns of the coast, and
perhaps Miletos itself, under their power. The Ionian
cities returned decisively again to the Greeks when

captured by Alexander the Great as a prelude to his
invasion of Asia which destroyed the already tottering
Persian Empire. Thereafter they shared in the
vicissitudes of Alexander's successors, an account of
which is well beyond the scope of this book.

There is evidence that during the fourth century BC,
the Ionian cities increased in wealth and began to assume
the appearance which the present-day archaeological
remains suggest. The new city of Priene was laid out on
the slope of a hill in neat Hippodameian plan and new city
building was undertaken at Erythrai, Smyrna and Kolophon.
Ionia was probably the Greek pioneer in the new Hellenistic urbanisation of Greek cities, resembling the
'teeming cities with beautiful towers by the salt sea'
anachronistically introduced by Euripides in the
'Bacchae'.(61) Newer cities, such as Pergamon, lying back
from the sea, and hardly heard of in the fifth century,
became the lavishly appointed capitals of extensive
kingdoms in the period of Alexander's successors. The
older cities of the Asia Minor coast, although subject to
the arbitrary overlordship of Hellenistic kings, retained
a great deal of personal and political freedom in external
affairs, while the moving of the economic focus of the
Greek world eastwards undoubtedly helped their commercial
prospects.

Yet political power, like cultural identity, can be
subjective; for the Ionian cities, as for the Greek world
in general, what autonomy they had was exercised in a
world whose frontiers were far wider and whose culture was
much more homogeneous than that of earlier times. Corresponding to this, we see during this period the development
of a common language, the 'koine', based upon fourth-
century Attic, modified by occasional Ionic forms, which
formed the basis of the Greek of the Scriptures and
medieval and modern Greek.(62) The Greek dialects swiftly
disappeared in all but limited local affairs, and as an
artificial medium sanctified by tradition for certain
literary genres. In the same way, culture became
increasingly homogeneous, showing a common heritage based
upon Attic models and leavened by assimilation to non-
Greek peoples, to whom Greek culture became increasingly
the path of civilisation, and, indeed, remained so for
more than a millennium. In this amalgam whatever was
Ionian was not really distinct enough to merit the name.
The philhellenism of the Karians and their powerful rulers
was, in the mid-fourth century, directed towards the long-
Hellenised Ionian cities to the north; but what Mausolos
was imbibing was not Ionian culture but Greek. It is in
this sense that we may refer to the end of Ionia as a

distinct influence upon Hellenism and the beginning of her
new historical role in the wider and culturally homogeneous world of later antiquity.

For G.L. Huxley, the early failure of the Ionians is
associated with the inability 'in their own cities to join
thought with action, philosophy with politics'.(63) That
this was not a moral failure, as the ancients tended to
suppose, has, I trust, been sufficiently shown in the
foregoing pages. Nor, in one sense, was the decline
permanent. In the broadest perspective of the history of
western Asia Minor, the period here discussed represents
merely the first phase of a long and fruitful development
which, in the case of some cities, extends right up to the
present day (see chapter 1, p. 3).
    Yet, culturally, the Ionian contribution to Hellenism
belongs essentially to the archaic period, and, like much
of archaic Greek culture, suffered the fate of assimilation or destruction. For the fifth and later centuries,
the Ionians are seen through a perspective which we
ourselves have inherited - the art and literature largely
assimilated and the early Ionian thinkers individuals
whose isolated, brilliant and often bizarre utterances
provoked amused respect but rarely understanding. The
reasons for this are, as we have seen, numerous. In the
case of the philosophers, Ionia's greatest product,
perhaps the fundamental reason was their apparent
inability to start humbly and systematically at the
beginning, as later ages felt they ought to have done.
Instead, they surveyed with great brilliance and arresting
simplicity the territory which their successors were
content to cultivate with greater caution but without that
indefinable sense of heroic adventure which we associate
with the fellow citizens of Homer.

Abbreviations

ABSA	Annual of the British School at Athens
AJA	American Journal of Archaeology
AJP	American Journal of Philology
Ath.Mitt.	Mitteilungen des deutschen archäologischen Instituts in Athen
BICS	Bulletin of the Institute of Classical Studies
BM	British Museum
CAH	Cambridge Ancient History
CP	Classical Philology
CQ	Classical Quarterly
DK	Diels-Kranz Fragmente der Vorsokratiker
FGH	Fragmente der griechischen Historiker ed. F. Jacoby
GRBS	Greek, Roman and Byzantine Studies
HSCP	Harvard Studies in Classical Philology
JHS	Journal of Hellenic Studies
KR	G.S. Kirk and J.E. Raven, The Presocratic Philosophers
LSJ	Liddell-Scott-Jones, A Greek-English Lexicon 9th edn.
Mus.Helv.	Museum Helveticum
PCPS	Proceedings of the Cambridge Philological Society
Proc.Am.Phil.Soc.	Proceedings of the American Philological Society
RE	Realencyclopädie des Klassischen Altertums, ed. Wissowa, Kroll et al.
TAPA	Transactions of the American Philological Association
YCS	Yale Classical Studies

Notes

CHAPTER 1 INTRODUCTION

1 Hippokrates, 'Airs, Waters, Places', XII.
2 Herodotos I,142; Pausanias VII,5,4.
3 Hipp., op.cit., XVI.
4 Ibid., XIV.
5 The name is also used (and was used in antiquity) to
   indicate a dialect-group of the Greek language and a
   racial subdivision of the Greeks which embraced many
   peoples living in the Aegean islands and on the Greek
   mainland, including the Athenians. Cf. Hdt. I,142-7.
6 Strabo XIV,1,2.
7 Catullus XLVI,6. Cf. also Horace, 'Epistles',I,11.
8 Acts of the Apostles esp. chapter XIX.
9 Hdt. I,5,4.
10 Strab. XII,8,19.
11 Almost certainly a false attribution (see below,
   chapter 7, p.171).
12 G.M.A. Hanfmann, 'Ionia: Leader or Follower?', HSCP 61
   (1953), 2.
13 E. Akurgal, Die Kunst Anatoliens, ix. See further,
   chapter 3.
14 U. von Wilamowitz, Nordionische Steine, 64ff.(1909)
   quoted, with approval, by M.N. Tod in 1933 (Greek
   Historical Inscriptions, 2nd edn, 1946, 2-3.) The
   Chios inscription has since been down-dated to c.550
   BC in e.g. R. Meiggs and D.M. Lewis, A Selection of
   Greek Historical Inscriptions to the End of the Fifth
   Century BC., 14-17 (see further, chapter 2, p.20).
15 Prominent in early modern scholarship on the Pre-
   socratics were F.E.D. Schleiermacher, J. Bernays and,
   of course, Hermann Diels. On Ephesos cf. J.T. Wood,
   Discoveries at Ephesus (1877) and D.G. Hogarth,
   Excavations at Ephesus: the Archaic Artemisia (2 vols,

179

1908). On Miletos cf. T. Wiegand, Milet: Ergebnisse
der Ausgraben und Untersuchungen seit dem Jahre 1899
(1906-29).

16 R.M. Cook, 'Ionia and Greece in the Eighth and Seventh
Centuries B.C.', JHS 66 (1946), 67-98. Cf. also
Hanfmann op.cit., on Ionian art.

17 See below, chapter 2, p. 25.

18 See below, chapter 2, p. 14.

19 Progress reports for the whole of Asia Minor appear
every year in AJA (M. Mellink) and, for a more limited
geographical area, every few years in JHS Archaeological Reports (J.M. Cook and D.J. Blackman) and there
are detailed discussions in Istanbuler Mitteilungen
and Anatolia.

20 Notably by G.L. Huxley, The Early Ionians.

21 See Akurgal, op.cit. and, e.g., R.D. Barnett,
'Early Greek and Oriental Ivories', JHS 68 (1948),
1-25.

22 For detailed discussion and bibliography, see G.S.
Kirk and J.E. Raven, The Presocratic Philosophers: A
Critical History with a Selection of texts; Cambridge,
1957. For a most original and interesting discussion
of the origins of philosophy, including criticism of
earlier work, see Kirk's recent study, The Nature of
Greek Myths, esp. chapter 12.

23 For discussion and some account of the vast biblio-
graphy, see J.B. Hainsworth, Homer (Greece and Rome
Surveys in the Classics no.3, 1969) and F.M.
Combellack, 'Contemporary Homeric Scholarship',
Classical Weekly 49 (1955), 17ff.

CHAPTER 2 THE IONIAN CITIES

1 Strabo XIV,1,3.

2 Pausanias VII,4,8ff.

3 Herodotos I,141-70.

4 Ibid., V,28 -VI,43.

5 See A.R. Burn, Persia and the Greeks, 5-13.

6 The Suda, s.v. Κάδμος Πανδίονος. But its authenticity
is suspected by F. Jacoby, Kadmos(6), RE cols 1474-5.

7 Athenaios XII,525 e-f. See below, p. 20.

8 Paus. VII,4,1.

9 F. Jacoby, Atthis, 363-4,n.62. This is not to deny
Jacoby's basic thesis, i.e. the absence of a 'pre-
literary chronicle' in archaic Ionia (178-85).

10 See F. Jacoby, FGH IA.1(Hekataios von Milet), fr.228-
54. (For a detailed discussion of Hekataios see
chapter 5 below.)

11   Thukydides VIII,5ff.
12   See J.M. Cook, 'Greek Settlement in the Eastern Aegean
     and Asia Minor', CAH 3, II(2), 773-96.
13   Hdt. I,146; Strab. XIV,1,1-3; Paus. VII,2-4.
14   Hdt. I,147.2.
15   On this question see further chapter 7, below.
16   For a recent and detailed sceptical examination, see
     M.B. Sakellariou, La Migration grecque en Ionie.
17   Cf. Huxley, The Early Ionians, 30-2.
18   See V.R.d'A. Desborough, The Greek Dark Ages, 179-80
     and J.N. Coldstream, Geometric Pottery, 264.
19   See J.M. Cook, JHS Arch. Rep. 1959/60, 40 for Proto-
     geometric pottery at Pygela and modern Mordoğan. Cf.
     also Strab. XIV,1,20.
20   So J.M. Cook, CAH 3, II(2), 786. But see the case of
     e.g. Myous and Lebedos (below, p.24).
21   See J.T. Hooker, 'The Coming of the Greeks', Historia,
     25 (1976), 136.
22   I,146,1. Cf. Cook, 'Greek Settlement...', 784.
23   Desborough, loc.cit.
24   Cf. F. Cassola, La Ionia nel mondo miceneo. See also
     the critical review of A.B. Graham in JHS 81 (1961),
     196-7.
25   See J.T. Hooker, Mycenaean Greece, 115.
26   See D.L. Page, History and the Homeric Iliad, 1-40 for
     a full discussion. In the thirteenth century BC
     Miletos may have become a Hittite dependency after
     destruction, cf. JHS Arch. Rep. 1970/1, 44 (J.M. Cook
     and D.J. Blackman).
27   See further, chapter 4 below.
28   Thuk. I,2,8. Desborough, op.cit., 354-5.
29   Conon, FGH 26fr.1; Nicholas of Damascus, FGH 90fr.52-3.
30   Strab. XIV,I,3.
31   Paus. VII,2,8.
32   Ibid., VII,4,2-3.
33   Ibid., VII,4,9-10.
34   Polyainos, VIII,66.
35   Strab. XIV,1,6; Paus. VII,2,5. Cf. J.M. Cook, JHS
     Arch. Rep. 1959/60, 48ff.
36   Hdt. I,146,2-3.
37   Huxley, loc.cit.
38   See C. Roebuck, 'Tribal Organisation in Ionia', TAPA
     92 (1961), 495-507.
39   A standard accusation; see e.g. Ath. XII,524ff. and
     further, chapter 7.
40   See above, n.29.
41   For the question of Ionian pottery styles in the
     Protogeometric period, see below, chapter 3, pp. 40-2.
42   Vitruvius, 'De Architectura', IV,1,3-5. 'Inschriften

von Priene', 37.

43   C. Roebuck ('The Early Ionian League', CP 50 (1955),
     26-40) has suggested that the league was a survival of
     the old Ionian kingdom which had its royal seat in
     Ephesos (see above, n.30), a view which has not won
     wide acceptance, if only for lack of evidence, and
     seems to be fairly conclusively disproved by the more
     recent archaeological excavation of the site of Melie
     which indicates a *floruit* for Melie of the eighth
     century BC and destruction soon after (JHS Arch. Rep.
     1964/5, 49). On the other hand it seems rather
     extreme to suppose (J.M. Cook, CAH 3, II(2), 803) that
     the common religious festival only originated after
     the destruction of Melie (possibly early seventh
     century BC). Evidence for the later habitation of the
     site of Melie cannot at present be squared with the
     historical tradition (Arch. Rep. 1959/60, 47). The
     reference in the 'Homeric Hymn to Delian Apollo' to an
     Ionian gathering at Delos (147-55) contains no
     reference to the Asia Minor Ionians as a group
     separate from the general Ionian family.

44   Arch. Rep. 1964/5, 50.

45   Hdt. I,141,4.

46   Anakreon fr.426 (Page); cf. Aristophanes 'Ploutos',
     ℓ.1002.

47   Furniture: Ath. I,28; Wool: ibid., XII,540d; Dye:
     Aristotle, 'Hist.Anim.', V,15,3.

48   On Phokylides, see below, chapter 5.

49   Paus. VII,2,6. See R.A. Tomlinson, Greek Sanctuaries,
     132; B.C. Dietrich (The Origins of Greek Religion,
     Berlin, 1974, 217) argues strongly for continuity in
     religious cult here and at Samos and Ephesos, even
     when a break in the archaeological settlement pattern
     is indicated.

50   Arch. Rep. 1964/5, 52-3.

51   Hdt. VI,19,4. Strabo attributes the sack to Xerxes
     (XIV,1,5.) Cf. Arch. Rep. 1964/5, 52-3. The
     equivocal attitude of the shrine is earlier
     illustrated in its reception of the renegade Lydian
     Paktyes and the surrender of him to the Persians (Hdt.
     I,154ff.).

52   Hdt. I,26.

53   Hdt. I,92,1. British Museum, B.16. See chapter 3,
     below.

54   Paus. VII,2,7-8.

55   See R.D. Barnett, 'Early Greek and Oriental Ivories',
     JHS 68 (1948), 20-1. The Ephesian ivories will be
     discussed in more detail below, chapter 3. On
     possible reflection of a Hittite cult of the Ephesian

Artemis, see J. Boardman, The Greeks overseas, 111.
56 On Hipponax, see below, chapter 4.
57 Hdt. I,147,2.
58 On Samian Geometric see below, chapter 3. On the
    early Heraion, see J.M. Cook, The Greeks in Ionia and
    the East, 75-8.
59 Desborough, op.cit., 281ff.
60 Hdt. III,60. There are difficulties in assigning
    these feats to the time of Polykrates himself. M.
    White (The Duration of the Samian Tyranny, JHS 74
    (1954), 36-43) suggests that they may belong to an
    earlier generation of tyranny established by
    Polykrates' father, although this view has been
    disputed more recently by B.M. Mitchell ('Herodotus
    and Samos', JHS 95 (1975), 75-91). See further below,
    chapter 4, on Anakreon.
61 Ath. XII, 525f.
62 Here the text has a lacuna.
63 On the inscription and its contents, amid a large
    bibliography, see especially L.H. Jeffery, 'The Courts
    of Justice in Archaic Chios', ABSA 51 (1956), 157-67.
64 E.g. M.N. Tod, Greek Historical Inscriptions, 2nd ed.,
    1946, 2-3.
65 Thuk. VIII,24,4.
66 See G.Kleiner in RE Supplementband IX, cols 1181-221.
67 Paus. VII,2.10.
68 Herakleitos DK 22 B.104. On Herakleitos see chapter 6.
69 Hdt. I,170,1-2.
70 Paus. VII,3,3.
71 Arist., 'Politics', 1290b15, on estates; Strab. XIV,1,
    28, on cavalry.
72 Xenophanes DK 21 B.3.
73 See C.M. Bowra, 'Xenophanes Fr.3', CQ 35 (1941), 119-
    26.
74 The question of the Ionians and effeminacy will be
    discussed in the final chapter of this book (chapter
    7).
75 'Hymn to the Delian Apollo', 40. See also Strab. XIV,
    1,27.
76 Ibid.
77 JHS Arch. Rep. 1959/60, 41-3; 1964/5, 46.
78 Arch. Rep. 1959/60, 41. Excavation by E. Akurgal
    revealed monochrome pottery characteristic of Aeolic
    occupation underneath the more usual Geometric.
79 Paus. VII,3,10.
80 See A. Langlotz, 'Die kulturelle und künstlerische
    Hellenisierung der Küsten des Mittelmeeres durch die
    Stadt Phokaia', Cologne, 1966, and F. Bilabel, Die
    ionische Kolonisation, 240-3.

81 Hdt. I,164-5.
82 Strab. XIV,1,3; Paus. VII,3,6.
83 Arch. Rep. 1964/5, 45.
84 Hdt. I,170,3.
85 Strab. XIV,1,30.
86 See D.W.S. Hunt, 'Feudal Survivals in Ionia', JHS 67 (1947), 68-76.
87 Paus. VII,3,8. On early archaeological settlement, see Arch. Rep. 1959/60, 40 and Desborough, op.cit., 184.
88 On the Lydian defeat, Hdt. I,16,2. On later history, Paus. VII,3,9.
89 Aristotle, 'Politics', 1305b,18-22.
90 Thuk. I,138,5.
91 Hdt. I,150.
92 JHS 72 (1952), 104 (J.M. Cook on the Smyrna excavations).
93 JHS 71 (1951), 247-9 (J.M. Cook on the Smyrna excavations). On Smyrna and Homer, see below, chapter 4.
94 Strab. XIV,1,37.
95 The fullest account of literary sources may be found in Huxley, op.cit., 47-54. A general picture emerges from Cook, CAH 3, II(2), 796-804.
96 The hypothesis of two waves of migration, the first establishing the southern Ionian cities, the second expanding northwards with the 'calling in' of sons of Kodros and take-over of Aeolic cities like Phokaia and Smyrna, has been supported by C. Roebuck (Ionian Trade and Colonisation, 23) and more recently by C.G. Thomas, 'The Roots of Homeric Kingship'. Historia 15 (1966), 402-3.
97 CAH 3, II(2),804. See also Thomas, op.cit., 404-5. Both authorities speculate that the changes in the tribal system of the Ionians at Ephesos and elsewhere in order to incorporate non-Ionian elements, Greek and native, may have weakened tribal loyalties and strengthened civic feeling.
98 The complex questions touched upon here will be discussed more fully below in chapter 4.
99 See R.S. Young, report in Proc.Am.Phil.Soc. 107 (1963), 348-64).
100 For illustration, see J.M. Cook, JHS 71 (1951), 248, fig.8.
101 The question remains undecided (cf. Young, in Anatolian Studies 14 (1964), 29-33) and Boardman, op. cit., 101-11. See now J. Coldstream, Geometric Greece, 301.
102 Hdt. I,19-21.

103   On this subject, see below, chapter 5.
104   See e.g. 'Iones', RE IX,2, col.1877.
105   See the seminal article of R.M. Cook 'Ionia and
       Greece in the Eighth and Seventh Centuries B.C.',
       JHS 66 (1946), 80-7.
106   Hdt. II,178. On the site in general, see Boardman,
       op.cit., 134-50.
107   The most detailed study of this subject (in some
       respects now out of date) is C. Roebuck, Ionian Trade
       and Colonisation (1959) which can be supplemented
       with the relevant sections of Boardman (op.cit.) and
       the same author's detailed account of Black Sea
       colonies in JHS Arch. Rep. 1962/3, 34-51.
108   See R.M. Cook, op.cit., 70-80, and for a recent
       archaeological and economic survey, Boardman, op.cit.,
       245-67(esp.253ff.).
109   The question of the earliest Greek penetration of the
       Black Sea is the object of a current controversy, cf.
       A.J. Graham, 'The Date of the Greek Penetration of
       the Black Sea', BICS 5 (1958), 25-42. R. Drews, 'The
       Earliest Greek Settlements on the Black Sea, JHS 96
       (1976), 18-31, argues contra Boardman et al. for an
       eighth-century BC date for earliest Greek penetration.
110   Pliny, 'Natural History', V,112.
111   Contra W.W. How and J. Wells, A Commentary on
       Herodotus, Oxford, 1912, II,10 (note on V,28). On
       'Gergithes', cf. Hdt. V,122 and Ath. XII,524a.
112   Hdt. V,92,6. Aristotle ('Politics' 1284a and 1311a)
       makes Periander the giver of the advice.
113   Hdt. VI,21,1.
114   Aelian, 'Varia Historia', III,26.
115   In Athenaios (see above, n.111).
116   Ibid.
117   Hdt. V,28-9
118   In Aristotle, 'Politics', 1295b,28.
119   See below, chapter 5.
120   Hdt. I,6,2-3. For possible favourable treatment of
       Miletos by Croesus, see Diogenes Laertius I,25.
121   Hdt. I,92,1-2.
122   Ibid., 84-90. For the historical record, see Burn,
       op.cit., 42 and n.9.
123   Hdt. I,141,1-2.
124   Ibid., 141,4.
125   Ibid., 159.
126   Boardman, The Greeks Overseas, 77.
127   Though, as we saw above (p. 20 and n.60) there are
       arguments, on historical and economic grounds, for
       placing the major achievements, or at least, their
       inauguration, earlier than Polykrates (d.c.522 BC).

M. White (op.cit., 41) believes that the tunnel, which must have taken at least fifteen years to construct, was started before Polykrates.

128   Hdt. IV,89ff. The bridge was built by a Samian called Mandrokles.

129   Hdt. III,90,1.

130   Hdt. V,28, VI,8. See C Roebuck, 'The Economic Development of Ionia', CP 48 (1953), 9-16. The possibility cannot be ruled out, however, that Herodotos has his own dramatic reasons for emphasising the prosperity of Miletos on the eve of its great fall.

131   Hdt. V, 37,2.

132   The question of motivation and the individual responsibility for the Ionian Revolt as well as the relationship between its protagonists, Histiaios and Aristagoras, his son-in-law, is a very controversial one. Amid a large bibliography, see M. Lang ('Herodotus and the Ionian Revolt', Historia 17 (1968), 24-36) who is sharply critical of Herodotos and sees the Revolt as a general movement with definite political aims; hence the generous Persian settlement afterwards, which attempted to settle genuine grievances. However the picture of Aristagoras as a patriotic hero whose Naxian adventure was an attempt, legitimately, to mobilise the Ionian fleet, since it rejects Herodotos, has nothing better to rest on, as later critics have been quick to point out. See e.g. K.H. Waters (Herodotus and the Ionian Revolt', Historia 19 (1970), 504-8) who perhaps goes to the other extreme, while making the valuable point that personal, and even discreditable, motives on the part of the leaders are not incompatible with genuine reasons for popular revolt. The question is further complicated by a variety of possible relationships between Aristagoras and Histiaios ranging from close co-operation to rivalry (P.B. Manville, 'Aristagoras and Histiaios: The Leadership Struggle in the Ionian Revolt', CQ n.s. 27 (1977), 80-91). Attempts to show Herodotos as not always anti-Ionian (J.A.S. Evans, 'Herodotus and the Ionian Revolt', Historia 25 (1976), 31-7 (esp.34) seem beside the point in view of his clear inability to see the Revolt except from hindsight as an inevitable disaster. It is difficult to avoid Lang's original point that a great deal of Herodotos' account contains the material for its own refutation.

133   On the general question of anti-Ionian bias, in Herodotos and others, see below, chapter 7. It has

been suggested (Evans, op.cit., 33-4) that he may
have inherited his pessimistic view of the Revolt
from the Milesian geographer Hekataios, who' was
against it (Hdt. V,36), or from the Samians, whose
role he was trying to place in as favourable a light
as the facts would permit. (VI,13).

134 See M. Cary in CAH 1, IV,225 and Burn, op.cit., 198.
135 Hdt. V,38,2. On common coinage, see P. Gardiner ('The
Coinage of the Ionian Revolt', JHS 31 (1911), 151-60),
who believed that each city minted its own coins
rather than surrender this privilege to a central
mint, a view supported recently by R. Meiggs (The
Athenian Empire, 441-2) who nevertheless emphasises
the remarkable degree of co-ordination required in
the individual issue of common coinage.
136 Hdt. VI,10-16.
137 Hdt. IV,22,1. There is some evidence of possible
continuity in the list of eponymous priestly
officials from the Milesian Delphinion, which has no
gap corresponding to the period of supposed collapse
(Milet, Heft III (1914) 230ff.) though the reservations of F. Jacoby (Atthis, 359,n.27) concerning the
antiquity and reliability of such lists, should be
noted.
138 Hdt. IX,103.
139 JHS Arch. Rep. 1964/5, 50.
140 For a Milesian inscription at Susa, the Persian
capital, see Jeffery, Archaic Scripts, 334.
141 Hdt. VI,20.

CHAPTER 3 THE CHARACTER OF IONIAN ART

1 For example, R.M. Cook's dismissal of extant Ionian
'korai' as 'rather plain' (Greek Art, London, 1972,
100), and a generally low estimate of Ionian vase-
painting (e.g. Greek Painted Pottery, 115) may be
compared with the rather over-enthusiastic
description of 'Wild Goat' pottery as 'one of the
most successful Greek creations in the field of fine
arts' (E. Akurgal, 'The Early Period and the Golden
Age of Ionia', AJA 66 (1962), 374).
2 J.N. Coldstream, Geometric Pottery, 262ff.
3 See R.M. Cook, Greek Painted Pottery, 130, on the
Louvre kylix. In the case of the 'Cheramyes Hera',
the survival of similar 'korai' from the Samian
Heraion makes the existence of a tradition more
likely.
4 For differing views of Ionian influence on the

Caeretan hydriai see e.g. J. Boardman, Pre-Classical:
From Crete to Archaic Greece, 150 and R.M. Cook,
Greek Art, 159-60.

5 See e.g. J. Beazley and B. Ashmole, Greek Sculpture
and Painting, 8ff.

6 Boardman, op.cit., 169.

7 Vitruvius IV,1,4-8.

8 G.M.A. Richter, Kouroi: Archaic Greek Youths, 5.

9 Athenaios XII,524f-525a.

10 See below, chapter 7.

11 G.M.A. Hanfmann, 'Ionia: Leader or Follower?', HSCP
61 (1953), 23.

12 Ibid.

13 For details of finds, see V.R.d'A. Desborough, The
Greek Dark Ages, 179-84.

14 Cf. the agreement on this point between R.M. Cook,
Greek Painted Pottery, 35, and Desborough, op.cit.,
181.

15 For good photographs of about a dozen of the Dipylon
vases, see M. Hirmer and P.E. Arias, A History of
Greek Vase Painting, trs. and rev. B.B. Shefton,
London, 1962, pls 1-10. For Samos, the site of the
most distinguished Ionian Geometric to date, see
Coldstream, op.cit., pl.64 and H. Walter in Samos 5
(Frühe samische Gefässe), 1968. For illustrations of
Milesian examples, see Istanbuler Mitteilungen 7
(1957), pl.36, and 9-10 (1959-60), pls 53,3 and 55,1.
For Smyrna, see JHS 70 (1950), 13; 71 (1951), 248,
and 72 (1952), 103. For Chios, see J. Boardman,
Greek Emporio (1967), 101-47.

16 For Samian Geometric, see R. Eilmann, 'Frühe Griechische Keramik im Samischen Heraion', Athenische
Mitteilungen 58 (1933), 47-145. For Samos and Chios
see references in previous note.

17 For Miletos, see Coldstream, op.cit., 296-7.

18 Hanfmann, op.cit., 14.

19 Ibid., 20. Boardman (The Greeks Overseas, 105) is
sceptical about Phrygian influence on Greek Geometric.
See also E. Akurgal, Phrygische Kunst, Ankara, 1955,
40ff.

20 See chapter 1, p. 6. It cannot be too strongly
emphasised how localised Greek culture in Ionia must
have been in the archaic period. Anatolian influences
are to be found in the language of inscriptions,
religion and personal names (Hanfmann, op.cit., 2-3).
Cf. also Herodotos' account of intermarriage (chapter
2, p.16).

21 See chapter 2, p.26 and n.100. For Terpander's
invention see Pindar fr.100 (Bowra). The oriental

lyre has no canonical number of strings (Akurgal, Die
Kunst Anatoliens, 14).

22   See E. Akurgal, The Birth of Greek Art, 173 and pl.49.
23   Boardman, The Greeks Overseas, 70ff.
24   Akurgal, Die Kunst Anatoliens, 177, for illustration.
25   See Hirmer and Arias, op.cit., pl.26 for a Rhodian
     example and Akurgal, Die Kunst Anatoliens, 178-9 for
     one from Old Smyrna.
26   E. Buschor, Griechische Vasen, Munich, 1940, 51.
27   See Akurgal's remarks cited in n.1 above.
28   See Boardman, Greek Emporio, 102-53 and 156-75.
29   Discussion and illustration of later Ionian Black
     Figure by R.M. Cook can be found in Fasc. XIII of the
     Corpus Vasorum Antiquorum, British Museum, 8 (1954).
     See also the same author's 'Fikellura Pottery', ABSA
     34 (1936), 1-98.
30   In the British Museum, 64.10-7.156.
31   For a full discussion and illustration of Ionian
     Little Master Cups, see E. Kunze, 'Ionische Klein-
     meister', Athenische Mitteilungen 59 (1934), 81-122.
     See Taf. VI-X and Beil. VI-XI, illustrating the
     article comprehensively.
32   See Kunze, op.cit., 101-4 and Beil. VIII.
33   Kunze, op.cit., 101 and n.4. The kylix probably
     comes from Samos.
34   Kunze, op.cit., 103.
35   'Iliad', IX, 323-4.
36   G.M.A. Richter, Archaic Greek Art, 110.
37   See Boardman, The Greeks Overseas, 160-1. R.M. Cook
     ('Origins of Greek Sculpture', JHS 87 (1967), 24-32)
     does not think the influence was a direct or specific
     one.
38   Richter, Archaic Greek Art, suggested the possible
     primacy of Ionia.
39   See the Attic 'kouros' in Boardman, Greek Sculpture:
     The Archaic Period, pl.63.
40   Akurgal, Die Kunst Anatoliens, pls 137-8(187).
41   For an illustration, see Boardman, Greek Sculpture,
     pl.50.
42   An ivory youth from Samos dates to the late seventh
     century, see Boardman, Greek Sculpture, pl.54.
43   See R.D. Barnett, 'Early Greek and Oriental Ivories',
     JHS 68 (1948), 20.
44   Also with Hittite, see Barnett, op.cit., 20 and fig.
     19. The shape of the ivory tusk may not be
     irrelevant here.
45   'Il.', IV, 141-5. For the historical implications,
     see Barnett, op.cit., 18.
46   See Barnett, loc.cit.

47   Akurgal, Die Kunst Anatoliens, 196-7.
48   Strabo XIV,1.23. Barnett, op.cit., 20, n.130.
49   Barnett, op.cit., 7 (fig.6).
50   Akurgal detects what he feels to be 'Wild Goat'
     ornamentation around the bottom of the priest's robe
     (Die Kunst Anatoliens, 198).
51   See ibid., pls 160-1(200).
52   Ibid., 206-9.
53   See E. Buschor, Altsamische Standbilder, II,24ff. and
     G.M.A. Richter, Korai: Archaic Greek Maidens, no.55.
     In the Louvre.
54   Buschor, Altsamische Standbilder, 26ff. In Vathy
     Museum, Samos.
55   Buschor, Altsamische Standbilder, III, Abb.160-2.
56   See the East Greek groups distinguished by Richter in
     Korai.
57   For four examples see Akurgal, Die Kunst Anatoliens,
     pls 203-6(236-7).
58   Richter, Archaic Greek Art, 110.
59   B.271.
60   Ibid., pl.189(225). (B.27).
61   Ibid., pls 190-1(226-7). (B.275 and 276).
62   B.280.
63   B.281.
64   On Ionian epigraphic styles, see below, chapter 5.
65   Akurgal, Die Kunst Anatoliens, pl.244(275).
66   Ibid., pl.245(275).
67   See chapter 2, p.19 and n.53. Three of these column
     bases are in the British Museum, with Croesus'
     personal dedication.
68   B.89. (It is not certain whether it actually
     belonged to the drums.)
69   Akurgal, Die Kunst Anatoliens, pls 212-13(248-9).
70   See e.g. the Athenian 'Peplos kore' (540-530 BC),
     possibly the work of an immigrant Ionian, and a head
     of a young man from Rhodes.
71   Akurgal, Die Kunst Anatoliens, 256.
72   Lyra Graeca Selecta (ed.D.L.Page), 191,14.
73   Paus. VIII,14,8.
74   By G.M.A. Richter, Archaic Greek Art, 106.
75   Excavation took place immediately after the Second
     World War, led by E. Akurgal and J.M. Cook; for a
     full account, see E. Akurgal, Bayrakli, Ankara, 1950,
     and J.M. Cook, 'Old Smyrna: 1948-51', ABSA 53-4
     (1958-9), 1-34. Summaries in JHS 67 (1947), 41-3;
     70 (1950), 10-13; 71 (1951), 247-9; 72 (1952), 104-7;
     73 (1953), 124-5 - all by J.M. Cook.
76   Akurgal, Die Kunst Anatoliens, pl.1(10), estimates
     that this building dates from c.900 BC.

77 J.M. Cook, JHS 72 (1952), 104.

78 On the historical associations of this house see W.B.
    Stanford, The Odyssey of Homer, 2 vols, London, 1947,
    note to XXII,459 and Appendix B. For diagrammatical
    illustration, see Akurgal, Die Kunst Anatoliens, fig.
    2(301).

79 For an illustration of a section of the wall, see
    ibid., pl.136(186) and Boardman, The Greeks Overseas,
    fig.5(50) for a reconstruction of late seventh-
    century Smyrna.

80 Akurgal, pls 131-3(182-3).

81 See R.A. Tomlinson, Greek Sanctuaries, 124-7.

82 See ibid., 127-36 for details of the Ephesian
    Artemision and the Sanctuary of Apollo at Didyma (and
    pls 45-6, for an illustration of the latter).

83 Suggested by Tomlinson, ibid., 122.

84 W.B. Dinsmoor, The Architecture of Ancient Greece,
    139.

85 For illustration, see Akurgal, Die Kunst Anatoliens,
    pls 251-2.

86 See D.S. Robertson, Greek and Roman Architecture, 2nd
    edn, Cambridge, 1943, figs 46,40 and 41.

87 See Akurgal, Die Kunst Anatoliens, pl.253.

88 See ibid., pl.257.

89 Ibid., 108.

90 Barnett, op.cit., 18ff.

91 Boardman, The Greeks Overseas, 83ff.

92 See Akurgal, The Birth of Greek Art, pl.14.

93 Ibid., pl.37.

94 G.M.A. Richter, Greek Art, 7th edn, London, 1974, pl.
    66(65).

95 Ibid., pls 89 and 90(78-9).

96 Richter, Korai, 9-10.

97 For examples see Akurgal, Die Kunst Anatoliens, pls
    200,205,207,216,221,226-8 and 229-32.

98 British Museum, B.325.

99 Boardman, The Greeks Overseas, 139 and pl.9b.

100 The Ionian connection is disputed, see R.M. Cook,
    Greek Painted Pottery, 160-1. See above, p.37.

101 Boardman, Pre-Classical, 151.

102 Dinsmoor, op.cit., 92-6.

103 Boardman, Pre-Classical, 172.

104 Boardman, The Greeks Overseas, 109.

105 Pliny, 'Natural History', XXXIV,68.

106 See G.M.A. Richter, 'Greeks in Persia', AJA 50 (1946),
    15-30. See Boardman, The Greeks Overseas, fig.33
    (121).

107 See Boardman, Greek Sculpture, pl.175 (date c.490-
    480).

108   See, on its limitations, K. Friis Johansen,
      'Clazomeneian Sarcophagus Studies', Acta Archaeologia
      13,1-3 (1942), 1.
109   For an illustration of the Alexander sarcophagus, see
      Richter, Greek Art, pl.205 (154).

CHAPTER 4   HOMER AND THE IONIAN POETIC TRADITION

1   Homer, 'Od.', VI, 57-70.
2   The exact meaning of ὑπερτερίῃ is not certain; see
    W.B. Stanford, The Odyssey of Homer, 2 vols, London,
    1947, ad loc.
3   On the subject of epithets, see below pp. 70f. In
    this particular passage the translator is faced with
    the problems of rendering (a) θαλερόν (66). E.V.
    Rieu, whose translation succeeds particularly in
    conveying the light, urbane quality of the original,
    omits it. (Rieu fails in general to come to terms
    with the problems of epithets, either omitting them,
    as here, or giving them more significance than the
    context seems to warrant.) Lattimore's 'joyful' has
    been adopted here, *faute de mieux*. The word seems to
    indicate 'blooming', 'rich' or 'fruitful'.   (b)
    φίλος (57,62,67), whose range of meanings (in later
    literature as well as Homer) covers possession as
    well as affection (see LSJ φίλος 2c.).
4   A blend of wish and question, as Stanford notes, ad
    loc.
5   Lattimore, assuming in his translation strong
    punctuation in the middle of 59 and none at the end,
    spoils the effect of καὶ δὲ σοὶ αὐτῷ κτλ. in 60.
6   Teasing, that is, if we are correct in seeing
    Alkinoos' words in 69-70 as a playful repetition of
    those of Nausikaa in 57-8. This, however, raises the
    major question of the aesthetic significance of
    formulaic language, on which see below p.80 and n.87.
7   On this, see the interesting remarks of H. Fränkel,
    Early Greek Poetry and Philosophy, 1f.
8   See ibid., x.
9   On the remains of non-Homeric epic poetry, see G.L.
    Huxley, Greek Epic Poetry: Eumelos to Panyassis.
10 'Od.', I,325-7; VII,256-369; 487-521.
11 On the complicated question of post-Ionic 'corrup-
    tion', see G.S. Kirk, The Songs of Homer, 203-10.
12 The original theory was put forward in 1883 by A.
    Fick (Die homerische Odysee in ihrer ursprünglichen
    Sprachform wiederhergestellt).
13 See M. Parry, 'The Epic Technique of Oral Verse-

Making, II: Homeric Language as the Language of an
Oral Poetry', HSCP 43 (1932), 26ff. (Reprinted in
The Making of Homeric Verse ed. A. Parry, 345ff.)

14   The case against an Aeolic phase has been argued
forcibly by K. Strunk, Die sogennanten Äolismen der
homerischen Sprache. See also the review by O.
Szemerényi in JHS 79 (1959), 191-3.

15   See the generally cautious summary of Kirk, op.cit.,
113-20.

16   Kirk (op.cit., 108ff.) does not regard a Mycenaean
poetic tradition as a *sine qua non*; he cites the
(admittedly inconclusive) evidence of the epics
themselves that, at least in the long stories told by
Nestor, Menelaos and Eumaios, a tradition of prose
narrative existed.

17   V.R.d'A. Desborough, The Greek Dark Ages, 24-7.

18   C. Whitman, Homer and the Heroic Tradition.

19   See Huxley, op.cit., pp. 113-22.

20   Kirk, op.cit., 105-25.

21   Ibid., 199.

22   For the former cf. the story of Meleagros in 'Il.',
IX, where compression makes the narrative barely
intelligible (cf. esp. 553-72) and for the latter,
cf. Nestor's reminiscences esp. XI,669-761, where
characterisation of the garrulous old man may not be
unintentional (cf. 'Od.', III,103-200, where, however,
the material is more interesting to us.).

23   J. Griffin, The Epic Cycle and the Uniqueness of
Homer', JHS 97 (1977), 39-53.

24   Kirk, op.cit., 316ff.

25   'Hymn to Delian Apollo', 172-3.

26   Thukydides III,104,4-6.

27   'Il.', XIII,685.

28   See G.P. Shipp, The Language of Homer.

29   'Il.', II, 459-66.

30   See the edition of W. Leaf, note on 463.

31   'Il.', II,144-6.

32   'Il.', IX,4-7. For possible evidence from wind
direction, see 'Od.', VII,119 and XIX,205-8.

33   'Il.', XXIV, 614-17.

34   'Il.', IV, 141-5, the simile of a Maionian or Karian
woman staining ivory (see chapter 3, p.47 for text and
translation); XX,404, a sacrifice to Poseidon
Helikonios (also a simile). For Homer and the Troad,
see C.M. Bowra, 'Homeric Epithets for Troy', JHS 80
(1960), 16-23 (esp.22).

35   A pitfall not entirely avoided by J.M. Cook, The
Greeks in Ionia and the East, 36ff.

36   See chapter 3, p.42.

37. See P. Walcot, Hesiod and the Near East, for a different explanation. The question of when and how eastern ideas entered Greek culture is by no means settled. J.T. Hooker (Mycenaean Greece, 120) has recently suggested that eastern elements could have entered Greek traditions possibly via Neo-Hittite.

38 See Kirk, The Homeric Poems as History, CAH 3, II(2), 820ff.

39 See C.G. Thomas, 'The Roots of Homeric Kingship', Historia 15 (1966), 404-5. Thomas pursues the argument, rather speculatively, into details of tribal structure.

40 Thomas (ibid., 390) seems to me to go too far when, quoting T.B.L. Webster, he sees the 'Odyssey''s Scherie as a reflection of Ionian town-planning. The reminiscences of 'gridiron' do not go beyond Alkinoos' grounds. On the other hand, the likeness of Scherie to an Ionian coastal site is unmistakable.

41 F.A. Wolf, Prolegomena ad Homerum (1795).

42 The edition of the 'Iliad' by W. Leaf, one of the later of the 'analysts', is only just, in English, being replaced by that of M. Willcock (Books I-XII have been published, the remainder are in preparation). For a short account of the nineteenth-century Homeric Question, cf. A. Parry's introduction to The Making of Homeric Verse (the collected papers of Milman Parry), pp. xiv-xix.

43 See previous note.

44 In 'L' Épithète traditionelle dans Homère; Essai sur un problème de style homérique' and 'Les Formules et la métrique d'Homère' (trans. in The Making of Homeric Verse, 1-239).

45 Ibid., 109-13.

46 See esp. 'Studies in the Epic Technique of Oral Verse-Making I and II', HSCP 41 (1930), 73-147 and 43 (1932), 1-50 (The Making of Homeric Verse, 266-364). These, as Parry's first well-known articles in English, received the earliest attention from scholars.

47 The Making of Homeric Verse, 276-7.

48 Ibid., 277.

49 Ibid., 279-301.

50 Ibid., 271.

51 See A.B. Lord, The Singer of Tales and periodic publications of Serbocroation Heroic Songs (1953-).

52 B. Fenik, Typical Battle Scenes in the Iliad.

53 T. Krisher, Formale Konventionen der homerischen Epik.

54   This was suggested as early as 1923 by A. Meillet,
     Les Origines indo-européennes des mètres grecs.
55   One of the most penetrating of criticisms of Parry,
     that of M.W.M. Pope ('The Parry-Lord Theory of
     Homeric Composition', Acta Classica 6 (1963), 1-21)
     does not really deal with the more recent discussions
     of oral poetry, especially in the assumption that
     shortcomings in the 'length and thrift' of systems
     radically undermine the theory, or that it really
     describes the process of oral composition to suggest
     that Homer had 'a store of formulae' in the 'index of
     his mind' (19).
56   J.B. Hainsworth, The Flexibility of the Homeric
     Formula.
57   A. Hoekstra, Homeric Modifications of Formulaic
     Prototypes.
58   For the song as οἴμη cf. 'Od.', VIII,481; XXII,347.
59   Hainsworth, op.cit., 3.
60   The 'Wedding of Smailagić Meho' sung by Avdo
     Međedović and running to more than 12,000 lines (and
     regarded by Parry as the prize of his collection) has
     recently been published (1974) in Serbocroatian
     Heroic Songs, III.
61   Cf. the critical exchanges between A.B. Lord ('Homer
     as Oral Poet', HSCP 72 (1967), 1-46) and the late Ann
     Amory Parry, 'Homer as Artist', CQ 21 (1971), 1-15.
62   On the relations between tradition and individual
     creation in Homer, see most recently M.N. Nagler,
     Spontaneity and Tradition (1975).
63   See the short introduction of E.A. Speiser in Ancient
     Near Eastern Texts Relating to the Old Testament, ed.
     J.B. Pritchard, 72-3.
64   Ibid., 90.
65   E.g. Odysseus in 'Od.', XVIII, 130-7; Achilles in
     'Il.', XXIV, 525ff.
66   Pritchard, op.cit., 79.
67   In the sense intended by Bruno Snell in the book Die
     Entdeckung des Geistes (The Discovery of the Mind,
     trans. E. Rosenmayer).
68   See especially the work of 'neo-analytic' critics
     such as W. Schadewaldt (Iliasstudien and Von Homers
     Welt und Werk).
69   See above p.62 and n.10.
70   Lord, The Singer of Tales, 65.
71   See Aias' remarks in 'Il.', IX, 632-6.
72   See D.L. Page, History and the Homeric Iliad,
     Appendix I, pp.297-315 for a full statement of the
     problems (albeit without a very convincing solution).
73   One supposes, gradually; there is, however, no way of

disproving the theory that 'Homer' was entirely
responsible for the more developed story, improbable
though that hypothesis may seem.

74 'Il.', IX,318-22.

75 Ibid., 607-10.

76 At no time does Achilles resemble the later tragic
hero in his consciousness of what he has done or
basic regret for it.

77 This passage has been exhaustively dealt with by
scholars, see Kirk, op.cit., 216.

78 'Il.', III,161-90.

79 'Il.', XXII,33-78.

80 See Kirk, op.cit., 320-1.

81 The Greek, πυκινή = 'dense', 'crowded'.

82 'Il.', XXIV,477-84.

83 I.e. both Achilles and Priam continue to recognise
the code through which they have momentarily
penetrated; Achilles grants Priam's request for a
truce, which, they both know, will be followed by
fighting again. Moreover, during the interview,
Achilles has trouble in controlling his anger.

84 'Il.', VI, 119-236. Homer makes a joke of the
inequality in value of the gifts exchanged (234-6).

85 Ransom of living captives takes place on a number of
occasions, esp. Book I, where the priest Chryses
tries to ransom his daughter (11-42).

86 Of Achilles' hands, 'Il.', XVIII,317; The word is a
regular epithet of Hektor (cf. 'Il.', XXIV,724,etc.).

87 Cf. φυσίζοος αἶα ('Il.', III,243) the 'lifegiving
earth' which covers the bodies of Kastor and
Polydeukes (an 'effect' admired by Ruskin).
ornamental epithets, see the differing viewpoints of
F.M. Combellack, 'Milman Parry and Homeric Artistry',
Comparative Literature 11 (1959), 193-208 and W.
Whallon, 'The Homeric Epithets', YCS 17 (1961), 97-
142.

88 For Homeric 'objectivity' of style, see the famous
essay of E. Auerbach, in Mimesis, trans. W.R. Trask,
Princeton, 1968, chapter 1.

89 Modern criticism tends to echo Longinus' rather
dismissive comments in On the Sublime, IX,11, see
Kirk, op.cit.,355-71. See a fairer assessment by
J.B. Hainsworth, Homer (Greece and Rome Surveys in
the Classics no.3, 1969), 40-1.

90 See Kirk's unnecessarily harsh strictures of 'Od.',
XIV and XV, the books in which Odysseus (disguised as
a beggar) and Eumaios the swineherd, exchange life
histories to while away the time (op.cit., 358-61).
We may find them unnecessarily long, but there is no

reason to suppose Homer's audience reacted similarly.

91 Whitman, op.cit.,304.

92 'Od.', XXIV,226-350.

93 For the arguments see the edition of Stanford, note
on XXIII,296ff. Page's arguments on grounds of taste
seem to me largely irrelevant (The Homeric Odyssey,
111-12).

94 Lord, The Singer of Tales, 169-85.

95 Hdt. II,53.

96 See Matthew Arnold, 'On Translating Homer', On the
Classical Tradition (vol.1 of Complete Prose Works),
ed. R.H. Super, Michigan, 1960.

97 'Il.', I,517-30.

98 'Od.', VIII,335-43.   There are some linguistic
features which suggest that the story as a whole is
late; see Stanford note to 266ff.

99 'Il.', III,399-412.

100 'Od.', XIII,291-5.

101 'Od.', XIII,312-13.

102 'Il.', XIV,346-51. For the only other example of
this style, see 'Il.', XIII,27-31. It is much more
common in the Homeric Hymns and may, as Kirk suggests
(op.cit., 173), reflect the 'sophisticated taste of
Ionian audiences towards the end of the oral period'.

103 See C.M. Bowra, Tradition and Design in the Iliad,
114ff.

104 'Il.', VI,506-11 = XV,263-8.

105 A basic work on the Homeric similes is H. Fränkel,
Die homerischen Gleichnisse. The most recent
contribution is W. Scott, The Oral Nature of the
Homeric Simile (1974).

106 'Il.', XV,361-6.

107 'Il.', XVIII,207-14.

108 'Od.', V,432-5.

109 'Il.', XI, 113-21.

110 A motif which frequently recurs in the similes (see
C. Moulton, 'Similes in the Iliad', Hermes 102 (1974),
381-97, on 'parent-child' relationships).

111 One of Virgil's most striking similes is of a Roman
senator quelling a mob ('Aeneid', I, 148-56) and
Milton ('Paradise Lost', I,287ff.) describes the moon
as seen through Galileo's telescope.

112 'Il.', XII,432-6.

113 See below, chapter 5, pp.122-3.

114 See on this Snell, op.cit., 199-204, and G.E.R. Lloyd,
Polarity and Analogy, 183-92.

115 In the Iliad example, the use of πορφύρῃ, κωφῷ and
ὀσσόμενον, words normally used of mental states, to
describe the sea, is odd - almost as if elements of

the dilemma were entering into the concrete image
itself. Lloyd (op.cit., 188) points out how the use
of individual words (e.g. 'Od.', XX,13f. ὑλάκτει,
used both in the simile of a bitch snarling to
protect her cubs and metaphorically of Odysseus'
heart 'barking within him') has the effect of
extending knowledge of the inner psychological state.

116   'Il.', XVIII,483-607.

117   As Kirk has demonstrated (op.cit., 135ff.) there is
no overwhelming need to suppose an elaborate
material environment either for the transmission of
the poems, or their final delivery. Circumstances of
modern oral performance suggest quite the reverse
(for what the analogy is worth, see Lord, The Singer
of Tales, 13-29).

118   For an exhaustive discussion of the whole question,
see L. Jeffery, The Local Scripts of Archaic Greece,
43ff.

119   T. Wade-Gery, The Poet of the Iliad, 111ff.

120   The 'Peisistratean recension' is a matter of great
scholarly controversy not immediately relevant to our
concern here. Amid a vast bibliography, see J.A.
Davison, 'Pisistratus and Homer', TAPA 86 (1955), 1-
21; Kirk, op.cit., 306ff.

121   See C. Lévi-Strauss, The Savage Mind, London, 1966,
passim.

122   On this, see G.S. Kirk, 'Homer and Modern Oral
Poetry: Some Confusions', CQ n.s.10 (1960), 271-81.

123   Amid a large bibliography on this controversial
subject, see A.B. Lord, 'Homer's Originality: Oral
Dictated Texts', TAPA 84 (1953), 124-34 and A. Parry,
'Have we Homer's Iliad?', YCS 20 (1966), 177-216, for
both sides of the argument.

124   The question of Alkman's eastern origins was disputed
in antiquity and has never been resolved (see C.M.
Bowra, Greek Lyric Poetry, 2nd edn, 17-19, and D.A.
Campbell, Greek Lyric Poetry: A Selection, 192-3).

125   D.L. Page, in Archiloque (Entretiens sur l'Antiquité
Classique) X,119ff.

126   So M.L. West, 'Greek Poetry, 2000-700 BC', CQ n.s.23
(1973), 182.

127   Clement, 'Stromateis', I,144, puts Kallinos a little
earlier than Archilochos on the (rather dubious)
grounds that the latter speaks of Magnesia as
destroyed, while for Kallinos it is still flourishing.

128   For stylistic dependence on Homer, see Campbell, op.
cit., 162.

129   J.M. Edmonds, Elegy and Iambus, 2 vols, London 1931,
I,96 (fr.10.6). See above, chapter 2, p.25 for the

historical event.
130 For the sun fragment, see G.S. Kirk and J.E. Raven,
     The Presocratic Philosophers, Cambridge, 1957, 14.
131 Edmonds, op.cit., 88-90 (fr.1).
132 Ibid., 90 (fr.2).
133 D.A. Campbell, 'Flutes and Elegiac Couplets', JHS 84
     (1964), 63-8.
134 The opinion of Boardman, from the viewpoint of Greek
     art, in The Greeks Overseas, 119.
135 [Plato], 'Hipparchos', 228b.
136 Edmonds, Lyra Graeca, 3 vols, rev.edn, London, 1952,
     II,144-6 (fr.15). Edmonds bowdlerises to ἄλλον in
     the last line, which spoils the risqué joke. The
     Lesbian woman follows the traditional proclivities of
     her city of origin.
137 On this element, see A.E. Harvey, 'Homeric Epithets
     in Greek Lyric Poetry', CQ n.s.7 (1957), 213.
138 Edmonds, Elegy and Iambus, 192 (fr.104).
139 Ibid., 174 (fr.72). Bowra (op.cit., 282) reads ἐμῶν
     in ℓ.1. The reading makes no material difference to
     the sense of the fragment.
140 'Il.', XIV,183. For descriptions of dress, see the
     fragments of Asios and Xenophanes quoted above
     (chapter 2, pp.20 and 22).
141 Edmonds, Elegy and Iambus, 138 (fr.4). Bergk reads
     οὐ κοεῖς (ℓ.2). The epic verb (ℓ.4) is effectively
     employed in an unexpected metaphor.
142 Schol. on Pindar, 'Isthmians', II,1 (Edmonds, Elegy
     and Iambus, 126).
143 Ibid., 138 (fr.2).
144 κυανῶπις is used of Amphitrite in Homer, 'Od.', XII,
     60.
145 Bowra, op.cit., 268.

CHAPTER 5 MYTH AND REASON: THE IONIAN ORIGIN OF GREEK
PHILOSOPHY

1 Hdt. I,74,2.
2 See especially the polemic of D.R. Dicks, 'Solstices,
   Equinoxes and the Presocratics', JHS 86 (1966), 26-40
   and C.H. Kahn, 'On Early Greek Astronomy', JHS 90
   (1970), 99-116, with a reply by Dicks in JHS 92
   (1972), 175-7.
3 See O. Neugebauer, The Exact Sciences in Antiquity,
   136.
4 W.K.C. Guthrie, A History of Greek Philosophy, I,48,
   quotes the relevant early Assyrian text which makes
   it clear that the important thing, from the religious

point of view, was not to miss the possibility of an
eclipse of sun or moon.

5 Dicks' dismissal of Herodotos' story as a 'hoary
   fable' (JHS 86 (1966), 37) shows undue scepticism of
   the only source remotely near the event in question.

6 B. Farrington, Greek Science, 36. Eclipses did have
   divine significance for the Greeks, as we know from
   Nikias' misplaced superstition in the Sicilian
   Expedition of the Peloponnesian War (Thuk. VII,50,4).

7 G.S. Kirk and J.E. Raven, The Presocratic Philosophers, 82-4 (hereafter referred to as KR).

8 Aristotle, 'Metaph.', A 3, 983b6ff.

9 The basic motivation for research in these two fields
   was identical, see Kahn, op.cit., 116, contra Dicks,
   op.cit., 38.

10 Aristotle, 'Metaph.', A 2, 982b11.

11 Plato, 'Theaetetus', 174a.

12 Aristotle, 'Politics', A 11, 1249a9ff.

13 Plato, 'Republic', IX, 581c. Cicero, 'Tusc. Disp.',
   V, 9, has a similar anecdote, in which Pythagoras
   likened human beings to the different types to be
   seen at the Olympic games.

14 Hdt. I, 75.

15 Athenaios, XII, 524a, quoting Herakleides of Pontos.

16 Guthrie, op.cit., 75, based on Aelian, 'VH', III,7.

17 See F. Bilabel, Die ionische Kolonisation, 57.

18 See A. Andrewes, The Greek Tyrants, London, 1956.

19 A.R. Burn, The Lyric Age of Greece, 3.

20 J.M. Edmonds, Elegy and Iambus, 2 vols, London, 1931,
   I, 120 (fr.5).

21 See, e.g. 'Il.', IX, 502-12, where the effect of
   prayers is developed allegorically.

22 Edmonds, op.cit., 118-20 (fr.4, 27-30; 33-40).

23 See the inscription on the Dipylon oinochoé
   illustrated in L.H. Jeffery, The Local Scripts of
   Archaic Greece, pl.1,1, dated to the last quarter of
   the eighth century BC.

24 The earliest Ionian writing may well be the Samian
   inscribed pentameter mentioned in chapter 4, p. 91,
   illustrated in Jeffery, op.cit., pl.63,1, dated to
   the latter half of the seventh century. However, see
   now L.H. Jeffery, 'Old Smyrna: Inscriptions on Sherds
   and Small Objects', ABSA 59 (1964), 39-49.

25 Hdt. V, 58,3.

26 Jeffery, The Local Scripts, 57-64. This is a view
   recently given some support by J.N. Coldstream,
   Geometric Greece, 301.

27 E.G. Turner, Greek Papyri: An Introduction, Oxford,
   1968, 1-16.

28 Eupolis fr. 304K; Plato, 'Apology', 26d-e.
29 L.D. Reynolds and N.G. Wilson, Scribes and Scholars, London, 1968, 5.
30 H.J. Chaytor, From Script to Print, 5-11.
31 This excludes Linear B, a script used in the Bronze Age palaces of Knossos in Crete and Pylos on the mainland of Greece. Yet the difficulty of inter-pretation and the apparently limited subject-matter of the tablets discovered renders this omission unimportant for the present argument. If the Mycenaeans had a literate class of scribes for the organisation of their bureaucracy, neither the bureaucracy nor the script survived into the Hellenic 'polis'.
32 See especially on Anakreon (chapter 4, pp.93-6).
33 G.S. Kirk, The Nature of Greek Myths, 279ff.
34 Hesiod, 'Works and Days', 220-1, 264.
35 Demades, in Plutarch, 'Solon', 17. Cf. Aristotle, 'Politics', B, 1274b17f.
36 C.D. Buck, The Greek Dialects, no.62 (p.261) with full translation.
37 Jeffery, The Local Scripts, 20.
38 Ibid. On μνήμονες see R.F. Willetts, The Civilis-ation of Ancient Crete, 167-8.
39 Jeffery, The Local Scripts, 59.
40 Homer, 'Od.', I, 32-4.
41 Hdt. I, 94. See above, chapter 2, p.28.
42 See the important conclusions of E.S.G. Robinson, 'The Coins from the Ephesian Artemision Reconsidered', JHS 71 (1951), 165-6.
43 See C. Kraay, 'Hoards, Small Change and the Origin of Coinage', JHS 84 (1964), 76-91.
44 DK 22 B.90. On Herakleitos see below, chapter 6.
45 The independence of Aristotle's pupil Theophrastos (an important source for early thought in his 'Opinions of the Physicists') maintained by H. Diels (Doxographi Graeci) has been decisively questioned by J.B. McDiarmid, 'Theophrastus on the Presocratic Causes', HSCP 61 (1953), 85-156 (reprinted in D.J. Furley and R.E. Allen, eds, Studies in Presocratic Philosophy, I, 178-238).
46 H.F. Cherniss, Aristotle's Criticism of Presocratic Philosophy. Cherniss is sometimes extreme, especially when suggesting intellectual dishonesty as a charge to be answered by Aristotle (352, 'wilful misrepresentation').
47 Guthrie lists four possible charges against Aristotle (Aristotle as a Historian of Philosophy: some Prelim-inaries', JHS 77, Part I (1957), 35-41.

48 Cherniss, op.cit., xi.
49 I have discussed the whole question at length in Some Aspects of Traditional Opposites in Archaic Greek Thought (unpublished thesis accepted by the University of Birmingham for the degree of PhD 1972), 15-46.
50 Hekataios, FGH, 1A1. See L. Pearson, The Early Ionian Historians, 96-106.
51 See above, chapter 2, p.11.
52 Hdt. V, 36.
53 Hdt. V, 49,1. This may well be an example of Ionian cartography despised by Herodotos, IV, 36. See How and Wells, A Commentary on Herodotus, Oxford, 1912, note ad loc.
54 See A.B. Lloyd, Herodotus Book II: A Commentary, Leiden, 1975, I, 138.
55 See T.S. Brown, 'The Greek Sense of Time in History as Suggested by their Accounts of Egypt', Historia 11 (1962), 269-70.
56 Aristotle, 'Metaph.', A 3, 983b27; Homer, 'Iliad', XIV, 246.
57 The title is, conventionally, the first two words of the poem which mean in Akkadian 'when on high' (see E.A. Speiser in J.B. Pritchard, ed., Ancient Near Eastern Texts Relating to the Old Testament, 60).
58 See Speiser in ibid.
59 See H. Frankfort (ed.), Before Philosophy, 182-99. The following section relies very heavily upon this study of Near Eastern myth and speculation.
60 See especially an Egyptian creation myth, in which the earth arises out of Nun, the primordial waters which are beneath and around it. The waters sink to reveal a small hillock, which becomes the seat of life (Frankfort, op.cit., 59-62).
61 Frankfort, op.cit., 12-14.
62 See my discussion (ref.n.49 above), 53-6.
63 For a full translation, with textual comment, see Speiser in Pritchard, op.cit., 60-72. See also W.A. Heidel, The Babylonian Genesis. A pioneer work in the relating of Eastern myths to Greek thought was F.M. Cornford's unfinished Principium Sapientiae (see below, n.75).
64 A closer model for Hesiod is the more recently discovered 'Epic of Kumarbi' from the royal library of the Hittite emperors at Bogaz-köy, which includes the castration motif and the swallowing by Kumarbi of a stone as a substitute for his son (see R.D. Barnett, 'The Epic of Kumarbi and the Theogony of Hesiod', JHS 65 (1945), 100-1).

65   See P. Walcot, Hesiod and the Near East, 27-54.
66   Hesiod, 'Theogony', 116-28. Text of M.L. West. For
     a summary of textual problems see West's notes ad
     loc., and my discussion, op.cit., 67-8.
67   On this question see G.S. Kirk, The Structure and Aim
     of the Theogony (in Fondation Hardt, Geneva, 1962,
     63-94).
68   A meaning attested for the archaic period from Homer
     onwards, cf. LSJ, γίγνομαι II (normally, though not
     invariably, with predicate).
69   West, note to 119, takes Tartaros as a separate
     element (nominative plural) and not a continuation of
     the formulaic 118.
70   See Cornford, op.cit., 194 followed by KR, 26-32.
     Against this, and in favour of Chaos as a yawning
     space beneath the earth filled with murky darkness,
     see West, note to 116.
71   Various forms of the Separation myth have been
     collected by W. Staudacher, Die Trennung von Himmel
     und Erde, Darmstadt, 1968.
72   Hesiod, 'Theogony', 26-8.
73   Cf. Aristotle, 'Metaph.', 984a.
74   Guthrie, A History of Greek Philosophy, I,29.
75   The most distinguished of the former was J. Burnet,
     the first great British historian of the Presocratics;
     he made an unequivocal distinction between science
     and philosophy on the one hand, and myth and religion
     on the other, in the context of ancient Greece (see
     Greek Philosophy: Thales to Plato, London, 1924, 4).
     The Cambridge school's most famous representatives
     were Jane Harrison in the field of religion and F.M.
     Cornford in the field of philosophy. The latter
     leaned heavily, in his earlier work, upon Emile
     Durkheim (cf. From Religion to Philosophy, 1912) but
     later modified his views considerably in Principium
     Sapientiae, a work which pioneered the investigation
     of the mythical origins of Greek philsophy (see my
     critical summary, op.cit., 48-51).
76   Guthrie, A History of Greek Philosophy, I,26-8.
77   Kirk, The Nature of Greek Myths, 287ff. The final
     chapter of Kirk's book contains an acute analysis of
     the question of the transition from myth to
     philosophy.
78   E. Fränkel, Early Greek Poetry and Philosophy, 61.
79   Hesiod, 'Works and Days', 47-89.
80   'Od.', III, 255-75; 303-12. I, 298ff. (Orestes as
     model) and XXIV, 192-202 (Penelope contrasted with
     Klytemnestra).
81   The problem of Euripides' intentions is too big for

discussion here. Amid the very great controversy which surrounds the interpretation of many of his plays it can perhaps safely be said that the view of Euripides as a thoroughgoing sceptic now commands little adherence. See, amid a large bibliography, R.F. Willetts, 'Action and Character in the Ion of Euripides', JHS 93 (1973), 201-9.

82   Conclusively demonstrated by C.H. Kahn, Anaximander and the Origins of Greek Cosmology.

83   E.G. in 'De Caelo', III, 5, 303b10f.

84   Aristotle, 'Physics' III, 4, 203b6 (DK 12 A.15). For a summary of the problem of whether Aristotle correctly attributed divinity to the 'apeiron' see my discussion op.cit., 86-7. 'Enquirers into nature' is a clumsy translation of φυσιόλογοι, but it avoids the anachronism of 'physical scientists' or 'physicists'.

85   Aristotle, loc.cit.

86   Guthrie, A History of Greek Philosophy, I, 404.

87   See KR, 109 and esp. n.1(110).

88   Pritchard, op.cit., 61. M.C. Stokes ('Hesiodic and Milesian Cosmogonies', Phronesis 7 and 8 (1962-3), 1-37 and 1-34) attempts to relate Hesiodic Tartaros ('Theogony', 736ff. 807-14) to the 'apeiron' of Anaximander and the 'air' of Anaximenes.

89   Burnet, Greek Philosophy: Thales to Plato, 60-1. But see further H.B. Gottschalk, 'Anaximander's Apeiron', Phronesis 10 (1965), 37-53.

90   P. Seligman, The Apeiron of Anaximander.

91   DK 12 A.10.

92   DK 12 A.11(4).

93   KR, 132.

94   Cornford, Principium Sapientiae, 163.

95   The abstracts θερμότης and ψυχρότης, etc. (heat and cold) can be found in the Hippocratic 'On Ancient Medicine', chapter XVI, but do not occur in early Presocratic texts.

96   Aristotle, 'Physics', A 4, 187a20ff.

97   Ibid.

98   A thorny and inconclusive question; see my discussion, op.cit., 102.

99   Aetius II, 20,1 (KR, 135).

100   See KR, 134 for texts.

101   Aristotle, 'De Caelo', III, 295b10.

102   It need hardly be explained that the word 'primitive' is here devoid of any association of 'underdeveloped' or 'crude'. The word is used here more in the sense frequently applied to certain periods of art (see A.R. Burn, The Lyric Age of Greece, 11, for an elucidation in a not dissimilar context).

103   DK 12 B.1.
104   See my detailed summary of the problems, philological
      and philosophical, op.cit., 90-5.
105   For the full context, see DK 12 A.9.
106   For the first point see Burnet, op.cit., 53f.,
      followed by KR, 117f. contra Cornford, 'Innumerable
      worlds in Presocratic Cosmogony', CQ 28 (1934), 11,
      n.2. On the second point it has been pointed out
      that while the first clause appears to refer to the
      'apeiron', the second clause obviously doesn't,
      making the logical connection (διδόναι γάρ...)
      difficult to understand. On this, see G.S. Kirk,
      'Some Problems in Anaximander', CQ n.s.5 (1955),
      32-8.
107   See DK 22 B.126.
108   This is now the generally accepted interpretation.
      Another interpretation, originating from Diels (and
      based upon a text without the restoration of ἀλλήλοις
      (to each other)) sees the mutual injustice as
      cumulative rather than regulative, resulting in an
      ultimate return to the ἄπειρον (see G. Vlastos,
      'Equality and Justice in Early Greek Cosmologies',
      CP 42 (1947), 172). Part of the motivation for this
      interpretation, the attempt to reconcile both clauses
      of the fragment to each other, does not now seem
      compelling. In any case, as Kirk ('Some Problems',
      34) points out, it is hard to see how the dissolution
      of the world could square with the cycle of mutual
      reparation (see further my discussion, op.cit., 92-5).
109   The idea of Anaximander's philosophy as a solution to
      a problem raised by earlier myth is explored (and
      perhaps made too explicit) by Seligman, op.cit.
110   See R. Radcliffe-Brown, 'The Comparative Method in
      Social Anthropology', Journal of the Royal
      Anthropological Institute, 81 (1951), 21, who makes
      an explicit connection between the 'polar unity' of
      dualist organisations and some characteristics of
      early Greek polarity. Despite shortcomings in method
      (see my survey of a wide variety of anthropological
      examples and reservations on method, op.cit., 50-6)
      the remarkable similarity in these phenomena is of
      importance, provided the analogy is not taken too
      far. G.E.R. Lloyd (Polarity and Analogy, 31ff.)
      quotes the anthropological evidence of the polarity
      of dualist classifications as a 'striking reminis-
      cence' of Greek ideas, but neglects just that aspect
      of dynamism and unity in antagonism emphasised by his
      anthropological sources (cf. my criticisms, op.cit.,
      51-3).

111   Fr. 36,3 (Edmonds, Elegy and Iambus, I, 148).
112   This is clear in Solon, e.g. fr. 12 (Edmonds, op.cit.,
      124-5) where the sea, not stirred by winds, πάντων
      ἐστι δικαιοτάτη (is the justest of all things). The
      explicit separation of the physical and moral order
      was achieved in the fifth-century BC debates on the
      relative status of φύσις (nature) and νόμος (law);
      associated with the Sophists.
113   Vlastos, op.cit., 166-7.
114   G.D. Thomson, Studies in Ancient Greek Society II;
      The First Philosophers, 231.
115   Alkmaion DK 24 B.4. Vlastos, op.cit., 173ff., for
      the theory. See my more detailed historical
      objections (op.cit., 101-4).
116   Kahn, op.cit., 168-9. It is hard to know how, with
      the loss of almost all texts, Kahn can conjecture
      this.
117   W. Jaeger, The Theology of the Early Greek Philo-
      sophers, 34.
118   The title Περὶ φύσεως may be a later, and conventional
      label (although by the time of Gorgias (who wrote a
      work Περὶ τοῦ μὴ ὄντος ἢ περὶ φύσεως (on the non-
      existent or on nature)) the element of parody in the
      title seems to suggest that it was applied generally
      to scientific works).
119   Aristotle ('Meteorologica', B 3, 357a24) objects to a
      description of sea as the 'sweat of the earth', as
      'not advancing our knowledge of nature in any way'.
120   B. Snell ('Die Ausdrücke für den Begriff des Wissens
      in der vor-Platonischen Philosophie', Philologische
      Untersuchungen, 29, 8) thinks that verse-writers
      among the older Presocratics chose their medium
      despite the fact that the time had long passed when
      it would have been necessary to render an idea of
      literary significance in verse-form. How, in the
      absence of a philosophical prose tradition of any
      significance before the mid-fifth century BC, can
      Snell possibly know this?
121   DK 28 B.1. See L. Tarán, Parmenides, Princeton,
      1965, 18-31.
122   On the question of poetry and philosophy, see further
      chapter 6.
123   Cf. KR, 159.
124   See the admirable account in KR, 48-72.
125   DK 7 B.2 (col.1).
126   Jacoby, FGH, I (Hekataios von Milet) T.I.
127   These are conveniently collected in FGH, T.16-20.
128   See LSJ, 'πεζός' II (compare the dates of authors in
      1 and 2) and III,2.

129   Strabo I, 2,6. See also E. Norden, Die antike
      Kunstprosa, I, 30ff.
130   Plato, 'Sophist', 242D. On the whole question of
      poetry and prose in early Greece, see E. Zarnke,
      Über die Entstehung der griechischen Literatur-
      sprachen.
131   J.D. Denniston, Greek Prose Style, 2.

CHAPTER 6 XENOPHANES AND HERAKLEITOS: THE INTERACTION OF
LANGUAGE AND THOUGHT

1   Xenophanes DK 21 B.7, 3-5.
2   The vast and complicated historical problems con-
    nected with the history of Orphism and the early
    doctrines of Pythagoras are, thankfully, not our
    immediate concern here. On the whole question, see
    W.K.C. Guthrie, A History of Greek Philosophy I,
    148ff.
3   According to Aristoxenos (quoted by Porph. 'VP',9)
    DK 14.8.
4   See E.L. Minar, Early Pythagorean Politics in
    Practice and Theory, Baltimore, 1942.
5   DK 21 B.8.
6   So KR, 163. There is also a problem in the trans-
    lation of φροντίδ'. The majority of translations
    prefer the less precise 'worry' or 'care' (Freeman,
    Guthrie, DK, etc.) but there is no compelling argu-
    ment against KR since the word has clear currency as
    'thought','meditation' in the Presocratics (see DK
    Register φροντίς) which becomes canonical in the
    ridicule of Aristophanes' 'Clouds', ℓℓ.94, 233, etc.
7   Diogenes Laertius, IX, 18.
8   This tradition seems to stem from Plato, 'Sophist',
    242D (DK 21 A.29) and was based upon the superficial
    similarity between Xenophanes' 'one god' (see below,
    p.139) and Parmenides' Sphere of Being (see KR, 165-
    6).
9   It is important not to read too much back into
    Xenophanes from later and more formal theories of
    scepticism; see J.H. Lesher, 'Xenophanes' Scepticism',
    Phronesis 23 (1978), 1-21. See also below, p.141.
10 Athenaios XII, 526b.
11 DK 21 B.2.
12 B.11. See also B.12, which repeats the criticism.
13 Χρηστός is difficult to render into English. It is
    regularly used, from the fifth century BC onwards as
    the opposite of κακός (bad, evil) in a moral sense.
    See LSJ, 'Χρηστός' I, 2.

14   B.1,14.
15   B.15.
16   B.16.
17   Taken as a separate poem in DK (frs 23-41). On the
     genuineness of the title in archaic thought in
     general, see chapter 5, n.118.
18   B.23.
19   B.24.
20   B.25.
21   B.26.
22   DL IX, 18.
23   E.A. Havelock in a suggestive article, 'Pre-literacy
     and the Presocratics', BICS 13 (1966), 44-67 sees
     Xenophanes (51-3) as still strongly influenced by the
     'thought forms' and style of oral epic.
24   Havelock (op.cit., 53) seems to be suggesting that
     Xenophanes did recite these verses at symposia!
25   Guthrie (op.cit., 375 and n.2) seems to make rather
     heavy weather of the contradiction. To suggest that
     Xenophanes was guilty of 'surprising carelessness' is
     to ignore the problems of expression which undoubt-
     edly faced him.
26   Homer, 'Il.', IX, 600; XXII, 235 (cf. KR, 171, n.2).
27   The position is complicated by the existence of a
     treatise 'On Melissus, Xenophanes and Gorgias' (MXG)
     a pseudo-Aristotelian work written some time after
     the first century BC (DK 21 A.28), giving an account
     of Xenophanes' thought which presumes a familiarity
     with later Eleatic argument - an obvious historical
     anachronism.
28   KR, 171.
29   Guthrie, op.cit., 376ff.
30   Ibid., 382.
31   Cf. Guthrie, op.cit., 381-3.
32   Hence KR, 'One god' implies the more restricted
     interpretation offered there; likewise Guthrie's 'God
     is one' might be thought to anticipate his more
     radical interpretation (op.cit., 374).
33   KR pertinently remarks that Aristotle's puzzlement
     over Xenophanes' god ('Metaph.', A 5, 986b18ff.) and
     especially his complaint that he οὐδὲν διεσαφήνισεν
     (made nothing clear) would not accord well with a
     clear elaboration of his views (171).
34   B.34.
35   Lesher (op.cit., 13-16) gives B.34 a much more
     precise reference. He thinks that Xenophanes is
     speaking against divine revelation implied in
     divination, augury, etc., and that τὸ σαφές =
     'revealed truth'. This, he feels, may be related to

Xenophanes' general position with regard to
traditional religious practices.

36 An apparent contradiction of monotheism, but not to
be taken too seriously; Xenophanes did not jettison
entirely the traditional thought forms of his age,
any more than did Parmenides (here the 'illogicality'
becomes more acute).

37 For texts and comment, see KR, 141-2.

38 B.27. For the theory, see KR, 177-8.

39 See Guthrie, op.cit., 390-4.

40 For Hekataios, see chapter 5, pp.110-4.

41 Nietzsche mentions Herakleitos with enthusiasm in
The Birth of Tragedy (see W. Kaufmann, Basic Writings
of Nietzsche, 729). This high regard can also be
found in Heidegger.

42 G.S. Kirk, in Heraclitus: The Cosmic Fragments, xiv.

43 See [Aristotle], 'De Mundo', 396b20.

44 Hdt. VI, 16,2. Earlier, the Ephesians had furnished
guides for the Athenians and Eretrians on their
journey inland to burn Sardis (Hdt. V, 100). The
fact that the fleet was left in Ephesian territory
seems to suggest friendly neutrality.

45 See G.L Huxley, The Early Ionians, 33. The exact
date for Ephesos is not known - its dating to the
sixth century BC is merely a conjecture.

46 For the fragments of Hipponax, see A.D. Knox, ed. and
trans. Herodes, Cercidas and the Greek Choliambic
Poets, London, 1924 , 14-63.

47 Hermodoros is said to have assisted the Romans in the
drawing up of the Twelve Tables, see Pliny, 'NH',
XXIV, 21.

48 DK 22 B.121. Attempts to date Herakleitos' philosophical activity after 479 BC, on the grounds that
this fragment implies self-government for the
Ephesians, founder on two counts: first, from the
fragment it is not clear what political status the
Ephesians enjoyed, and second, internal self-
government would not have been inconsistent with
Persian rule, especially since Ephesos may have been
friendly. Moreover, Herodotos explicitly tells us
that, after the Ionian Revolt, Mardonios ejected
Ionian despots and set up democratic institutions
(Hdt. VI, 43). Perhaps this is what Herakleitos was
complaining about! (See Kirk, op.cit., 1.)

49 DL, IX, 1ff. See Kirk, op.cit., 3ff. M.L. West's
attempt to rehabilitate late biography of
Herakleitos (Early Greek Philosophy and the Orient,
196-201) is not convincing.

50 Strabo XIV, 1,3.

51 B.29.

52 B.1.

53 The relation of ἀεί (always) in the first line may be either forwards, backwards or deliberately ambivalent (cf. Kirk, op.cit., 34 and n.1, who dismisses the idea of deliberate ambivalence, on not very convincing grounds).

54 B.2.

55 B.34.

56 B.40.

57 Aristotle, 'Rhet.', Γ 5, 1407b14 (DK A.4).

58 DL IX,6 (DK A.1).

59 DL II,22 (DK A.4).

60 Plato, 'Theaetetus', 179e-180b.

61 B.67. This fragment will be discussed further below, p.157. On Herakleitos' style, see S. Lilja, On the Style of the Earliest Greek Prose, 45-9, 65-9 and 93-8.

62 B.56.

63 See H.W. Parke, The Delphic Oracle, II (The Oracular Responses), Oxford, 1956.

64 Ibid., 24.

65 Apollodoros III,5.7ff.

66 Sophokles, 'OT', ℓℓ.711ff.

67 See Kirk, op.cit., 7.

68 For Aristotle see ref. above, n.57, on which Guthrie (op.cit., 406ff.) seems to base his argument for a formal book.

69 Kirk, op.cit., 8.

70 Havelock, op.cit., 54.

71 See my article, 'Heraclitus and the Identity of Opposites', Phronesis 21 (1976), 89-114. Much of the argument of the present chapter originated in ideas presented in this article in a more compressed form.

72 DL IX 6,8.

73 See Guthrie's extensive analysis (op.cit., 421-4).

74 But not identified, as M.L. West, op.cit., 124-30 unconvincingly argues. All attempts to banish the Logos as a principle from Herakleitos founder on B.50 where he urges people to listen not to him ἀλλὰ τοῦ λόγου (but to the Logos). J. Barnes, The Presocratic Philosophers, I, 59, n.7, follows West without stating any further arguments against the traditional view.

75 See W.J. Verdenius, 'Notes on the Presocratics', Mnemosyne 13 (1947), 277. See also my summary of the question, op.cit., 96-7.

76 Kirk, op.cit., 39.

77 See also B.72.

78 See B.1, last sentence (p.146 above).
79 The translation of P. Wheelwright (Heraclitus, Princeton, 1959, 83) which maintains the pun.
80 B.28, first sentence.
81 B.18.
82 See my discussion with bibliography, op.cit., 99-100.
83 See my discussion of sacred and profane in Some Aspects of Traditional Opposites in Archaic Greek Thought (PhD thesis, Birmingham, 1972), 52-3, with full bibliography.
84 This does not exhaust the significance of the fragment (see further ref. at n.82 above).
85 B.123 and 54.
86 In Agnostos Theos, Leipzig, 1913.
87 E. Norden, Die Antike Kunstprosa, I, 18-19.
88 DK 90.
89 Notably in the Just and Unjust Arguments (Aristophanes, 'Clouds', ℓℓ. 889ff.).
90 Plato, 'Apology', 18b9, etc.
91 Aristotle, 'De Soph.El.', 165b30ff. and 166a7ff.
92 Aristotle, 'Rhet.', 1404b2.
93 Aristotle, 'De Soph.El.', 165a11ff.
94 See my summary, in Some Aspects..., 1-10 and chapters 4,5,7 and 8 passim.
95 B.42 commenting, doubtless on a line such as 'Il.', XVIII,107 (DK A.22).
96 Or, reading παλύντονος, 'backward-stretched'.
97 B.51. For details of text and interpretation see Kirk, op.cit., 203-21.
98 B.60.
99 B.61.
100 B.57. Usually seen as a criticism of 'Theogony', 123ff. where Day is said to be born from Night.
101 B.5 (first half).
102 See Guthrie, op.cit., 443, M. Marcovich, 'Herakleitos', RE suppl.10, cols 286f. Kirk, op.cit. 94.
103 If we assume, following K. Reinhardt (supported by Kirk, op.cit., 109-12), 'Heraklits Lehre vom Feuer', Hermes 77 (1942) 16ff., that the cosmological interpretation derived from Theophrastos (DL IX, 8-9) is incorrect, contra G. Vlastos, 'Equality and Justice in Early Greek Cosmologies', CP 42 (1947), 165. This assumption is by no means certain.
104 Lack of space compels me to assert this somewhat dogmatically; for arguments, see my discussion, including treatment of similar fragments B.59 and 103 (Phronesis, 1976, 102-3).
105 Textual difficulties make the exact meaning

uncertain; Herakleitos could be saying that doctors complain that they do not receive a worthy fee for what they do - see my summary in ibid., 104 n.70.

106 Ibid., 105.

107 A pun on ὁμολογεῖν (to agree) is probably intended, since the word could be seen to mean 'bring the Logos into conformity'.

108 B.50.

109 B.80.

110 The question of whether Herakleitos proposed a 'Flusslehre' is still controversial and centres around the question of whether Plato correctly derived his attribution of the flux doctrine to Herakleitos from the original fragments or from the more extreme position of Kratylos, one of his followers (see G.S. Kirk, 'The Problem of Cratylus', AJP 72 (1951), 239ff., opposed by G. Vlastos, AJP 76 (1955), 338ff.).

111 Guthrie, 452, n.1. The question is too detailed to be taken very far here.

112 B.30.

113 See e.g. Aristotle, 'Metaph.', A.984a7-8.

114 DK 22B.64.

115 Kirk has shown conclusively (Heraclitus: The Cosmic Fragments, 335-8) that Herakleitos contains no ecpyrosis (periodic consumption of the world by fire and its subsequent regeneration). For subsequent argument see R. Mondolfo, 'The Evidence of Plato and Aristotle Relating to the Ekpyrosis in Heraclitus', Phronesis 3 (1958), 75-82, and Kirk's reply ('Ecpyrosis in Heraclitus: some comments', Phronesis 4 (1959), 73-6).

116 See my fuller discussion, in Phronesis, 1976, 108-9.

117 Although this is not, as Vlastos seems to suppose ('Equality and Justice in Early Greek Cosmologies', CP 42 (1947), 165) to reduce the identity of opposites to a merely cosmological doctrine.

118 My view on this point is fundamentally opposed to that of Kirk, who feels strongly that a 'personal criterion' enters into Herakleitos' opposites doctrine, and that the human view of things as opposed is superficial in contrast to the underlying unity which is more important (Kirk, op.cit., e.g. 176-9). The question is a complicated one which I have examined in detail elsewhere (Phronesis, 1976, 102-9). It suffices to say here that: (1) In no fragment does Herakleitos introduce human experience as a determining factor in the recognition of the identity of opposites; this is presented as an

objective fact which humans merely observe. (2) Far
from emphasising unity over diversity, Herakleitos
(B.10) seems to be stating the equal importance of
either, and, on occasions (e.g. B.80) stresses the
latter.

119   See e.g. M.L. West, op.cit., 131-6. It is hardly
coincidence that Herakleitos' meteorology seems less
coherent than that of the Milesians.

120   DL (quoting Diodotos) IX,12, says that one of the
titles of Herakleitos' book was ἀκριβὲς οἰάκισμα πρὸς
σταθμὴν βίου (a genuine rudder for the rule of life).

121   A pun on the similarity between the Greek for 'with
intelligence' and 'common' is not translatable.

122   B.114.

123   B.45.

124   See DK 13 B.2, although the genuineness of the
macrocosm/microcosm argument is not universally
accepted (cf. Kirk, op.cit., 312).

125   B.107. See also B.101: ἐδιζησάμην ἐμεωυτόν (I
searched myself).

126   B.36.

127   B.118.

128   B.103.

129   Almost universally accepted as younger, despite some
attempts (notably K. Reinhardt, Parmenides und die
Geschichte der griechischen Philosophie, 2nd edn,
Frankfurt, 1959) toereverse the order of thinkers.

130   That this is a serious problem would be denied by
those who see the Proem of Parmenides' 'Way of Truth'
(DK 28 B.1) as a literary device (e.g. L. Tarán,
Parmenides, Princeton, 1965, p.31), but see the
remarks of Guthrie, op.cit., II, 10-13.

131   On the survival of Ionian philosophical texts, see
chapter 7, p.175.

132   See further, chapter 7, pp.172f.

133   C.H. Kahn, Anaximander and the Origins of Greek
Cosmology, pp.3ff.

134   It is also only fair to point out that very little
systematic work has been attempted in this enormously
difficult field. Until the immense historical
problems have been more carefully worked out, any
conclusions are bound to be highly speculative.

CHAPTER 7 THE AFTERMATH: THE IONIAN LEGACY TO HELLENISM

1   Hdt. VI,26.2.

2   See chapter 6, p.144 for the incident.

3   Hdt. VI,17.

4   Ibid., 13-14.
5   Ibid., 25,2.
6   Ibid., 22ff.
7   Hdt. V,124,1.
8   Aristagoras was killed before Lade (Hdt. V,126,2) and Histiaios after (VI,30).
9   Hdt. VI,43,3.
10 See the scepticism of How and Wells, A Commentary on Herodotus, Oxford, 1912, II, 80, note ad loc.
11 See J.M. Cook, 'The Problem of Classical Ionia', PCPS 7 (1961), 9.
12 See B. Merritt and T. Wade-Gery, The Athenian Tribute Lists, Cambridge, Mass., 1939-53, I, 342-3 and R. Meiggs, The Athenian Empire, 270.
13 M.N. Tod, (Greek Historical Inscriptions, I, 68) remarks on the smallness of the fines imposed and of rewards offered in an inscription concerning political expulsions from Miletos c.450 BC.
14 See chapter 2, p.33 and n.130.
15 Hdt. VI,42,2.
16 Amid a large bibliography, see How and Wells, note on Hdt. VI, 42,2, with a summary of older views; A.W. Gomme, CQ 20 (1926), 97-8; J.M. Cook, op.cit.; Meiggs, op.cit., 273; O. Murray, 'Ο Ἀρχαῖος Δασμός', Historia, 15 (1966), 142-56.
17 See R. Meiggs and D.M. Lewis, A Selection of Greek Historical Inscriptions, 89-94.
18 See A.J. Earp, 'Athens and Miletus c.450 B.C.', Phoenix 8 (1954), 142-7; J. Barron, 'Milesian Politics and Athenian Propaganda c.460-440 B.C.', JHS 82 (1962), 1-6; Meiggs, op.cit., app.15, 562-5.
19 Thuk. I,115,2 -117,3. Meiggs and Lewis, op.cit., 151-4;
20 See R. Meiggs, 'The Dating of Fifth-Century Attic Inscriptions', JHS 86 (1966), 86-98.
21 Cf. Thuk. I, 19 on the conversion by the Athenians of the allied naval contribution to the league into a financial one.
22 Hdt. V,97,2.
23 The literary record extends back to Solon, who refers to Attica as the πρεσβυτάτην ... γαῖαν Ἰαονίας (Edmonds, Elegy and Iambus, 2 vols, London, 1931, I, 142 (fr.28a)).
24 Hdt. IX,106,3.
25 Thuk. I,95.
26 See Barron, op.cit., 6.
27 Hdt. VI,21,2.
28 Hdt. I,143,3. See the studied insult of the Athenians in Aristophanes, 'Acharnians', ℓ.104.

29   The Persians knew all Greeks as 'Yauna', but this does
     not entirely explain Aeschylus' purpose here.
30   See also ℓℓ.563, 950-1, 1011. See the notes of A.J.
     Podlecki in his translation of the play in the
     Prentice Hall Greek drama series and his The Political
     Background of Aeschylean Tragedy, 17-21.
31   Hdt. VIII,10,2-3.
32   Ibid., 90;3.
33   Hdt. I,170.
34   Hdt. VI,19,2.
35   Made by Hekataios (I,36,3-4).
36   Hdt. IV,142.
37   Aristophanes, 'Ecclesiazusae', ℓ.883. Later in the
     same play (ℓℓ.918ff.) the 'Ionian manner' of love
     indicates perversion (see the edition of R.G. Ussher,
     note ad loc.).
38   Athenaios, 620e.
39   Ibid., 524f-526d. For the association of Ionia with
     'soft' musical modes, see C.M. Bowra, Greek Lyric
     Poetry, 269. Ionic poetic metre was early connected
     with a plaintive, languishing effect.
40   Hdt. IX,122,3.
41   Plutarch, 'Pericles', XXIV,1.
42   Ibid.,6; Aristophanes, 'Acharnians', ℓℓ.526ff. See
     further 'Aspasia' (1), RE II, 2 cols 1716-22.
43   See G.L. Huxley, 'Ion of Chios', GRBS, 6 (1965), 29-
     46.
44   See R.E. Wycherley, How the Greeks Built Cities, 46ff.
45   Strabo XIV,2,9. For scepticism concerning the first
     of these achievements see A. Burns, 'Hippodamus and
     the Planned City', Historia 25 (1976), 414-28.
46   Aristotle, 'Pol.', II,8,1267b30ff.
47   Ibid., b.22ff.
48   DL IX,28.
49   For chronological difficulties concerning Anaxagoras'
     life, see W.K.C. Guthrie, A History of Greek Philo-
     sophy, II,322-3.
50   See the remarks of K.J. Dover in the Introduction to
     his edition of the play, lvi.
51   See Guthrie's valuable chapter, op.cit., II, ch.6,
     345-54.
52   DK 59 B.11. For the considerable controversy
     surrounding this fragment, see my summary and
     discussion with bibliography, Some Aspects of
     Traditional Opposites in Archaic Greek Thought (PhD
     thesis, Birmingham, 1972), 206-12.
53   Aristotle, 'Metaph.', A.985a18ff.
54   See the reservations about the authenticity of DK 13
     B.2 in KR, 158-62.

55 Diogenes, in his choice of air as the primary
    substance, is probably one of the chief objects of
    Aristophanes' satire in the 'Clouds', ℓℓ.227ff., along
    with Anaxagoras and others.
56 See Guthrie, op.cit., II, 339 and n.2.
57 DK 80 B.1.
58 Plato, 'Theaetetus', 179d-180c. It is hardly
    necessary to mention the use made by Plato of a
    version of Herakleiteanism in the development of his
    own epistemology.
59 Thuk. VIII,5,5.
60 Xenophon, 'Hell.', II,2,6. For the decrees, see
    Meiggs and Lewis, op.cit., 283-7 and Tod, op.cit., II,
    1-4.
61 Euripides, 'Bacchae', ℓℓ.17-19.
62 See R. Browning, Medieval and Modern Greek, London,
    1969, 27ff. It was in the fourth century BC also that
    Hellenism gradually began to extend to the interior of
    Asia Minor.
63 G.L. Huxley, The Early Ionians, 155.

Bibliography

AKURGAL, E., Die Kunst Anatoliens von Homer bis Alexander, Berlin, 1961.

AKURGAL, E., 'The Early Period and the Golden Age of Ionia', AJA 66 (1962), 369-79 (pls 96-103).

AKURGAL, E., The Birth of Greek Art: the Mediterranean and the Near East, London, 1968.

AKURGAL, E., Ancient Civilisations and Ruins of Turkey, Istanbul, 1970.

BALDRY, H.C., 'Embryological Analogies in Presocratic Cosmogony, CQ 26 (1932), 27-34.

BARNES, J., The Presocratic Philosophers (The Arguments of the Philosophers Series, ed. T. Honderich), 2 vols, London, 1979.

BARNETT, R.D., 'The Epic of Kumarbi and the Theogony of Hesiod', JHS 65 (1945), 100.

BARNETT, R.D., 'Early Greek and Oriental Ivories', JHS 68 (1948), 1-25.

BARRON, J.P., 'Milesian Politics and Athenian Propaganda c.460-440 B.C.', JHS 82 (1962), 1-6.

BARRON, J.P., 'The Sixth-Century Tyranny at Samos', CQ n.s.14 (1964), 210-29.

BARRON, J.P., 'Religious Propaganda of the Delian League', JHS 84 (1964), 35-48.

BEAN, G.E., Aegean Turkey: an Archaeological Guide, London, 1966.

BEAZLEY, J. and ASHMOLE, B., Greek Sculpture and Painting to the End of the Hellenistic Period, reprint, Cambridge, 1966.

BECHTEL, F., Die griechische Dialekte, vol. III, Berlin, 1924.

BEYE, C.R., The Iliad, the Odyssey and the Epic Tradition, London, 1968.

BILABEL, F., Die ionishche Kolonisation (Philologus Supplementband 14) Leipzig, 1921.

BOARDMAN, J., 'A Greek Vase from Egypt', JHS 78 (1958),
4-12.
BOARDMAN, J., 'Chian and Early Ionic Architecture',
Antiquaries' Journal 39 (1959), 170-218.
BOARDMAN, J., 'Greek Archaeology on the shores of the
Black Sea', JHS Arch. Reports, 1962-3, 34-51.
BOARDMAN, J., The Greeks Overseas, London, 1964.
BOARDMAN, J., Pre-Classical: From Crete to Archaic Greece,
London, 1967.
BOARDMAN, J., Greek Sculpture: The Archaic Period, London,
1978.
BOWRA, C.M., Tradition and Design in the Iliad, Oxford,
1930.
BOWRA, C.M., Early Greek Elegists, Cambridge, Mass., 1938.
BOWRA, C.M., 'Xenophanes Fr.3', CQ 35 (1941), 119-26.
BOWRA, C.M., Heroic Poetry, London, 1952.
BOWRA, C.M., 'Asius and the Old-fashioned Samians', Hermes
85 (1957), 391-401.
BOWRA, C.M., 'Homeric Epithets for Troy', JHS 80 (1960),
16-23.
BOWRA, C.M., Greek Lyric Poetry, 2nd edn, Oxford, 1961.
BOWRA, C.M., Homer, London, 1972.
BROADHEAD, H.D., The Persae of Aeschylus, ed. and comm.,
Cambridge, 1960.
BROWN, T.S., The Greek Sense of Time in History as
Suggested by their Accounts of Egypt, Historia 11 (1962),
257-70.
BUCK, C.D., The Greek Dialects, 2nd edn, Chicago, 1955.
BURN, A.R., The Lyric Age of Greece, London, 1960.
BURN, A.R., Persia and the Greeks, London, 1962.
BURNET, J., Early Greek Philosophy, 4th edn, London, 1948.
BURNS, A., 'Hippodamus and the Planned City', Historia 25
(1976), 414-28.
BURY, J.B., The Ancient Greek Historians, London, 1909.
BUSCHOR, E., Altsamische Standbilder, Berlin, 1934-.
CAMPBELL, D.A., Greek Lyric Poetry: A Selection, London,
1967.
CAMPBELL, D.A., 'Flutes and Elegiac Couplets', JHS 84
(1964), 63-8.
CASKEY, J.L. 'The Trojan War' (with M.I. Finley, G.S. Kirk
and D.L. Page), JHS 84 (1964), 1-20.
CASSOLA, F., La Ionia nel mondo miceneo, Naples, 1957.
CHADWICK, J., 'The Greek Dialects and Greek Prehistory',
Greece and Rome, 2nd series 3 (1956) 38-50. (Reprinted in
The Language and Background of Homer, ed. G.S. Kirk, 106-
18.)
CHADWICK, J., The Prehistory of the Greek Language, CAH
rev.edn, II, 1963, ch.39.
CHAPMAN, G.A.H., 'Herodotus and Histiaeus' Role in the

Ionian Revolt', Historia 21 (1972), 546-68.

CHAYTOR, H.J., From Script to Print. An Introduction to Medieval Vernacular Literature, 2nd edn, Cambridge, 1950.

CHERNISS, H.F., Aristotle's Criticism of Presocratic Philosophy, Baltimore, 1935.

COLDSTREAM, J.N., Geometric Pottery, London, 1968.

COLDSTREAM, J.N., 'Hero Cults in the Age of Homer', JHS 96 (1976), 8-17.

COLDSTREAM, J.N., Geometric Greece, London, 1977.

COMBELLACK, F.M., 'Milman Parry and Homeric Artistry', Comparative Literature 11 (1959), 193-208.

COOK, J.M., 'Excavations at Old Smyrna' in JHS 67 (1947), 41-3; 70 (1950), 10-13; 71 (1951), 247-9; 72 (1952), 104-7; 73 (1953), 124-5.

COOK, J.M., 'Archaeology in Western Asia Minor', JHS Arch. Reports, 1959-60, 39-50; 1964-5 (with D.J. Blackman) 43-53; 1970-1 (with D.J. Blackman) 38-46.

COOK, J.M., 'The 'palai' Names', Historia 4 (1955), 40-5.

COOK, J.M., 'Old Smyrna: 1948-51', ABSA 53-4 (1958-9), 1-34.

COOK, J.M., 'The Problem of Classical Ionia', PCPS 7 (1961), 9-18.

COOK, J.M., 'Some Sites of the Milesian Territory', ABSA 56 (1961), 90-101.

COOK, J.M., The Greeks in Ionia and the East, London, 1962.

COOK, J.M., 'Old Smyrna: Ionic Black-Figure and other Sixth-Century Figured Wares', ABSA 60 (1965), 114-42.

COOK, J.M., 'Greek Settlement in the Eastern Aegean and Asia Minor', CAH 3, II(2), 1975, 773-804.

COOK, R.M., 'Fikellura Pottery', ABSA 34 (1936), 1-98.

COOK, R.M., 'Ionia and Greece in the Eighth and Seventh Centuries B.C.', JHS 66 (1946), 67-98.

COOK, R.M., Corpus Vasorum Antiquorum, BM Fasc.VIII (1954) (East Greek Pottery).

COOK, R.M., 'Origins of Greek Sculpture', JHS 87 (1967), 24-32.

COOK, R.M., Greek Painted Pottery, 2nd edn, London, 1972.

CORNFORD, F.M., Before and After Socrates, Cambridge, 1932.

CORNFORD, F.M., 'Innumerable Worlds in Presocratic Cosmogony', CQ 28 (1934), 1-16.

CORNFORD, F.M. The Unwritten Philosophy and other Essays (ed. W.K.C. Guthrie), Cambridge, 1950.

CORNFORD, F.M., Principium Sapientiae: The Origins of Greek Philosophical Thought (ed. W.K.C. Guthrie), Cambridge, 1952.

CROIX, G.E.M.de Ste, The Origins of the Peloponnesian War, London, 1972.

DAVISON, J.A., 'Pisistratus and Homer', TAPA 86 (1955), 1-21.

DAVISON, J.A., 'Literature and Literacy in Ancient Greece', Phoenix 16 (1962), 141-56; 219-33.

DEICHGRÄBER, K., 'Hymnische Elemente in der philosophischen Prosa der Vorsokratiker', Philologus 88 (1933), 347-61.

DEICHGRÄBER, K., 'Rhythmische Elemente im Logos des Heraklit', Akademie der Wissenschaften und der Literatur, Mainz (1962), 479-553.

DENNISTON, J.D., Greek Prose Style, ed. H. Lloyd Jones, Oxford, 1965.

DESBOROUGH, V.R.d'A., Protogeometric Pottery, Oxford, 1952.

DESBOROUGH, V.R.d'A., The Last Mycenaeans and their Successors, Oxford, 1964.

DESBOROUGH, V.R.d'A., The Greek Dark Ages, London, 1972.

DICKS, D.R., 'Solstices, Equinoxes and the Presocratics', JHS 86 (1966), 26-40.

DIELS, H. and KRANZ, W., Die Fragmente der Vorsokratiker, 10th imp., Berlin, 1961.

DIMOCK, G.E., 'From Homer to Novi Pazar and Back', Arion, 2 (1963), 40-57.

DINSMOOR, W.B., The Architecture of Ancient Greece, rev. edn, New York, 1970.

DOVER, K.J., 'The Poetry of Archilochus' in 'Archiloque' (Entretiens Hardt 10) Geneva, 1964, 193ff.

DREWS, R., The Greek Accounts of Eastern History, Publications of the Centre for Hellenic Studies, Washington, 1973.

DREWS, R., 'The Earliest Greek Settlements on the Black Sea', JHS 96 (1976), 18-31.

DUNBABIN, T.J., The Greeks and their Eastern Neighbours (JHS Suppl.8), 1957.

DUNHAM, A.G., The History of Miletus, London, 1915.

EARP, A.J., 'Athens and Miletus c.450 B.C.', Phoenix 8 (1954), 142-7.

EISENSTADT, M., 'Xenophanes' Proposed Reform of Greek Religion', Hermes 102 (1974), 142-50.

EVANS, J.A.S., 'Herodotus and the Ionian Revolt', Historia 25 (1976), 31-7.

FARRINGTON, B., Greek Science: Its Meaning for Us, rev. edn, London, 1961.

FENIK, B., Typical Battle Scenes in the Iliad (Hermes Einzelschriften 21), Wiesbaden, 1968.

FINLEY, M.I., The World of Odysseus, 2nd edn, London, 1977.

FINLEY, M.I., The Trojan War (see under J.L. Caskey).

FINLEY, M.I., Early Greece: the Bronze and Archaic Ages,

London, 1970.

FRÄNKEL, H., Die homerischen Gleichnisse, 2nd edn,
Göttingen, 1921.

FRÄNKEL, H., 'A Thought Pattern in Heraclitus', AJP 59
(1938), 309-37.

FRÄNKEL, H., 'Heraclitus on God and the Phenomenal World',
TAPA 69 (1938), 230-43.

FRÄNKEL, H., Wege und Formen frühgriechischen Denkens, 2nd
edn, Munich, 1960.

FRÄNKEL, H., Early Greek Poetry and Philosophy (transl. of
Dichtung und Philosophie des frühen Griechentums by
M. Hadas and J. Willis), London, 1975.

FRANKFORT, H., Before Philosophy: the Intellectual
Adventure of Ancient Man, Chicago, 1946.

FREEMAN, K., Companion to the Presocratic Philosophers,
2nd edn, Oxford, 1949.

FURLEY, D.J. and ALLEN, R.E., eds, Studies in Presocratic
Philosophy, Vol.I The Beginnings of Philosophy, London,
1970.

GIGON, O., Untersuchungen zu Heraklit, Leipzig, 1935.

GIGON, O., Der Ursprung der Griechischen Philosophie von
Hesiod bis Parmenides, Basle, 1945.

GOETZE, A., Kleinasien 2nd edn, Munich, 1957.

GOOLD, G.P., 'Homer and the Alphabet', TAPA 91 (1960),
272-91.

GRAHAM, A.J., 'The Date of the Greek Penetration of the
Black Sea', BICS 5 (1958), 25-42.

GRANET, M., La Pensée Chinoise, Paris, 1934.

GRIFFIN, J., 'The Epic Cycle and the Uniqueness of Homer',
JHS 97 (1977), 39-53.

GRONINGEN, B.A.van, La Composition littéraire archaique
Greque, Amsterdam, 1956.

GUTHRIE, W.K.C., 'The Presocratic World Picture', Harvard
Theological Review 45 (1952), 87-104.

GUTHRIE, W.K.C., Aristotle as a Historian of Philosophy,
JHS 77 Part 1 (1957), 35-41.

GUTHRIE, W.K.C., The Religion and Mythology of the Greeks,
CAH 3, II(2), 1975, 851-905.

GUTHRIE, W.K.C., A History of Greek Philosophy, I. The
Earlier Presocratics and the Pythagoreans, Cambridge,
1962.

HAINSWORTH, J.B., 'Structure and Content in Epic Formulae:
The Question of the Unique Expression, CQ n.s.14 (1964),
155-64.

HAINSWORTH, J.B., The Flexibility of the Homeric Formula,
Oxford, 1968.

HAINSWORTH, J.B., 'The Criticism of an Oral Homer', JHS 90
(1970), 90-8.

HALL, J.J., 'Πρηστῆρος Αὐλός', JHS 89 (1969), 57-9.

HANFMANN, G.M.A., 'Ionia: Leader or Follower?' HSCP 61
(1953), 1-37.

HARRIS, A.E., Ionia Under Persia 547-477 B.C. dissertation,
North-Western University, Evanston, Ill., 1971.

HARVEY, A.E., 'Homeric Epithets in Greek Lyric Poetry',
CQ n.s.7 (1957), 206-23.

HAVELOCK, E.A., 'Pre-literacy and the Presocratics', BICS
13 (1966), 44-67.

HEIDEL, A., The Gilgamesh Epic and Old Testament Parallels,
Chicago, 1946.

HEIDEL, A., The Babylonian Genesis, 2nd edn, Chicago, 1951.

HEIDEL, W.A., 'Qualitative Change in Presocratic Philosophy', Archiv für Geschichte der Philosophie, 12 (1906),
333-379.

HIGGINS, R.A., Greek Terracottas, London, 1967.

HILLER von GAERTRINGEN, F., 'Miletos', RE XV 2, cols 1586-
1622.

HOEKSTRA, A., Homeric Modifications of Formulaic Prototypes, Amsterdam, 1965.

HOGARTH, D.G., Excavations at Ephesus: the Archaic
Artemisia, London, 1908.

HÖLSCHER, U., 'Anaximander und die Anfänge der Philosophie,
Hermes 81 (1953), 257-77 and 385-418. (Reprinted and
translated in Furley and Allen (above), 281-322.)

HÖLSCHER, U., Anfängliches Fragen, Gottingen, 1968.

HOMANN-WEDEKING, E., Die Anfänge der griechisches Gross-
plastik, Berlin, 1950.

HOMANN-WEDEKING, E., Archaic Greece, trans. J.R. Foster,
London, 1968.

HOOKER, J.T., Mycenaean Greece, London, 1976.

HOOKER, J.T., 'The Coming of the Greeks', Historia 25
(1976), 129-45.

HUNT, D.W.S., 'Feudal Survivals in Ionia', JHS 67 (1947),
68-76.

HUXLEY, G.L., Achaeans and Hittites, Oxford, 1960.

HUXLEY, G.L., 'Ion of Chios', GRBS 6 (1965), 29-46.

HUXLEY, G.L., The Early Ionians, London, 1966.

HUXLEY, G.L., Greek Epic Poetry: Eumelos to Panyassis,
Harvard, 1969.

IOANNIDI, H., 'Essai de reconstruction de la logique
archaïque', Eirene 3 (1964), 5-50.

IOANNIDI, H., 'La place d'Heraclite dans l'histoire de la
pensée grecque', Eirene 5 (1966), 17-41.

JACOBSTAHL, P., 'Date of the Ephesian Foundation Deposit',
JHS 71 (1951), 85-95.

JACOBY, F., Atthis, The Local Chronicles of Ancient Athens,
Oxford, 1949.

JACOBY, F., Die Fragmente der griechischen Historiker,
Erster Teil a., Leiden, 1957.

JAEGER, W., The Theology of the Early Greek Philosophers, Oxford, 1947.

JEFFERY, L.H., 'The Courts of Justice in Archaic Chios', ABSA 51 (1956), 157-67.

JEFFERY, L.H., The Local Scripts of Archaic Greece, Oxford, 1961.

JEFFERY, L.H., 'Old Smyrna: Inscriptions on Sherds and Small Objects', ABSA 59 (1964), 39-49.

JEFFERY, L.H., '"Αρχαια Γράμματα: Some ancient Greek views' (Sonderdr. Europa: Festschrift für E. Grumach, ed. W.C. Brice), Berlin, 1967, 152-66.

JEFFERY, L.H. and MORPURGO-DAVIES, A., 'ποινικαστάς and ποινικάζεν: BM 1969 4-2.1. A New Archaic Inscription from Crete', Kadmos 9 (1970), 118-54.

JEFFERY, L.H., Archaic Greece: The City States c.700-500 B.C., London, 1976.

JOHANSEN, K.F., 'Clazomeneian Sarcophagus Studies', Acta Archaeologia, 13 (1942), 1-64.

JONES, A.H.M., The Cities of the Eastern Roman Provinces, 2nd edn, Oxford, 1971.

JONES, A.H.M., The Greek City from Alexander to Justinian, 2nd edn, Oxford, 1966.

KAHN, C.H., Anaximander and the Origins of Greek Cosmology, New York, 1960.

KAHN, C.H., 'On Early Greek Astronomy', JHS 90 (1970), 99-116.

KIRK, G.S., 'Natural Change in Heraclitus', Mind 60 (1951), 35-42.

KIRK, G.S., 'Some Problems in Anaximander', CQ n.s.5 (1955), 21-38.

KIRK, G.S.,'Men and Opposites in Heraclitus', Mus.Helv. 14 (1957), 155-63.

KIRK, G.S.,'Objective Dating Criteria in Homer', Mus. Helv. 17 (1960), 189-205.

KIRK, G.S., 'Homer and Modern Oral Poetry: Some Confusions', CQ n.s.10 (1960), 271-81.

KIRK, G.S., Heraclitus: The Cosmic Fragments, 2nd edn, Cambridge, 1962.

KIRK, G.S., The Songs of Homer, Cambridge, 1962.

KIRK, G.S., The Trojan War (see under J.L. Caskey).

KIRK, G.S., 'Formular Language and Oral Quality', YCS 20 (1966), 153-74.

KIRK, G.S., The Nature of Greek Myths, London, 1974.

KIRK, G.S., The Homeric Poems as History, CAH 3 II(2) 1975, 820-50.

KIRK, G.S., Homer and the Oral Tradition, Cambridge, 1976.

KIRKWOOD, G.M., Early Greek Monody: The History of a Poetic Type, Cornell, 1974.

KLEINER, G., Alt-Milet, Wiesbaden, 1966.

KLEINER, G. with HOMMEL, P. and MÜLLER-WIENER, W.,
Panionion und Melie, Berlin, 1967.

KNOX, M.G., 'Huts and Farm Buildings in Homer', CQ n.s.21
(1971), 27-31.

KRAAY, C., Hoards, Small Change and the Origin of Coinage,
JHS 84 (1964) 76-91.

KRISHER, T., Formale Konventionen der homerischen Epik,
Munich, 1971.

KUNZE, E., 'Ionische Kleinmeister', Ath.Mitt. 59 (1934),
81-122.

LANG, M., 'Herodotus and the Ionian Revolt', Historia 17
(1968), 24-36.

LESKY, A., 'Homeros', RE suppl.XI, cols 687-846.

LEVI, P., Pausanias' Guide to Greece, trans. with
introduction. (vol.I), London, 1971.

LILJA, S., On the Style of the Earliest Greek Prose (Soc.
Sci Fennica; comm. hum. litt. 41,3), Helsinki, 1968.

LLOYD, A.B., Herodotus Book II, Leiden, 1975 (vol.I).

LLOYD, G.E.R., 'Hot, Cold, Wet and Dry in Greek Philosophy, JHS 84 (1964), 92-106.

LLOYD, G.E.R., Polarity and Analogy: Two types of
Argumentation in Early Greek Thought, Cambridge, 1966.

LLOYD, S., Early Anatolia, London, 1956.

LORD, A.B., The Singer of Tales, Oxford, 1960.

LORD, A.B., 'Homer as Oral Poet', HSCP 72 (1967), 1-46.

McDIARMID, J.B., Theophrastus on the Presocratic Causes,
HSCP 61 (1953), 85-156.

MANVILLE, P.B., 'Aristagoras and Histiaios: The Leadership
Struggle in the Ionian Revolt', CQ n.s.27 (1977), 80-91.

MARCOVICH, M., Heraclitus: Greek Text with Short Commentary, Venezuela, 1967.

MARCOVICH, M., 'Herakleitos', RE suppl.X, cols 286ff.

MEIGGS, R., The Athenian Empire, Oxford, 1972.

MEIGGS, R. and LEWIS, D.M., A Selection of Greek Historical Inscriptions to the End of the Fifth Century B.C.,
Oxford, 1969.

MELLINK, M., Yearly reports on archaeology in Asia Minor,
AJA 59 (1955-).

MELLINK, M., 'Anatolia: Old and New Perspectives', Proc.
Am.Phil.Soc. 110 (1966), 111-29.

MERLAN, P., 'Ambiguity in Heraclitus', Actes du Xième
Congrès international de philosophie 12 (1953), 56-60.

MITCHELL, B.M., 'Herodotus and Samos', JHS 95 (1975), 75-91.

MOULTON, C., 'Similes in the Iliad', Hermes 102 (1974),
381-97.

MURRAY, O., ''Ο 'Αρχαῖος Δασμός', Historia 15 (1966), 142-
56.

NAGLER, M.N., 'Towards a Generative View of the Oral
Formula', TAPA 98 (1967), 269-311.

NAGLER, M.N., Spontaneity and Tradition, California, 1975.
NEUGEBAUER, O., The Exact Sciences in Antiquity, 2nd edn, Providence, 1957.
NORDEN, E., Die antike Kunstprosa I, 5th imp., Stuttgart, 1958.
NOTOPOULOS, J., 'Continuity and Interconnection in Homeric Oral Composition', TAPA 82 (1951), 81-101.
NOTOPOULOS, J., 'Studies in Early Greek Oral Poetry' (I and II) HSCP 68 (1964), 1-77.
PAGE, D.L., History and the Homeric Iliad, 2nd imp., California, 1963.
PAGE, D.L., The Homeric Odyssey, Oxford, 1955.
PAGE, D.L., The Trojan War (see under J.L. Caskey).
PARRY, A., 'The Language of Achilles', TAPA 87 (1956), 1-7.
PARRY, M., The Making of Homeric Verse (ed. and trans. A. Parry, with introduction), Oxford, 1971.
PEARSON, L., The Early Ionian Historians, Oxford, 1939, repr. Connecticut, 1975.
PODLEĆKI, A.J., The Political Background of Aeschylean Tragedy, Ann Arbor, 1966.
POPE, M.W.M., 'The Parry-Lord Theory of Homeric Composition', Acta Classica 6 (1963) 1-21.
PRITCHARD, J.B., ed., Ancient Near Eastern Texts Relating to the Old Testament, 2nd edn, Princeton, 1955.
QUINN, T.J., Political Groups at Chios 412 BC, Historia 18 (1969), 22-30.
RAMNOUX, G., Vocabulaire et structures de penseé archaïque chez Héraclite, Paris, 1959.
REINHARDT, K., 'Heraklits Lehre vom Feuer' Hermes 77 (1942), 1-27.
RICHTER, G.M.A., 'Greeks in Persia', AJA 50 (1946), 15-30.
RICHTER, G.M.A., Archaic Greek Art, Oxford, 1949.
RICHTER, G.M.A., Korai: Archaic Greek Maidens, London, 1968.
RICHTER, G.M.A., Kouroi: Archaic Greek Youths, London, 1970.
RIVIER, A., 'L'homme et l'expérience humaine dans les fragments d'Héraclite', Mus.Helv. 13 (1956), 144-64.
ROBINSON, E.S.G., 'The Coins from the Ephesian Artemision Reconsidered', JHS 71 (1951), 156-67.
ROEBUCK, C., 'The Grain Trade between Greece and Egypt', CP 45 (1950), 236-47.
ROEBUCK, C., 'The Economic Development of Ionia', CP 48 (1953), 9-16.
ROEBUCK, C., 'The Early Ionian League', CP 50 (1955), 26-40.
ROEBUCK, C., Ionian Trade and Colonisation (Monographs on Archaeology and Fine Arts 9) New York, 1959.
ROEBUCK, C., 'Tribal Organisation in Ionia', TAPA 92

(1961), 495-507.

ROSE, P.W., 'Class Ambivalence in the Odyssey', Historia 24 (1975), 129-49.

RUSSO, J.A., 'A Closer Look at Homeric Formulas', TAPA 94 (1963), 235-47.

RUSSO, J.A., 'The Structural Formula in Homeric Verse', YCS 20 (1966), 217-40.

SAKELLARIOU, M.B., La Migration grecque en Ionie, Athens, 1958.

SCHADEWALDT, W., Iliasstudien, 2nd edn, Darmstadt, 1966.

SCHADEWALDT, W., Von Homers Welt und Werk, 2nd edn, Stuttgart, 1959.

SCOTT, W., The Oral Nature of the Homeric Simile, Leiden, 1974.

SELIGMAN, P., The Apeiron of Anaximander, London, 1962.

SHIPP., G.P., The Language of Homer, rev. edn, Amsterdam, 1966.

SNELL, B., 'Die Sprache Heraklits', Hermes 61 (1926), 353-81.

SNELL, B., 'Heraklits Fr.10', Hermes 76 (1941), 84-7.

SNELL, B., The Discovery of the Mind: The Greek Origins of European Thought, trans. T.G. Rosenmeyer, Oxford, 1953

SNODGRASS, A.M., The Dark Age of Greece, Edinburgh, 1971.

SOLMSEN, F., Aristotle's System of the Physical World, Cornell, 1960.

STOKES, M.C., 'Hesiod and Milesian Cosmogonies', Phronesis 7 (1962), 1-37; 8 (1963), 1-34.

STOKES, M.C., One and Many in Presocratic Philosophy, Washington, 1971.

STRUNK, K., Die sogennanten Äolismen der homerischen Sprache, dissertation, Cologne, 1957.

THOMAS, C.G., 'The Roots of Homeric Kingship', Historia 15 (1966), 387-407.

THOMSON, G.D., Studies in Ancient Greek Society II; The First Philosophers, 2nd edn, London, 1961.

TOD, M.N., Greek Historical Inscriptions (vol.I) 2nd edn, Oxford, 1946.

TOMLINSON, R.A., Greek Sanctuaries, London. 1976.

TREU, M., Von Homer zu Lyrik, Zetemata 12, Munich, 1955.

TUCHELT, K., Die archaischen Skulpturen von Didyma, Berlin, 1970.

VERDENIUS, W.J., 'Homer, The Educator of the Greeks', Nederl. Akad. van Wet. Afd. Lett. 33 (1970), 207-31.

VERDENIUS, W.J., 'Callinus Fr.1: a Commentary', Mnemosyne 25 (1972), 1-8.

VLASTOS, G., 'Equality and Justice in Early Greek Cosmologies', CP 42 (1947), 156-78.

VLASTOS, G., 'Theology and Philosophy in Early Greek Thought', PQ 2 (1952), 97-123.

VLASTOS, G., 'Isonomia' AJP 74 (1953), 337-66.

VLASTOS, G., Review of Cornford's Principium Sapientiae,
Gnomon 27 (1955), 65-76.
VLASTOS, G., 'On Heraclitus', AJP 76 (1955), 337-68.
WACE, A.J.B. and STUBBINGS, F., A Companion to Homer,
London, 1962.
WADE-GERY, T., The Poet of the Iliad, Cambridge, 1952.
WALCOT, P., Hesiod and the Near East, Cardiff, 1966.
WATERS, K.H., 'Herodotus and the Ionian Revolt', Historia
19 (1970), 504-8.
WEBSTER, T.B.L., From Mycenae to Homer, London, 1958.
WEST, M.L., 'Greek Poetry 2000-700 B.C.' CQ n.s.23 (1973),
179-92.
WEST, M.L., Early Greek Philosophy and the Orient, Oxford,
1971.
WEST, M.L., 'Alcman and Pythagoras' CQ n.s.17 (1967), 1-15.
WHITE, M., 'The Duration of the Samian Tyranny', JHS 74
(1954), 36-43.
WHITMAN, C., Homer and the Heroic Tradition, Harvard,
1958.
WIEGAND, T., Milet: Ergebnisse der Ausgraben und Unter-
suchungen seit dem Jahre 1899, Berlin, 1906-29.
WILAMOWITZ, U.von, Nordionische Steine, Abh. Berlin, 1909.
WILLCOCK, M.M., 'Mythological Paradeigma in the Iliad',
CQ n.s.14 (1964), 141-54.
WILLETTS, R.F., Cretan Cults and Festivals, London, 1962.
WILLETTS, R.F., The Law Code of Gortyn, Berlin, 1967
WILLETTS, R.F., Some Characteristics of Archaic Cretan
Writing, Europa (Fest.E.Grumach), 320-31.
WILLETTS, R.F., The Civilisation of Ancient Crete, London/
California, 1977.
WYCHERLEY, R.E., How the Greeks Built Cities, 2nd edn,
London, 1976.
YOUNG, D., 'Never Blotted a Line? Formula and Premedit-
ation in Homer and Hesiod', Arion 6 (1967), 279-324.
ZARNKE, E., Über die Entstehung der griechischen
Literatursprachen, Leipzig, 1870.
ZELLER, E., Die Philosophie der Griechen, 6th edn by
W. Nestle, Leipzig, 1920.

Index